Frances Eales • Steve Oakes • Louis Harrison

speakout

Upper Intermediate
Flexi Course Book 2

with DVD-ROM

2ND EDITION

Pearson Education Limited
Edinburgh Gate
Harlow
Essex CM20 2JE
England
and Associated Companies throughout the world.

www.pearsonelt.com

First published 2015
Fifth impression 2019
This edition published 2016
ISBN: 978-1-292-14938-7
Set in Aptifer sans 10/12 pt
Printed in Slovakia by Neografia

Acknowledgements

The Publisher and authors would like to thank the following people and institutions for their feedback and comments during the development of the material:
Australia: Erica Lederman; **Hungary:** Eszter Timár; **Poland:** Konrad Dejko; **Spain:** Pilar Álvarez Polvorinos, Victoria O'Dea; **UK:** David Byrne, Lilian Del Gaudio Maciel, Niva Gunasegaran

Text acknowledgements

Extract on page 12 adapted from "30 Challenges for 30 Days" by Martijn Schirp, http://www.highexistence.com/30-challenges-for-30-days. Reproduced by kind permission of Martijn Schirp; Extract on page 32 adapted from "You Are Wonderful!", *Cultivate Life! magazine*, Issue 26 (Phil Evans, http://www.peoplestuff.com.au), http://www.trans4mind.com/cultivate-life-magazine/issue-026/Regular-Features-page-one.html, copyright © 1997-2014 Trans4mind Ltd. Reproduced with permission; Extracts on page 33 adapted from "What goes around comes around" by Stephen, 18 October 2008, http://academictips.org/blogs/what-goes-around-comes-around, and "The Falcon & The Branch" submitted by Hemendra Chanchani, 7 March 2014, http://academictips.org/blogs/the-falcon-and-the-branch. Reproduced with permission; Extract on page 35 adapted from Today (feature on 'Life in six words') by host Sarah Montague and guest Larry Smith, 28/06/2007, http://www.bbc.co.uk/radio4/today/reports/misc/sixwordlife_20080205.shtml, copyright © BBC Worldwide Limited; Extracts on pages 37, 44, 70, 107, 121, from *Longman Active Study Dictionary*, 5th edition, Pearson Education Ltd, copyright © Pearson Education Limited, 2010; Extract on page 71 adapted from 'Letters to myself', 22/02/2009, Audio interview on BBC Radio 4 copyright © BBC Worldwide Limited; Extract on page 86 adapted from 'Six topics that keep the tabloids in business', http://www.drewrys.com, copyright © John Drewry; Extract on page 92 adapted from "New York roommates find $40,000 in sofa and return cash to owner", *Associated Press*, 16/05/2014, copyright © 2105. Reproduced with permission of The Associated Press. All rights reserved; Extract on page 92 adapted from "Unemployed Brooklyn man misses job interview to save 9-month-old boy who was blown into path of oncoming subway train", *New York Daily News*, 27/06/2012 (Kerry Burke, Joe Kemp and Tracy Connor), copyright © Daily News, L.P. (New York). Used with permission; and Extract on pages 104-105 from "Memories on Trial" by Andy Ridgway, *BBC Focus*, January 2009, pp.58–61, copyright © Immediate Media Company Bristol Ltd.

Illustration acknowledgements

Fred Blunt: 18, 90, 150, 153, 155; Lyndon Hayes: 161, 162; Eric Smith: 156; Mark Willey: 107; Mariko Yamazaki: 72, 159.

Photo acknowledgements

The Publisher would like to thank the following for their kind permission to reproduce their photographs:

(Key: b-bottom; c-centre; l-left; r-right; t-top)

123RF.com: Arcady31 15t, Belchonock 92cr, Robert Churchill 55cr, 62, Iakov Kalinin 52-53b, Katre 15tc, Andrey Kiselev 99cl, Maska82 91cl, Igor Mojzes 151 (f), Kathawut Rueansai 12, Andrei Shumskiy 7b (icon), 19b (icon), 31b (icon), 43b (icon), 55b (icon), 67b (icon), 79b (icon), 91b (icon), 103b (icon), 115b (icon), Серей Тряпицын 43l, 44cr; **Alamy Images:** Adam Burton 40-41b, Age Fotostock 86-87t, Ammentorp Photography 110b, Art Directors & Trip 38tr, 55r, 64-65b, 152 (f), Ben Molyneux 38 (Life of Pi), Blend Images 31l, CBW 38 (The Hunger Games), 38 (The Kite Runner), Judith Collins 87cl, Caroline Cortizo 7l, Cultura Creative 99tl, Design Pics Inc 36bl, Dorling Kindersley ltd 119b, Chuck Eckert 156, Mark Harvey 19cl, 24, Image Source 79r, James Callaghan 58 (d), Keystone Pictures USA 69 (5), Marka 69 (1), Newscast 152 (e), Ben Nicholson 123 (e), Dale O'Dell 79cl, Pacific Press Service 67r, 76-77, PhotoAlto 74l, Pictorial Press Ltd 69 (4), Rafael Ben-Ari 67l, 70, Paul Rapson 95, Redsnapper 39cl, Ros Drinkwater 121b, Ross Gilmore 47c, Alistair Scott 162, Adrian Sherratt 149 (a), Marmaduke St.John 122 (b), Stocksearch 35 (car), Glyn Thomas 32tl, 158c, Maximilian Weinzierl 11tr, WENN Ltd 59br, Tim Whitby 103cl, ZUMA Press, Inc. 69 (2); **Ardea:** Thomas Marent 16tl; **BBC Photo Library:** Laurence Cendrowicz 31r, 40br, Rod Fountain 81b, Guy Levy 81tl, Jeff Overs 88-89b, Adrian Rogers 80br; **BBC Worldwide Ltd:** 28cl, 40cl, 52bl, 64l, 76, 88cl, 100cl, 112cl; **Corbis:** 167 / Ocean / Alex Treadway 43cl, Markus Altmann 91t, Ed Bock 98tr, Cardinal 11cr, Dpa / Marius Becker 23t, Monalyn Gracia 43t, 47bc, Henglein and Steets 8tl, David Sacks 82, Wavebreak Media Ltd 91cr; **Digital Vision:** 91r; **DK Images:** Dorling Kindersley 89 (snow globe); **Endemol UK:** 43r, 50-51t; **Exclusivepix:** 83 (a); **Eyewire:** 157 (c), Eyewire 157 (k); **Fotolia.com:** albphoto 122 (d), artzenter 58 (c), Bergamont 152 (a), Markus Bormann 152 (b), Diego Cervo 63t, Chones 55t, Christopher Dodge 57l, Timo Darco 26tr, Esebene 31cl, Gajus 67cl, Georgerudy 151 (e), Kletr 57cl, Markus Mainka 58 (b), Martincp 63l, Mediagram 58l, Photomelon 89 (paperclip), Pioneer11 60, Piotr Adamowicz 56c, Production Perig 15tr, Rawpixel 15, Rebius 83 (plane), Savoieleysse 106, Sentello 56r, Sergemi 83 (Man hanging on rope), Trekandphoto 16tr, Winston 55cl, 59l, Xuejun li 152 (c); **Getty Images:** Ablestock.com 157 (j), Archive Photos 35tl, AWL Images / Nigel Pavitt 19l, 20tl, Blend Images / Stewart Cohen / Pam Ostrow 148 (a), Leland Bobbe 115l, Christopher Bierlein 122 (c), Cynthia Johnson 69 (3), E+ / Nikada 25c, E+ / Sjharmon 98tc, Don Farrall 92bl, FilmMagic / Shareif Ziyadat 37tr, Stephen Frink 16-17b, Christopher Furlong 124bl, Craig Holmes 115r, 124-125, Imagebroker / Uwe Umstatter 27tr, Daniel Ingold / RF 115cr, iStock / mamadela 35tc, Jupiter images 20cr, Carsten Koall 83 (flooded house), Rich Legg 105, Martha Holmes 58 (a), Stijn Nieuwendijk 8tr, 8cl, Photodisc / Arne Pastoor 94, Photodisc / James Lauritz 19t, Photolibrary / Spencer Grant 149 (b), Popperfoto 57r, Joe Raedle / Staff 115t, Dmitriy Shironosov 20tr, Stocktrex 103r, 112-113b, William Casey 67cr, 75, Alena Yakusheva 19r, 28-29b; **Gulf Images:** 148 (b); **Hartwood Films:** Hartwood Films 81tc; **Imagemore Co., Ltd:** 108, 157 (b), 157 (h), 157 (i); **Nature Picture Library:** Eric Baccega 79l, 80tr; **Pearson Education Ltd:** Steve Shott 27tl; **PhotoDisc:** Tony Gable. C Squared Studios 157 (g), McDaniel Woolf 126; **Rex Features:** 51tl, 104, Endemol UK 50tl, Kevin Holt / Daily Mail 69 (6), Mark Large 121t, Geoffrey Robinson 79t, Karl Schoendorfer 38-39t; **Robert Harding World Imagery:** Jose Azel 47br, Jens Lucking 43cr, 47tr, Philippe Michel 48-49t; **Shutterstock.com:** Fabio Alcini 152 (d), Steve Allen 123 (f), amenic181 74bc, Arena Creative 15tl, Awe Inspiring Images 7t, 16c, Galina Barskaya 84, Beboy 149 (d), Bikeriderlondon 97, Natalia Bratslavsky 91l, 92tr, Jakub Cejpek 154bc, Christian Bertrand 115cl, Christophe Testi 89 (doorknob), Creatista 74r, De Visu 109, Goran Djukanovic 119t, Furtseff 157 (f), Icsnaps 151 (a), Iofoto 149 (c), Italianestro 157 (e), Jill Battaglia 35 (money), Julian Rovagnati 63r, Anna Jurkovska 31cr, Kachalkina Veronika 73l, Deborah Kolb 83 (shark fins), kornilov007 103cr, 110t, Sergey Krasnoshchokov 7r, 16tc, Piotr Krzeslak 103l, Labrador Photo Video 59tr, Liligraphie 67t, Isantilli 151 (c), Mangostock 19cr, Marie C Fields 34b, Minerva Studio 79cr, nanhatai 74tc, Nejron Photo 7cl, 11tl, Vitalii Nesterchuk 11tc, 16cr, Nito 47cr, Nneirda 154br, Jakkrit Orrasri 151 (d), Bombaert Patrick 157 (d), Pressmaster 9br, Primopiano 56l, Rawpixel 100-101b, Dario Sabljak 157 (l), Sabphoto 148 (c), scyther5 55l, 57cr, Stockelements 122 (a), TFoxFoto 103t, Toa55 33tr, 158br, Tatyana Vyc 151 (b), wavebreakmedia 71, Ivonne Wierink 157 (a), Zvonimir Atletic 73r; **SuperStock:** 31t, Blend Images 7cr, Fancy Collection 85; **The Kobal Collection:** 20th Century Fox 116t, Columbia / Tri-Star / Goldman, Louis 116b, Gravier Productions 118; **The Orion Publishing Group Ltd:** Cover Design Orionbooks, Image © Bernd Ott / Gallerystock 38 (Gone Girl)

All other images © Pearson Education

Every effort has been made to trace the copyright holders and we apologise in advance for any unintentional omissions. We would be pleased to insert the appropriate acknowledgement in any subsequent edition of this publication.

speakout 2ND EDITION

Upper Intermediate
Students' Book

with DVD-ROM

Frances Eales • Steve Oakes

CONTENTS

LESSON		GRAMMAR/FUNCTION	VOCABULARY	PRONUNCIATION	READING
UNIT 6 AGE page 67		BBC interviews | What was the best period of your life?			
6.1	The time of my life page 68	modal verbs and related phrases	age; word building: prefixes	connected speech: elision	read an article about early and late successes
6.2	Future me page 71	future perfect and continuous	optimism/pessimism	weak forms: auxiliaries	read emails making arrangements
6.3	So what you're saying is … page 74	persuading	collocations	intonation: persuading	
6.4	How To Live To 101 page 76				
UNIT 7 MEDIA page 79		BBC interviews | What kind of news stories interest you?			
7.1	TV globetrotters page 80	quantifiers	television; multi-word verbs	connected speech: linking	read about TV with a global appeal
7.2	The camera never lies page 83	reported speech	reporting verbs	word stress	read an essay on celebrities and the media
7.3	What's in the news page 86	adding emphasis	the press	sentence stress	read about tabloid topics
7.4	News Blunders page 88				
UNIT 8 BEHAVIOUR page 91		BBC interviews | What kind of behaviour gets on your nerves?			
8.1	It's a tough call page 92	past and mixed conditionals	collocations: decisions; compound adjectives	connected speech: weak forms	read three articles about life-changing decisions
8.2	Fair share page 95	*-ing* form and infinitive	values	connected speech: intrusive /w/	read the instructions for two games
8.3	Have you got a minute? page 98	handling an awkward situation	behaviour	sentence stress and intonation	read tips for handling awkward situations
8.4	The Human Animal page 100				
UNIT 9 TROUBLE page 103		BBC interviews | Do you have any phobias?			
9.1	Witness page 104	*-ing* form and infinitive	crime; dependent prepositions	connected speech: elision	read an article about memory
9.2	Scam page 107	past modals of deduction 演繹的な推論の	synonyms	connected speech: past modals	read an infographic about scams; read an advice leaflet about avoiding trouble on holiday
9.3	It's an emergency! page 110	reporting an incident	incidents	sentence stress	read reasons for calling the emergency services
9.4	Survival page 112				
UNIT 10 CULTURE page 115		BBC interviews | What areas of the Arts do you enjoy?			
10.1	Moving experiences page 116	relative clauses	adjectives to describe films	intonation: relative clauses	read a film review
10.2	Popular culture page 119	participle clauses	the Arts; two-part phrases	word stress; connected speech	read answers to popular cultu
10.3	On your left … page 122	giving a tour	dimensions	intonation in comments	
10.4	The People's Palace page 124				

DVD-ROM: DVD CLIPS AND SCRIPTS BBC INTERVIEWS AND SCRIPTS CLASS AUDIO AND SCRIPTS

IRREGULAR VERBS page 127 LANGUAGE BANK page 128 VOCABULARY BANK page 138

deduction (演繹的)
大きな1つの大前提から結論を推論すること.
ルールや法則に基づく物事に当てはめ、結果を導く
induction (帰納的)
複数の事実や事例から共通点を導き出し
一般論となる結論にたどりつく

CONTENTS

6
age

THE TIME OF MY LIFE p68

FUTURE ME p71

SO WHAT YOU'RE SAYING IS … p74

BBC

HOW TO LIVE TO 101 p76

BBC
INTERVIEWS

What was the best period of your life?

G modal verbs and related phrases
P connected speech: elision
V age; word-building: prefixes

SPEAKING

1 Work in pairs and discuss. What are the advantages and disadvantages of being the ages in the box?

| 10 | 15 | 20 | 30 | 45 | 65 |

VOCABULARY

AGE

2 A Match the words/phrases in bold in questions 1–8 with meanings a)–h).

1 If someone looks young **for their age**, is that good? *f*
2 When is someone **in their prime**?
3 If you tell a twenty-five-year-old person, '**Act your age!**' what kind of thing might they be doing?
4 At what age do people generally **come of age** in your country: seventeen, eighteen, twenty-one?
5 Are eighteen-year-olds too **immature** for university?
6 At what age does a person have the **maturity** to make a decision about marriage or a career?
7 At what age is a person **elderly**?
8 Does **age discrimination** affect people looking for jobs in your country?

   a) behave in a more adult way
   b) 'old' (said in a more polite way)
   c) in the best period of their life
   d) treating people unfairly based on age
   e) reach the age when legally an adult
   f) in relation to how old they are
   g) wisdom that comes with age
   h) childish

B Choose three questions that interest you from Exercise 2A and discuss them in pairs.

READING

3 A Work in pairs and discuss. What do you think it means to 'peak early' or to be a 'late bloomer'? Read the first two paragraphs of the article and check.

B Work in pairs and discuss the questions. Make notes on your ideas.

1 In the photographs, who do you think are late bloomers? Who peaked early?
2 In which of these fields is someone more likely to peak early: acting, singing, writing, sports, business?
3 One author says that sometimes a late bloomer seems to be a failure. Why do you think this is?
4 How do these change as one gets older: freedom, obligation, expectations? What is an example of each?

C Read the article and check your ideas.

EARLY PEAKERS AND LATE BLOOMERS: WHO HAS IT WORSE?

We're all familiar with the story of the film star or singer who peaks early, finds fame at a young age and then seems to disappear. Or the novelist whose brilliant debut at age 22 is followed by works of increasing **mediocrity**. Sports are particularly **biased** towards youth; how many teenagers have a moment of glory at the Olympics only to fade away in their 20s when they are no longer able to compete?

And then there are the late bloomers, who discover their talent relatively late in life: the actress who gets her first big part in her 40s, the office clerk who **pens** a bestseller at 50, and the businessman who starts a multi-million dollar **enterprise** in his 60s. Late bloomers might spend decades struggling to find their passion or be noticed, and that can be painful. As author Malcolm Gladwell wrote, 'On the road to great achievement, the late bloomer will resemble a failure.'

Wherever in the world you are born, society sets out a timeline for your life. You start out confronted by rules and restrictions: you mustn't cross at the red light; don't talk back to the teacher. There are **milestones** of freedom: the age at which your mother says you can stay out late, the point at which you're allowed to take public transport alone or to drive a car. Later, the fruits of your work give you other freedoms, for example you don't have to worry about money for a nice holiday or a meal at a fancy restaurant. And there are the **ever-shifting** sands of obligation and expectations. A teenager complains because her parents make her do her homework and don't let her stay out after 10 o'clock. The 30-year-old suffers because he's supposed to be earning more than his **peers** but he isn't; he has to work all hours but can't find himself in his profession, and meanwhile feels he should give everyone the impression that he's successful even if he isn't.

Early peakers and late bloomers have all made a name for themselves because in some way they managed to break out of the timeline that society had set for them. Perhaps we can all take a lesson from them and break out of our own timeline.

Director Ang Lee had his first global breakthrough at the age of 41 with *Sense and Sensibility* in 1995. Since then, with films like *Brokeback Mountain* and *Life of Pi*, he has become a worldwide success.

After working as a firefighter and insurance salesman, Colonel Sanders was 62 years old when he opened the first Kentucky Fried Chicken restaurant. When he sold the chain in 1964, there were 900 of them.

Wang Yani is a Chinese child prodigy whose work was first exhibited in China when she was four and later became a stamp. Her work now appears in galleries internationally.

It was in 1605, after a career as a soldier and then a tax collector, that Cervantes' novel *Don Quixote* was published, destined to become one of the greatest novels of all time. He was 58.

Romanian Nadia Comăneci, winner of three Olympic gold medals, was the first female gymnast to be awarded a perfect score of 10 in an Olympic gymnastic event. She was only 14. She retired at the age of 23.

As a child, Jocelyn Lavin was a natural mathematician and a gifted oboe and piano player. She later discovered she lacked the discipline for university work and eventually became a teacher.

4 A Work in pairs. Guess the meanings of the words in bold in the text.

B Check your ideas. Match meanings 1–7 with the words in bold.

1 a company or business .... *enterprise*
2 constantly changing .... *ever-shifting*
3 important events in the development of something *milestones*
4 average quality .... *mediocrity*
5 supporting one group in an unfair way .... *be biased towards*
6 writes .... *pens*
7 people who are the same age or have the same job as you *peers*

C Work in pairs and discuss.

• What timeline and milestones do you think society sets out for you?
• Do you feel pressured by this, or is it not a problem for you?
I think I'll be expected to … People tend to … It bothers me that …

GRAMMAR

MODAL VERBS AND RELATED PHRASES

5 A Check what you know. Complete the table with the modal and semi-modal verbs underlined in sentences 1–6 below.

1 You <u>mustn't</u> cross at the red light.
2 Your mother says you <u>can</u> stay out late.
3 You <u>don't have to</u> worry about money for a nice holiday.
4 He <u>has to</u> work all hours.
5 He <u>can't</u> find himself in his profession.
6 He feels he <u>should</u> give everyone the impression that he's successful.

RULES				
obligation (strong)	*has to* ~~must make somebody do st~~	prohibition	*mustn't*	
obligation (weak)	*should*	permission	*can* ~~let sb do st~~	
lack of obligation	*don't have to*	ability/lack of ability	*can't*	

B Look at the phrases in bold and think about their meanings. Which category in the table are they closest to?

1 They **are** no longer **able to** compete. *can't — lack of ability*
2 There are milestones of freedom: … the point when you **are allowed to** take public transport alone … *can — permission*
3 A teenager complains because her parents **make her do** her homework and don't **let her stay** out after 10 o'clock. *have to / can't / has (must)*
4 The 30-year-old suffers because he's **supposed to** be earning more than his peers … *should (weak obligation)*
5 … they **managed to** break out of the timeline that society had set for them. *can (ability)*

6 A ▶ 6.1 Listen and write the sentences you hear.

B CONNECTED SPEECH: elision Cross out a *t* or a *d* that isn't pronounced at the end of a word in each sentence. Then listen again and repeat.

We mus~~t~~ go home now.

▷ page 128 **LANGUAGEBANK**

7 A
Complete the sentences with a modal verb or related phrase in the correct form. In some cases there is more than one possibility.

1 Parents ___*should*___ be strict with babies or they _____ to control them later.
2 The worst thing about school was that I _____ do what I wanted to.
3 When I was a child, my parents often _____ me stay over at my friends' houses.
4 When I was younger, I _____ help clean our flat but I never did.
5 The best thing about being an adult is that no one can _____ you do something if you don't want to.
6 And the worst thing is that you just _____ to get the flat tidy and then the family messes it up again!
7 When I am older I _____ afford an apartment in the city centre.
8 A good thing about being retired is that you _____ work anymore.

B Choose four sentences and change them to give your opinion. Then discuss with a partner.

SPEAKING

8 A
Make notes on your answers to questions 1–3.

1 Are most of the people you spend time with your age or a different age? Why?
2 How is your generation different from older or younger ones? What sort of misunderstandings or conflicts can this cause?
3 Is the 'generation gap' greater or smaller than it used to be? Why?

B Work in groups and discuss the questions.

VOCABULARY **PLUS**
WORD-BUILDING: PREFIXES

9 A
Check what you know. Add a negative prefix to the words in bold to make them negative. Use *dis-, in-, il-, im-, ir-, mis-* or *un-*.

1 You have __un__ **realistic** expectations of life.
2 Your behaviour is _un_ **predictable** and sometimes _il_ **logical**.
3 You are _dis_ **satisfied** with how your life has turned out.
4 You aren't very keen on _un_ **familiar** situations.
5 You are _im_ **patient** with people who don't understand technology.
6 You think you are _im_ **mortal**.
7 You are _un_ **willing** to change your mind about your opinions.
8 You _mis_ **behave** to get people's attention. _mis_
9 You sometimes feel _in_ **secure** in groups and _mis_ **interpret** what people say to you.
10 How much money you have is _ir_ **relevant**. You're just happy not to be _un_ **healthy**.

B ▶ 6.2 Listen and check your answers to Exercise 9A. Then listen and repeat. Are the prefixes stressed or unstressed?

C Work in pairs and discuss. Are any of the sentences above truer for younger people and/or older people? Give examples to support your ideas.

speakout TIP

A dictionary can help you find which negative prefix a word takes. Look at this listing below for the adjective *mature*. How is the negative shown? How does your dictionary show negative prefixes?

> **M** **mature** *adj* **1** behaving in a reasonable way like an adult [≠ immature] *She's very mature for her age.*

From Longman Active Study Dictionary.

10 A
Answer each pair of questions with words that share the same prefix. Use the prefixes in the box and the words in bold to help.

> over- post- pre- under-

What do you call:

1 a) the generation who were born before the **war**? (adj)
   pre b) the period of **history** before written records? (adj)
2 a) the generation born after the **war**? (adj)
   post b) a university course taken after you **graduate** from your initial course? (adj)
3 a) the **time** you spend working in your job in addition to your *over* normal working hours? (n)
   b) people who are forced to **work** too much or too hard? (adj)
4 a) someone who isn't the minimum **age** to see an X-certificate *under* film? (adj)
   b) someone who doesn't have enough **qualifications** to get a job? (adj)

B Work with other students and brainstorm other words that begin with these four prefixes. Which group came up with the longest list?

▷ page 138 **VOCABULARYBANK**

FUTURE ME

G future perfect and continuous
P weak forms: auxiliaries
V optimism/pessimism

6.2

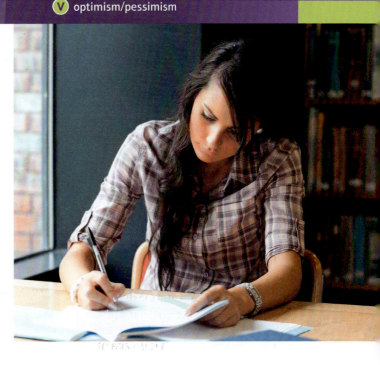

LISTENING

1 A Over the next four years, what are you definitely going to do, what do you think you might do and what do you hope you'll do? *100% / 50% / 0%*

B Work in pairs and compare your ideas. Do you have any plans or hopes in common?

2 Read the programme information below and answer the questions.

1 How does the website work? *happy*
2 Do you think it would be (uplifting) or depressing to get a letter from your younger self?

Letters to myself

The idea is simple:

write a letter to yourself, and futureme.org will keep it and send it back to you at a point in the future – you pick the date. What will you discover, looking back? In this BBC radio programme, people read aloud and comment on their letters.

3 A ▶ 6.3 Listen to Laura reading a letter she wrote to herself four years ago when she was sixteen. Answer the questions.

1 Which topics did she write about? *more realistic*
2 Is the letter down-to-earth or romantic? Is it generally optimistic or pessimistic? *you can see the future*

B Listen again and correct the mistakes.
1 I envisage myself at Oxford Uni, … sitting under a tree … and watching something floaty. *a collie / wearing*
2 I know, I'm practical. I hope that hasn't changed. *romantic*
3 I hope I'll have married someone.
4 … I think I'll have three children with long brown hair and blue eyes. *green*
5 … I have to write everything I can down, but I'm running out of time. *want*
6 Don't worry too much, and be happy with who you are. *change*

C ▶ 6.4 Listen to the second part of the programme and underline the two correct alternatives.
1 Laura now sees her sixteen-year-old self as *shallow/quite mature/unrealistic*.
2 She feels *very happy/ecstatic/amazed* at the way her life has turned out. *very happy*

not deep inside. *quite. = not very a little*

GRAMMAR

FUTURE PERFECT AND CONTINUOUS

4 A Look at sentences a) and b) from Laura's letter. Which one talks about:
1 things that will be completed before the moment she opens the letter? *a*
2 things that will be in progress around the moment that she opens the letter? *b*
a) I'll have changed so much.
b) I bet when I get this, it'll be raining.

B Complete the rules.

> **RULES**
> 1 To talk about something that will finish before a specific time in the future, use *will* + *have* + *p.p.* *(past participle)*
> 2 To talk about something that will be in progress at or around a specific time in the future, use *will* + *be* + ~~*continuous*~~ *verb+ing*

C Underline the correct alternative in the sentences and explain your reason.
1 In ten years' time, I expect *I'll be owning/I'll own* a flat. *state verb*
2 I'll have finished the report *by/until* 12 and certainly no later than that.

D ▶ 6.5 **WEAK FORMS: auxiliaries** Listen and write the sentences. Underline examples of the future perfect and future continuous. Circle the auxiliary verbs.

E Listen again and say the sentences at the same time as the speaker.

▷ page 128 **LANGUAGEBANK**

5 A Look back at the rules on page 71 and complete the questions with the correct form of the future perfect, future continuous or the future with *will*.

1 By the end of the day, do you think _you'll have received_ (you/ receive) more than fifty emails?

2 At 9p.m. tonight, _will you watch_ (you/watch) TV? If so, what?

3 Do you think _you'll have fallen_ (you/fall) asleep by midnight tonight?

4 This time next year, _you'll be still studying_ (you/still/study) English and _Will you have passed_ (you/pass) any English exams?

5 Do you expect _you'll still like_ (you/still/like) the same kind of music a few years from now?

6 In twenty years' time, **will you be living** (you/live) in the same town, do you think?

B Work in pairs and discuss the questions in Exercise 5A. Use words and phrases from the box.

Possibly	Yes, definitely
That's quite likely	I doubt it
No, definitely not	Perhaps
I expect so	I don't suppose so

SPEAKING

6 A Work alone and think about your plans for ten years' time. Make notes on three of the areas below.

studies or work   achievements

travel   **English**

relationships and/or family

home   *activities/experiences*

B Work with a partner and discuss your ideas.

A: What would you say about 'achievements'?

B: Well, in ten years' time, I hope I'll have become fluent in English. I'd like to be working abroad somewhere, maybe Australia. How about you?

C Work in pairs. Would you say you are generally an optimistic, 'glass half full' type of person or a pessimistic 'glass half empty' one? Give examples.

Glass half full or half empty?

1 How do you feel about your English?

a) It's going well.

b) You **have your ups and downs**.

c) You're stuck and **going nowhere**.

2 This weekend, you're going to a party with lots of people you don't know. How do you feel?

a) You're **looking forward to** it.

b) You **have mixed feelings about** it.

c) It's the last thing you feel like doing.

3 Your partner rings you and asks to meet as soon as possible as they have something important to tell you. What do you think?

a) You **look on the bright side**; the news will be good.

b) It'll just be news, nothing particularly positive or negative.

c) You're **dreading** it; you're sure they want to break up with you.

4 When you think about the next year or two in your life, how do you feel?

a) quite **upbeat** about it

b) cautiously hopeful

c) quite pessimistic about the prospects

5 How does the future in general make you feel?

a) It fills you with great hope.

b) It has its fair share of positive and negative prospects.

c) It **fills you with despair**.

VOCABULARY

OPTIMISM/PESSIMISM

7 A Work in pairs and read the quiz. Guess the meaning of the words/phrases in bold.

B Match the phrases in bold in the quiz with the meanings below. Put the phrase in the infinitive.

1 feel both positive *and* negative about something

2 think about a future event and feel good about it

3 sometimes go well and sometimes go badly

4 make no progress

5 be really worried and fearful about something

6 makes you feel extremely negative

7 optimistic

8 see things in a positive way

C Work in pairs and complete the quiz questions. Then read the key on page 143 and work out your partner's score. Do you think the analysis is accurate?

▷ page 138 **VOCABULARY**BANK

WRITING

AN INFORMAL EMAIL; LEARN TO FOCUS ON INFORMAL STYLE

8 A Imagine you could go anywhere and do anything you like on holiday next summer. Complete the sentence below, and then compare with other students. Did any of you have the same idea?

In the middle of next summer I'd like to be _____ -ing (activity) and _____ -ing (activity) in _____ (place).

B Read the email about someone's suggestion for next summer and the email reply from her friend. Does Corinna answer Louise's questions? What do you notice about the style?

Hi Corinna!

I've just heard there's an Irish dance and music festival in Dublin in July. ¹How about coming over to visit me and we can go to it together?

²Tickets are already on sale, and I'll get us some as soon as I know you're coming for sure. ³Check out the festival website (I'll paste the address below) and let me know which concerts you'd like to see.

⁴My cousin has a flat in Dublin – how about if we stay there? His family will have left for their summer holiday so it'll be just us staying there. Is there anything else you'd like to do in or around Dublin while you're over here?

⁵Let me know how many days you can stay. Can't wait to see you!

Louise

Dear Louise,

⁶I was **delighted to receive** your email **regarding** the music festival, and **I would like to accept the invitation**. I have always wanted to visit Dublin, and this seems like **the perfect occasion to do so**.

You asked me about concert choices but I didn't get the link. ⁷**I would be most grateful** if you could send it again. ⁸**My preference would be for** dance rather than music. **I will inform you** of my specific choices once I see the programme.

Your cousin's flat sounds excellent. ⁹**I would be interested to know** if it is in the city centre or on the outskirts.

¹⁰I'll be able to stay for three days, and I will book a flight once I know the concert dates. **I look forward to receiving further information** about it all.

Yours sincerely,

Corinna

C Read the emails again and write the number of the sentence next to the functions below. One sentence has two functions.

a) acknowledge email _____
b) request information (x4) _____
c) invite someone *1*

d) accept an invitation _____
e) make a suggestion _____
f) providing information (x3)

---

9 A Read Corinna's reply again. Work in pairs and discuss how to replace the formal phrases in bold with informal ones.

B Complete the table with the phrases in bold.

informal	formal
1 a great time for it	*the perfect occasion to do so*
2 about	
3 Can't wait to hear more	
4 Do you know	
5 happy to get	
6 I'd love to come	
7 I'd rather see	
8 All the best,	
9 I'll let you know	
10 It'd be great	

C Rewrite Corinna's reply in an informal style.

10 A Read the email extract from a friend. Write an informal reply accepting the invitation in 120–180 words.

I'm glad to hear that you're coming next month. This'll be only your second time in this city, won't it?

We could spend Wednesday walking in the hills nearby or perhaps just drive out and look at the scenery. Then would you like to go to the theatre in the evening?

On Thursday some friends of mine are having a party. We could go to that or if you like just stay in and watch a DVD, or walk around town.

Let me know what you prefer. Can't wait to see you!

B Swap your reply with your partner. Check each other's work using the table in Exercise 9B.

C Read other students' replies. Who sounds the most excited about their visit?

VOCABULARY

COLLOCATIONS

two guideline

1 A Underline the correct alternative.

1 *making*/*doing* a part-time job
2 *owning*/*belonging* a smartphone — *belongs to me.*
3 *wearing*/*putting* make-up — *put on make up*
4 *keeping*/*staying* home alone
5 *getting*/*making* your ears pierced — *make a hole*
6 *going*/*using* social networking sites — *horrible kids*
7 *having*/*signing up* your own credit card
8 *driving*/*riding* a scooter
9 *babysitting*/*taking care* for a toddler — *take care of*
10 *journeying*/*travelling* solo
11 *staying*/*keeping* up as late as you want — *not sleep. stay up late*
12 *being in charge*/*running* your own business — *— of*

B Work in pairs. Which of the activities above can you see in the photos?

C Work in pairs and discuss. What age is appropriate for someone to do activities 1–12?

D Tell the class anything you disagreed about.

FUNCTION

PERSUADING 說服

2 A ▶ 6.6 Listen to a radio phone-in and tick the three activities in Exercise 1A that the people discuss.

B Listen again and make notes about the callers' problems and the DJ's opinions. Then check with a partner.

problem	DJ's opinion

C Work in pairs and discuss. What's your opinion about each of the situations from the phone-in?

3 A Match examples 1–4 with meanings a)–d). Which two are often used to persuade people to agree with you?

1 Is it better to talk it over with her?
2 It's better to talk it over with her.
3 Surely it's better to talk it over with her.
4 Isn't it better to talk it over with her?

a) an opinion   2
b) a genuine question – the listener can answer *yes* or *no*   1
c) an opinion where the speaker is inviting the listener to agree with them   3
d) a strong opinion where the speaker thinks the listener *should* agree with them   4

B Complete the sentences from the phone-in.

1 _Surely it's_____ up to the parents to set guidelines. (Surely/it/be)
2 _Isn't_____ it better to talk it over with her? (not/be)
3 _Surely that's_____ just normal nowadays. (Surely/that/be)
4 _Don't you think_ it's just a stage he's going through? (you/not/think)
5 _Doesn't she simply want_ to be like her friends? (she/simply/not/want)

C ▶ 6.7 Listen and check.

D INTONATION: persuading Listen again and repeat. Copy the intonation pattern.

▷ page 128 **LANGUAGEBANK**

4 A Work in pairs. Do you know anyone who has had a 'gap year' either before they went to university or between university and work? What do you think of the idea?

B Work in pairs and role-play the situation. Use the flow chart to help.

Student A

> not / you / think / everyone / a gap year?

Student B

> I / not / agree. / not / be / better / start / work as soon as possible?

> Yes / but / not / gap year / give people / different kind of experience?

> gap year / just / long holiday. Surely / year / work / more useful?

> I / disagree. / year off / give / people / chance / think about / career.

> not / most 22-year-olds / decide / by that age?

> Not always. People / often / end up / job they hate. / Anyway, surely / worth trying?

> I / still / not convinced. / I think / a waste of time.

LEARN TO

CLARIFY IDEAS

5 A Read the extract from the radio phone-in. Find two phrases where people ask for clarification of an idea.

DJ: So basically you think she's too young for a phone.
Ed: Yeah, yeah, that's right.
DJ: Surely it's up to the parents to set guidelines.
Ed: So what you're saying is I should give her some rules?

B Read audio script 6.6 on page 148 and find two other phrases to ask for clarification.

speakout TIP

Clarify an idea by repeating something in your own words (paraphrasing). This also 'buys' time while you think about how to react.

C Complete the sentences to paraphrase 1–4.

1 It's unfair. Rich kids don't have to work.
So what you're saying is all kids should __*have to work*__.

2 Elderly people don't get enough respect from younger people.
So, in other words, younger people should _____.

3 Why is it that students who cheat in exams often don't get punished?
So basically you think students who cheat should _____.

4 It makes me angry that men are paid more than women.
So what you mean is women should _____.

D Work in pairs. Student A: read out a statement from Exercise 5C. Student B: cover the exercise and clarify the idea.

6 A Complete statements 1–4 with your own ideas.

1 The biggest problem with young people today is …
2 It's not fair that …
3 I think it was a mistake to …
4 One thing I learnt from my parents is …

B Work in pairs and swap your sentences. Write a paraphrase of your partner's sentences.

C Work in pairs. Student A: read out your idea. Student B: clarify the idea. Then practise again without looking.

A: *The biggest problem with young people today is they can't concentrate.*
B: *So, what you're saying is they can't focus on just one thing.*
A: *That's right.*

SPEAKING

7 A Work in pairs. For each statement, think of two points that support the opinion and two points against it.

• Thirteen is too young to join a social networking site.
• A sixteen-year-old shouldn't be allowed to get a tattoo.
• An eighteen-year-old who has just passed their driving test isn't ready to drive the family car alone.

B Student A: turn to page 143. Student B: turn to page 144. Student C: turn to page 146.

DVD PREVIEW

1 Work in pairs and discuss the questions.

1 Who is the oldest person you know or have known?

2 What do you think they would say is the secret to a long life?

2 A Match 1–8 with a)–h) to make collocations.

1 keep	**a)** some gentle exercise
2 follow	**b)** into monotonous routines
3 do	**c)** a sensible diet
4 don't fall	**d)** mentally active
5 avoid	**e)** a positive attitude
6 stay	**f)** healthy
7 maintain	**g)** depressed
8 don't become	**h)** stress

B Work in pairs and discuss. Which two factors do you think are the most important for a long life?

3 Read the programme information. Which three places are mentioned and what do they have in common?

◉)) Horizon: How to Live to 101

BBC

The quest to live longer has been one of humanity's oldest dreams, but while scientists have been searching, a few isolated communities have stumbled across the answer. On the remote Japanese island of Okinawa, in the Californian town of Loma Linda and in the mountains of Sardinia people live longer than anywhere else on earth.

A group of scientists who study the science of longevity have dedicated their lives to trying to uncover the secrets of these unique communities. Tonight's documentary travels to Okinawa to meet some of its long-living and remarkably healthy inhabitants.

DVD VIEW

4 A Watch the DVD. What are the two main reasons mentioned for why Okinawans live such long lives?

B Work in pairs. What does the underlined word refer to? Watch again and check your ideas.

1 <u>It's</u> four times higher than in Britain and America.

2 The Okinawans don't really think about <u>this</u>.

3 Bradley and Craig think that one of the main reasons for the Okinawans' longevity can be found <u>here</u>.

4 <u>They</u> contain antioxidants, which protect against cell damage.

5 The Okinawans only fill <u>it</u> to 80 percent of its capacity.

6 If you do <u>this</u>, you may die sooner than you might if you didn't do it.

C Watch the DVD again and underline the word you hear.

1 Without thinking about the latest diet or lifestyle *fad/fashion*, Mr Miyagi has developed his own way of slowing the ageing process.

2 The explanation for this extraordinary *phenomenon/miracle* begins in the most ordinary of places.

3 They've identified a number of important *qualities/properties* that protect the Okinawans from disease.

4 You go and you load up at the … at the, the all-you-can-eat restaurant and you, you walk away with this *swollen/bloated* feeling.

D Work in pairs and discuss. How easy do you think you would find it to live on Okinawa? Is there anything you would find difficult?

speakout a debate

5 A Look at the topic for a debate. Work in pairs and write two ideas in favour of the statement and two ideas against it.

Employers should give preference to younger applicants when hiring.

B ▶ **6.8** Listen to part of the debate. Did either speaker mention any of your ideas? Which speaker do you agree with most?

C Listen again and tick the key phrases you hear.

KEY PHRASES

The first point I'd like to make is that …
I would like to start off by saying that …
I would like to support the point made by …
Going back to what [Junko] said …
I would like to pick up on the point made by …
In [answer/reply] to the point made by …

6 A As a class, choose one of the topics for a debate.

1 Politicians should be young – younger adults understand the changing world better.
2 Junk food can shorten lives and should be made illegal.
3 Children should take care of their parents when they get old.
4 Workplaces should require employees to do an hour of exercise a day.
5 It's better to live at a very high standard for 50 years than at an average standard for 100.
6 Some younger people think they have nothing to learn from older people, and they're right.

B Work in pairs either for or against the statement. List at least four points to support your opinion.

C Work in groups and debate the topic. At the end, have a vote.

writeback a forum comment

7 A Read the forum comment and discuss in pairs. Do you agree with the writer?

I strongly feel that children should take care of their parents when they get old, and I'm shocked that anyone disagrees. I grew up in a traditional society, where my grandparents lived with us and were always in the house. When I came to this country, it surprised me how unusual it was for three generations to live together. I accept that most young people's lifestyles don't fit with those of grandparents. However, in my opinion, we are fully responsible for taking care of our ageing parents and grandparents. My reasons are that:

- our parents and grandparents invested a lot in caring for us, and it's our duty to do the same for them.
- elderly people can experience loneliness and helplessness. If we care about someone, we should protect them from these feelings.
- it's more expensive and wasteful for people to live in separate homes.

I definitely think that everyone should reconsider the way they live, and move towards a more traditional family structure, even in a modern context.

B Number parts a)–d) in the order they occur in the forum comment.

a) summary statement
b) reasons for opinion
c) statement of opinion
d) personal background

C Choose one of the topics from Exercise 6A and write a forum comment giving your point of view.

D Read other students' forum comments and tell them which parts you agree and disagree with.

Ⓥ AGE

1 A Add the vowels to complete the sentences.

1 Society, not families, should take care of the e_ld_erly.
2 People i_n the_i_r pr_i_m_e should simply enjoy life and not work.
3 The key sign of someone com_i_ng of _a_ge is when they earn enough money to pay their own rent.
4 It's embarrassing when an older man or woman dresses too young f_o_r the_i_r _a_ge. People should dress and act the_i_r _a_ge.
5 _A_ge d_i_scr_i_m_i_n_a_t_i_o_n is necessary in certain types of jobs.
6 M_a_t_u_r_i_ty comes from experience, not from age.

B Work in pairs and discuss. Which sentences do you agree with?

Ⓖ MODAL VERBS AND RELATED PHRASES

2 A Underline the correct alternatives in the website forum.

★ My worst job

My current job is the worst ever. I'm a waiter in an amusement park restaurant and the manager ¹*makes/ lets* us dress up as bears. The costume is the worst and when I'm wearing it I ²*can't/ I'm not able* to see properly. I can't believe some of the things children ³*are allowed to/should* do. We ⁴*don't have to/aren't supposed to* get angry with them but I'm sure one day I ⁵*can't/won't be able* to keep my temper and will do something awful! Thankfully, we ⁶*don't have to/ aren't allowed* wear the costumes for more than two hours at a time. Fortunately, because of the masks, my friends ⁷*don't have to/oughtn't to* know about my job. Once, I ⁸*could/managed to* serve two of my friends without them realising it was me!

32 answers • 2 days ago

B Work in pairs and discuss. What's the worst job you've ever had or that you can imagine? What was or would be so bad about it?

Ⓖ FUTURE PERFECT AND CONTINUOUS

3 A Complete the sentences with the correct form of the words in brackets.

1 Ten minutes from now, I _____ here. (not sit)
2 In two hours' time, the class _____. (definitely finish)
3 By the time you read this, I _____ in New York. I'll be in touch! (arrive)
4 A year from now, all of us in this group _____ regularly. (still communicate)
5 By 2025, the internet _____ by an alternative technology. (replace)

B Work in pairs and discuss. Which of the sentences above are true?

C Work in pairs and write five predictions about yourself/a classmate/a country/a famous person/the world.

D Work with another pair and discuss your ideas.

Ⓥ OPTIMISM/PESSIMISM

4 A Correct eight mistakes in the words/phrases in bold.

I've **had my downs and ups** at work, but I will never forget my first job: teaching French to a group of sixteen-year-olds in a state school. I **had fixed feelings** about taking the job, since I was very young myself, but I'd learnt to always **look on the light side** of things. I went in the first day feeling **beat-up** and really **looking backward to** meeting my group. But they turned out to be difficult, and for a long time I truly **dread** those lessons. No matter what I tried, I always felt I was **coming nowhere**, and it **filled me up with despair**. Then, one day, something amazing happened. One of the students brought a …

|Comment

B Work in pairs and discuss. How do you think the story ended?

Ⓕ PERSUADING

5 A Complete the conversation by adding the missing words from the box to the phrases in bold.

| what | surely | isn't | agree |
| can | clearly | shouldn't | |

A: **Don't you that** everyone should be vaccinated against flu?
B: **But** people ought to be able to choose for themselves.
A: **Why? Anyone see that** the community needs to be protected and that means everyone has to be vaccinated.
B: **But** parents decide what they think is best for their children? What about some of the side effects of vaccination?
A: **So you're saying is that** you think parents know more than the medical profession?
B: **But it obvious that** it's the companies who make the vaccines that are actually making money?
A: **Well**, we'll have to agree to disagree.

B Practise the conversation above in pairs. Look only at the phrases in bold to help.

C Work in pairs. Use the phrases in bold in Exercise 5A to discuss the following topics.

1 People who drink and drive should never be allowed to drive again.
2 The ideal world language is _____, not English.
3 Everyone should do one day a week of community service work.

A: *Don't you agree that everyone should do community service?*
B: *Why? Anyone can see that wouldn't be fair …*

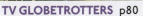

TV GLOBETROTTERS p80   **THE CAMERA NEVER LIES** p83   **WHAT'S IN THE NEWS?** p86   **NEWS BLUNDERS** p88

BBC
INTERVIEWS

What kind of news stories interest you?

G quantifiers
P connected speech: linking
V television; multi-word verbs

VOCABULARY

TELEVISION

1 A Work in pairs. Think of one similarity and one difference between the TV programmes. Use your dictionary to help if necessary.

1 a wildlife programme – a reality show
2 a costume drama – a soap opera
3 a sketch show – a sitcom
4 a documentary – a docudrama
5 a series – a serial
6 a thriller – a detective series
7 a game show – a quiz
8 a current affairs programme – the news

B Work in pairs and discuss. Which programme types above do you like the most/least? Give some examples.

READING

2 A Work in pairs and look at the photos of five programmes produced in the UK. What type of programme is each one? Why do you think each one is a global hit?

B Read the article and check your ideas.

C Why are sentences 1–8 false? Underline the relevant phrase or sentence in the article.

1 While nature programmes might be expected to be popular worldwide, costume dramas are only popular in the UK.
2 For a car programme, *Top Gear* has surprisingly few cars in it.
3 Viewers loved seeing the bullet train hit the supercar in *Top Gear*.
4 A lot of people thought *The Office* would be successful.
5 *The Office* is actually a serious documentary.
6 Everyone thought that people who liked Sherlock Holmes would welcome a new version.
7 Chinese viewers lost interest in *Sherlock* after the second season.
8 The only dancers on *Strictly Come Dancing* are professionals.

speakout TIP

Good writers use a range of vocabulary to refer to similar ideas, for example *quirky humour* and *slightly strange humour*. This makes a text more interesting for the reader.

D Find words in the article with similar meanings to the following. The numbers in brackets show the paragraph.

1 very good outcome(s) _successes_ (1) _____ (2)
2 mad or unconventional _____ (2) _____ 2)
3 worldwide extraordinary event _____ (2) _____ (3)
4 attracted _____ (2) _____ 4)
5 transmitted _____ (4) _____ (4)
6 brought back to life _____ (5) _____ (5)

E Discuss. Which of the programmes would you most like to watch?

NATURAL WORLD

UNLIKELY GLOBAL SUCCESSES

What sort of TV programme would you make if your goal was to appeal to the whole world? Obviously a well-made wildlife programme such as the BBC's *Natural World* series would travel well, with its visual content and cross-cultural appeal. Costume dramas and historical mini-series also seem to survive the transition to a different culture. But how about a car programme, a quirky British comedy or an old-fashioned dance competition? Recent years have seen **quite a few** unlikely successes for programmes with an appeal beyond their intended audience.

Would it surprise you to know that the most downloaded programme ever is *Top Gear*, which regularly attracts over 350 million viewers worldwide in 170 countries **every week**? And yes, we are talking about a car programme headed up by three middle-aged men. True, there are **a large number of** cars, very fast cars, but its appeal lies more in the jokey relationship between the three presenters and also in the crazy challenges that are a key feature of **each** programme. On one occasion, for example, the presenters' bizarre search for the source of the Nile pulled in millions of viewers, and a race between a supercar and a bullet train was **another** huge hit. Like it or loathe it, *Top Gear* truly is a global phenomenon.

THE OFFICE

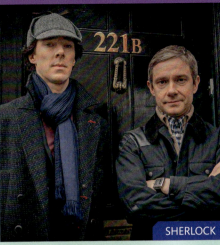

STRICTLY COME DANCING

SHERLOCK

Comedies rarely travel well and **many** people predicted *The Office* would flop because of its slightly strange British humour. Instead, the American version of the sitcom attracted 11.2 million viewers during its first showing in 2005. Since then, this 'mockumentary' has become an international sensation and has been copied **several** times. The French call it *Le Bureau* while those living in Chile have *La Ofis* and in Germany, it's *Stromberg*. It enjoys **a good deal of** popularity despite the fact that it features characters who aren't particularly funny and survive mundane office life by acting a little cooler than they really are. The boss is a deeply unattractive character who is respected by no one. However, *The Office* is a sitcom with a heart, centred around the romantic relationship between two main characters. Perhaps that's one reason why it has proved such a success.

There are **few** fictional characters as well known as Sherlock Holmes and when the BBC decided to give him a makeover, there was a real risk of alienating fans of the much-loved classic tales. The stories were updated to twenty-first century London, used state-of-the-art graphics and had two relatively unknown actors in the main parts. The BBC now has a worldwide hit on its hands. *Sherlock* is broadcast in more than 200 territories and the long-awaited first episode of the third season was viewed almost seven million times in China only a couple of hours after it was initially aired in the UK. As with *The Office*, people are drawn in by the intriguing relationships between the main characters, so maybe there's a theme developing here. However, this doesn't explain the appeal of our final programme.

Whoever could have imagined that *Come Dancing*, an old-fashioned dance competition popular in the 1960s, would be resurrected as *Strictly Come Dancing* in the UK and *Dancing With the Stars* in over forty-five countries who have bought the format? What's not to like? Show-stopping dances, celebrities, **plenty of** glamorous dresses, big band music, popular hosts and viewer participation, this programme has it all. Celebrity contestants with **little** or **no** experience of dancing pair up with professional dancers and perform in front of a live audience to impress the voting viewers and judges. A tired old format has been revitalised and gone global in a most unexpected way.

It all goes to show that when it comes to picking favourites, the audience will surprise you every time.

TOP GEAR

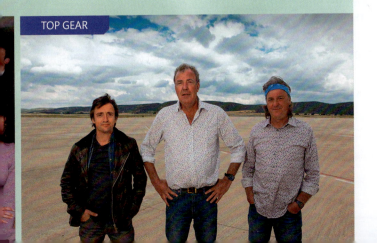

GRAMMAR

QUANTIFIERS

3 A Check what you know. Which of the quantifiers in bold in the article refer to: all; a lot; a moderate or small number/amount; an additional one; zero?

B Complete the rules with the type of noun: *singular*, *plural* or *uncountable*. Use the article to help.

> **RULES**
>
> 1 Use *several, few, a large number of, quite a few* + <u>Plural</u> noun.
> 2 Use *little, a good deal of* + _____ *uncountable* noun.
> 3 Use *every, each* + <u>singular</u> noun.
> 4 Use *plenty of, no* + <u>plu</u> or <u>uncountable</u> noun.
> 5 Use *another* + <u>singular</u> noun.

C In sentences 1–4 below, do the quantifiers *few* and *little* mean *some* or *not many/not much*?

1 There are <u>few</u> fictional characters that are as well known as Sherlock Holmes.
2 There are <u>a few</u> programmes I never miss, perhaps three or four every week.
3 Celebrity contestants with <u>little</u> or no experience of dancing …
4 I always try to spend <u>a little</u> time watching the news each day, at least half an hour.

▷ page 130 **LANGUAGEBANK**

4 A ▶ 7.1 Listen and write sentences 1–5 in your notebook.

B **CONNECTED SPEECH: linking** Draw links between final consonants and initial vowels in the quantifiers.

1 All_of_us watch lots_of TV.

C Listen and check. Then listen again and repeat.

5 A Find and correct one mistake in each sentence.

1 I watch very little sports programmes.
2 Every programmes have a commercial break every ten minutes.
3 The weekend schedules usually include few talent shows, at least three or four.
4 I like each programmes about hospitals or emergencies.
5 I once spent quite few days watching a box set of the series *24*.
6 I think a large number of TV has been dumbed down.
7 We have plenty detective shows; we don't need more.
8 I think little news is OK but not 24-hour news non-stop.

B Make the sentences true for you or your country.

C Work with other students and compare your answers. How many points do you have in common?

D Report back on three interesting results.

SPEAKING

6 A Work in pairs and discuss the questions.

1 What are the benefits of watching TV online as opposed to on a TV?

2 What types of TV shows do people tend to watch online?

3 What types do you watch online?

4 Would you allow a child online access to a TV or a computer? If not, how would you limit it?

B Work alone. Read the following statements and put a tick (✓) if you agree and a cross (✗) if you disagree.

1 TV and online news is the best way to stay accurately informed about current events.

2 TV programmes and online video hits are a vital part of people's shared cultural experience.

3 Watching TV is bad for you because it robs you of time you might spend exercising.

4 The negative effect of violence in TV programmes and online media is exaggerated. Violent people will do violent things anyway.

5 Watching online video or TV has a negative effect on your concentration span.

6 Sitcoms often provide positive role models for children.

C Talk to other students. Find out how many statements you disagree about. Give reasons.

VOCABULARY PLUS

MULTI-WORD VERBS
= phrasal verbs *(handwritten: 引用する, 짱?? , ex)*

7 A Which programmes in the box might the quotes below come from?

(handwritten numbers above box: 2 1 4 5 / 6 ... 3)

> Natural World   Top Gear   Dancing with the Stars   Sherlock
> The Office   World News

1 'The company has just brought out an electric version of the 408. It's superb! I take back everything I've said about electric models.'

2 'We've just come across a herd of elephants on our way through the jungle. The rain is making it difficult to film but we'll have to put up with it for a few more days.'

3 'Over five hundred turned out to cheer the runners to the finish.'

4 'A marvellous couple! And that dress! It takes me back to my teenage days! And it brings out the colour of your eyes.'

5 'He comes across as a helpful member of the public but it turns out that he's the mastermind behind the crimes. Clever!'

6 'I've lost the key to my flat. Could you put me up for the night?' Otherwise I'll have to sleep at my desk. Like I do most of the day!'

B Underline ten multi-word verbs in quotes 1–6.

C Match meanings 1–10 with the multi-word verbs in Exercise 7A. Add *something* (sth) or *somebody* (sb) in the correct place if the verb takes an object. One verb is a three-part verb.

1 introduce (a product) or make something available *bring sth out*

2 emphasise, or make something easier to notice *bring sth out*

3 tolerate *put up with sb/sth*

4 let someone stay in your home for a short time *put sb up.*

5 meet by chance *come across*

6 seem to have particular qualities *come across (as)*

7 make somebody remember *take sb back (to)*

8 accept you were wrong to say something *take sth back.*

9 go to watch or be involved in an event *turn out*

10 happen in the end *turn out*

8 A Cover the exercises above and complete the sentences.

1 What's one sound, smell or taste that takes you *back* to your childhood?

2 Do you think you come *across* as an extrovert or an introvert? *(handwritten: 외향성, 내향)*

3 What sort of person do you find it most difficult to put *up* with?

4 Do you always turn *out* to vote in an election?

5 What situation brings *out* the best – and worst – in your English?

6 Imagine you've been dating someone for a year and it turns *out* that they've lied about their age. What would you do?

7 Have you ever come *across* an old friend in an unexpected place?

8 When they brought *out* 3D films, did you think they were worth it?

9 Would you ever put *up* a stranger in your home?

10 If you criticised someone and later found out you were wrong, would you take *back* what you said and apologise?

B Work in pairs. Take turns asking and answering the questions.

▷ page 139 **VOCABULARY BANK**

THE CAMERA NEVER LIES

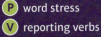

G reported speech
P word stress
V reporting verbs

7.2

A Abandoned bicycle swallowed up by tree

B Man survives cross-Channel journey in landing gear

C Sharks infest flooded suburban town

LISTENING

1 A Look at photos A–C. Do you think the news events really happened or are they hoaxes?

B ▶ 7.2 Listen to the interview and check.

C Listen again and tick the true statement(s) in each sentence.

1 The guest wants to remain anonymous because
  a) he thinks mystery is important.
  b) he doesn't want to get sued. *cold*

2 Police pay him to
  a) work out if a photo is a hoax.
  b) find out who did it.

3 He says the bike photo
  a) is easy to put together from two photos.
  b) was put together by a friend of his.

4 The guest says the plane photo
  a) could be real.
  b) is well done.

5 He laughs at the shark photo because
  a) hoax photos with sharks are common.
  b) this one looks so fake.

6 People who produce hoax photos do it because
  a) they can make good money.
  b) they feel excited when the hoax succeeds.

D Tick the statements you agree with. Then discuss your ideas with a partner.

1 When I see a photo in the media, I assume it's real.

2 It should be illegal to publish hoax photos. It's the same as publishing false news.

3 It's unfair to show a famous person in an embarrassing situation in a hoax photo.

4 It's more fun to be tricked by a hoax photo than to find out that it's fake.

GRAMMAR
REPORTED SPEECH

2 A Check what you know. Which sentences below report a) a statement, b) a request or c) a question?

C 1 I asked you before the show if you'd ever earned money for your hoax work.

a 2 A friend told me he had seen it with his own eyes a number of years before.

a? 3 You said that you often work with the police.

b 4 Sometimes the police ask me to look at it.

B For the sentences in Exercise 2A, write the exact words each person said.

1 *'Have you ever earned money for your hoax work?'*

C Work in pairs and complete the rules.

> **RULES**
>
> **1** In reported statements and questions the verbs usually shift back if the reporting verb (*say, tell*, etc.) is in the *past/present*.
>
> **2** This doesn't happen in sentence *1/2/3/4* because the reported information is *always true/still true*.
>
> **3** In reported questions the word order is the same as *a question/an affirmative statement*.
>
> **4** To report a request, use *ask somebody* + infinitive with *to/gerund*.

▷ page 130 **LANGUAGEBANK**

3 A Work in pairs. Who says each of these sentences, the presenter (P) or the hoaxer (H)?

1 Can you explain why you want to remain anonymous?

2 What exactly do you do for the police?

3 Talk us through the photographs if you would.

4 I wasn't sure myself, but I found out it was near Seattle, Washington.

5 Is there a technical reason why you know it's a hoax?

6 I'm thrilled when people believe one of my photos.

B Write the sentences in reported speech. Start with *He/She said/asked.*

83

VOCABULARY
REPORTING VERBS

4 A Read the news story and discuss with a partner. Do you think Les Brown is telling the truth?

Insurance hoax?

An insurance company has accused a Louisville man of faking injuries from an on-the-job accident in order to get a large insurance payment. Les Brown, 49, denies lying to authorities about his injuries, and has promised to prove that photos showing him playing tennis are fake. Brown has refused to speak to journalists about the matter.

B Read the update to the story below. Have you read about any similar stories in the news?

Faced with clear evidence, Les Brown has admitted faking his injuries to cheat the insurance company. His ex-wife persuaded him to stop lying about the situation after authorities warned Brown to tell the truth or face a long jail term. Brown has apologised for embarrassing his family and has agreed to pay a large fine.

C Look again at the texts and underline all the reporting verbs.

D Write each reporting verb next to the pattern that follows it.

1 -ing form	deny doing / admit doing
2 preposition + -ing form	apologise+ for + ing sth
3 object + preposition + -ing form	*accuse sb of doing sth*
4 infinitive	promise to + inf, agree / refuse to + inf,
5 object + infinitive	warm sb to+inf /not to+inf / persuad sb to do sth.

5 A Check what you know. Add the verbs in the box to the table above. If you are not sure, use examples in a dictionary to help.

tell   invite   suggest   advise   remind   threaten   offer

B ▶ 7.3   **WORD STRESS** Work in pairs. Which reporting verbs in the completed table have the stress on the first and which on the second syllable? Listen and check.

C Complete the sentences so they are negative.

1 He accused them of not taking (take) his injuries seriously.
2 He persuaded his doctor to not talk (talk) to the media.
3 His wife told him to not lie (lie) about the situation.
4 He apologised for not telling (tell) the truth.
5 The authorities warned him to not do (do) it again.

(• not to+inf
  • for not doing.

6 A Complete the questions with the correct form of the verb in brackets.

Questions of Trust

Situation 1

A colleague has a photo of you at an office party doing something embarrassing. He threatens to show it to your boss unless you pay him a small sum of money. Would you:

a) agree to pay (pay) the money since it's a small amount, just to avoid trouble?
b) deny doing (do) anything wrong and tell your colleague to do whatever he wants?
c) talk to your boss and apologise for acting (act) stupidly?

Situation 2

Someone shows you a printout of an email written by your best friend. It's full of negative comments about you and also contains a few secrets that you told your friend. Would you:

a) accuse your friend of betraying (betray) you?
b) refuse to believe (believe) that the email is real, and do nothing?
c) make your friend admit writing (write) the original email and warn him/her never to do it again (never do)?

Situation 3

A year ago, you promised to take a friend out to dinner for her birthday at an expensive restaurant. She's just reminded you, but now you don't really have the time or money. Should you:

a) promise to take (take) her but next year?
b) persuade her to go (go) to a cheaper restaurant?
c) tell her the situation and apologise for not keeping (not keep) your promise?

Situation 4

Your boss has offered to give you a bonus if you write a report that will have her name on it and that she will take full credit for. Would you:

a) offer to do (do) it but only if she gives you credit, too?
b) suggest asking (ask) someone else?
c) say no and threaten to report (report) your boss to her boss?

B Work in pairs. Take turns to ask and answer the questions in Exercise 6A.

SPEAKING

argument.

7 A Work in pairs. Look at statements 1–4. Choose two statements and write one reason for and one reason against each one. Give examples to support your ideas.

changing
1 Manipulation of images in advertising is justified in order to make a message stronger.
2 Idealised images of models in media can have a positive effect on ordinary people.
3 The media should be free to examine the lives of public figures.
4 The media should focus more on the lives of ordinary people rather than on famous people.

B Work with other students and compare your ideas.

WRITING

A DISCURSIVE ESSAY; LEARN TO USE LINKERS OF CONTRAST

8 A Read the essay and discuss. Which topic in Exercise 7A is it about? Do you agree with the writer's point of view?

These days the media is full of stories of celebrities' private lives: their relationships, rows, problems with weight and so on. In fact, the public seems to have a never-ending appetite for this type of gossip.

It could be argued that celebrities invite publicity despite knowing that this will leave them open to public attention. Therefore, it is hypocritical for them to complain when the media shows interest in other aspects of their lives. Also, celebrities are influential role models to many people and because of this, their private lives should be open to public examination. Additionally, the public have the right to know about the rich and famous since it is our money that supports them.

However, there are several reasons why celebrities deserve a certain level of privacy. Firstly, while some people actively seek fame, others do not. For example, a person might want to be a great tennis player but not wish to suffer media intrusion into their family's private life. Secondly, although reporters might claim an item is 'in the public interest' often, in fact, they are more interested in selling a sensational story. Lastly, the unwelcome attentions of reporters and photographers can put celebrities under great stress.

On balance, I believe that celebrities have the right to the same kind of privacy as anyone else. Just because on some occasions they invite interest in order to publicise their work, this does not mean that they should not be able to say 'no'.

Note.

B Read the essay again and underline the correct alternative.

1 The introductory paragraph *explains why the topic is of interest/gives the writer's opinion about the topic.*
2 Paragraph two gives points *for/for and against* the idea.
3 Paragraph three gives points *against/for and against* the idea.
4 The conclusion *asks the reader's/gives the writer's opinion.*

9 A Look at sentences 1–4. Circle the linker which is used to show a contrasting idea. *main.*

1 Celebrities invite publicity despite knowing that this will leave them open to public attention.
2 While some people seek fame, others never want or plan for it. *main*
3 Although a reporter might claim that a story is 'in the public interest', often they are more interested in selling a sensational story. *main.*
4 However, there are a number of reasons why celebrities deserve our sympathy. *main*

B Work in pairs and answer the questions. *comma.*

1 What punctuation follows *However*?
2 Which form follows *despite*? *verb + ing.*
3 In sentences 1, 2 and 3, which is the main clause?
4 Do the linkers in 1, 2 and 3 introduce the main clause or the subordinate clause?

C Use the linkers in brackets to connect the ideas in two different ways. *while = although*

1 some celebrities are good role models for young people / others set a negative example (however, although)
2 anonymously published internet news is unreliable / many people rely on it as a main source of information (despite, while)
3 false reports of celebrity deaths are common / some people still believe them (while, however)
4 the scandal damaged his reputation / he still has millions of fans (although, despite)

10 A Write notes for the four sections of a discursive essay on one of the other topics in Exercise 7A.

B Write the essay (250–300 words).

F adding emphasis
P sentence stress
V the press

VOCABULARY

THE PRESS

1 A What do you think are the most popular topics in newspapers? Read the article below and check your ideas.

Six topics that keep the tabloids in business

In an age when quality newspapers are seeing a serious drop in **circulation**, tabloid journalism is in no danger of dying out. Six topics always guarantee sales:

1 Scandal – the public loves glimpses into the lives of the rich, famous and powerful and scandal fuels **tabloid** sales.

2 Money – everyone wants it, and some people will stop at nothing to get it. Many tabloids have a regular **feature** about money.

3 Babies – whether it's because they were born in a taxi or can speak two languages from birth, it seems we can't get enough of them.

4 Animals – flip through any tabloid and you'll find a heart-warming story about a brave dog, or a cat that's befriended a mouse.

5 Royalty – hardly a day goes by that a 'royal' doesn't make an appearance in a morning **edition**.

6 Winners – from lottery winners to Olympic gold medallists, a winner on the front cover guarantees high sales.

Bold headlines, plenty of appealing photos, a low price and a colour **supplement** or two make tabloids the perfect escape from real life. They aren't afraid to be **biased** and show their opinion, most strikingly in the **editorial page**, which tends to be direct and aggressive in stating the editor's position on major issues. The public want excitement and **sensationalism**, and tabloids deliver.

B Match meanings 1–8 with the words in bold in the article.

1 a popular newspaper, half the size of a standard newspaper, with few serious stories *tabloid*

2 the section that gives the paper's opinion *editorial page* 社説

3 a special report or article about a topic *feature*

4 giving a single point of view, unfairly *biased*

5 an extra section of a newspaper which can be pulled out, often a magazine *supplement* 付録

6 reporting news to make it sound as exciting as possible *sensationalism*

7 the set of newspapers which are published at the same time *edition* 部数

8 the number of newspapers sold in a day or week *circulation* 発行部数

C Work in pairs and discuss the questions.

1 Which paper in your country is the most sensationalist/biased?

2 Which sections of a newspaper or online news do you read first, e.g. sports, etc.?

3 Which sections or stories do you never read?

▷ **page 139 VOCABULARYBANK**

A **Shop Clerk Cheats Lottery Winners**

B **MATCH FIXING SHOCK**

FUNCTION

ADDING EMPHASIS

2 A Work in pairs and look at tabloid headlines A–F above. What do you think the stories are about?

B ▶ 7.4 Listen to the conversations. Which headlines do they talk about?

C Listen again. What surprises the woman most in each story?

3 A Work in pairs. Underline the phrases that the speakers use to add emphasis.

1 The amazing thing is that the tiger ran off.

2 Wow, there's no way I'd do that!

3 You're the one who's always telling me to stop.

4 That is so wrong!

5 That's totally outrageous!

6 I do think they should do something about it.

7 That *is* a good idea.

8 How on earth did he catch it?

9 That's such an amazing thing!

10 Absolutely incredible!

B Work in pairs and discuss the questions.

1 What is the difference between *so* and *such*?

2 In sentence 6, what is unusual?

3 In sentences 5 and 10, what other modifiers could be used with the adjectives?

4 How is the beginning of sentence 3 different from 'You're always telling me …'?

5 In sentence 8, what expression is added to a question word to show surprise?

C ▶ 7.5 **SENTENCE STRESS** Work in pairs and mark the main stresses in the sentences in Exercise 3A. Listen and check. Then listen and repeat.

speakout TIP

The words that show surprise are usually stressed and said with high intonation (pitch). It's a good idea to exaggerate when you practise this to help you get it right.

▷ **page 130 LANGUAGEBANK**

C **Baby Saved From Ledge Fall**

D **Prince takes first steps**

E **WIFE'S LADLE SAVES MAN FROM TIGER**

F **POP STAR LOVE TRIANGLE**

4 A Rewrite the sentences to add emphasis using the words in brackets and making any other changes necessary.

Conversation 1

A: I'm *so* angry with you. Why didn't you tell me about the party? (so)

B: But I *did* told you. A few minutes ago. (did)

A: That's *really* helpful! How am I supposed to get ready in time? (really)

B: But *you're the one who* you said you never want to go to parties. (one)

Conversation 2

A: Dave's good-looking but she's *absolutely* crazy about Will. (absolutely)

B: ~~It's sad,~~ *The sad thing is* Dave adores her. (the sad thing)

A: Yeah, and he's really kind; *such* a nice man. (such)

B: What *on earth* shall I say if he asks me about Will? (earth)

Conversation 3

A: I'm quitting my job. It's *so* badly paid and it's *such a* hard work. (so, such)

B: I think you'll *do* regret it. (do)

A: ~~You~~ *You're the one who* always say I should do what I want. (one)

B: But you shouldn't just quit. (no way) *there's no way you sould just quite*

B Work in pairs and add two more sentences to each conversation. Add emphasis to one of your sentences in each conversation.

C Cover and practise the conversations.

LEARN TO

MAKE GUESSES

5 A Work in pairs and try to complete the extract. Then check your ideas in audio script 7.4 on page 149.

A: It's lucky the men noticed the baby.

B: Yeah, I ¹*think* they saw some movement.

A: Or ²*perhaps* they heard something.

B: What's that? The woman's bringing something.

A: It's ³*difficul* to say but it ⁴*seems* like a cushion.

B: Yeah, it ⁵*'s surely* be a sofa cushion.

A: I ⁶*imagine* they thought the baby might fall on it.

B: That ⁷*might* be the luckiest baby alive.

B Which words in 1–7 above could be replaced by words in the box?

> difficult   seems   perhaps   think   might
> 's surely   imagine

6 A ▶ 7.6 Listen to the sound. What do you think it is? Write down two ideas.

B Use the prompts to discuss the sound.

A: What / you / think / it / be?

B: hard / say / but / might / be (your first idea)

A: think / sound / like (your first idea)

B: suppose / could / be (another idea)

A: Or / perhaps / be (another idea)

B: Well / think / it / be (final decision)

C ▶ 7.7 Listen to five more sounds. Practise the conversation after each one.

SPEAKING

7 A Work in pairs and look at the categories. What do you think the top five are for each category?

The top five …
1 most dangerous animals
2 countries with the tallest people
3 cities for art lovers
4 friendliest countries

A: *I imagine the most dangerous animal is a tiger. What do you think?*
B: *I'm not sure. I suppose it could be, but …*

B Work in groups and take turns. Student A: turn to page 143, Student B: turn to page 144, Student C: turn to page 145, Student D: turn to page 146. Student A: tell the other students your category and see how many items they can guess. Tell them the answers they don't guess. Discuss which answers are the most surprising.

DVD PREVIEW

1 A Work in pairs and discuss the questions.

1 How often do you watch the news? Are the newsreaders in your country always serious?

2 What are the pros and cons of working as a TV newsreader?

3 The name of the programme you're going to watch is *The Funny Side of the News*. What do you think it's about?

B Read the programme information and answer the questions.

1 Why are there more mistakes on TV news than there used to be?

2 How many different types of mistakes are mentioned?

◗)) The Funny Side of the News

BBC

The Funny Side of … is a BBC series that looks at all the things that can go wrong on TV, from talent shows to wildlife programmes. Tonight it takes a look at TV news. As serious as news can be, mistakes and **blunders** are unavoidable. And with the introduction of 24-hour **rolling** news, mistakes have become more frequent and more visible with newsreaders **stumbling over their words** and endless **technical hiccups**. From microphones **malfunctioning** to the wrong guest being brought into the studio for an interview, disaster is waiting to **strike** at any moment.

C Look at the programme information again and match the words/phrases in bold with 1–6 below.

1 hesitating or making mistakes when speaking *stumbling over their words*

2 happen suddenly and cause damage *strike*

3 small problems with machines

4 continuous *rolling*

5 mistakes *malfunctioning*

6 going wrong (for a machine) *technical hiccups*

DVD VIEW

2 A Watch the DVD and make notes on which blunder:

• you found the funniest.

• you didn't find funny or didn't understand.

B Work in pairs. Number the blunders in the order they appear in the programme. Some have more than one example (there are seven). Then watch the DVD again and check.

Malfunctioning equipment *1*

People stumbling over their words

The wrong guest in an interview

An accident on a live programme

A: There was the bit where the woman …

B: Yes, and there was the part where the guy …

C Complete extracts 1–5 from the DVD. Then watch again and check.

1 So if it starts going _____, you're going to see it.

2 The _____ about rolling news _____ that you have to fill an awful lot of time …

3 I'm afraid we obviously have the wrong guest here. That's deeply _____ for us.

4 But the undisputed _____ of the wrong guest division is the BBC News 24 incident _____ the charming but inappropriate Guy Goma.

5 It goes to _____ just how much the public love a good news blunder.

D Discuss. Which incident do you think was the most embarrassing for the newsreader?

speakout a news story

3 A ▶ **7.8** Listen to someone retelling a news story about a man who swapped a paper clip for a house. Number the things he traded in the correct order.

a paper clip *1*
a snow globe
a pen shaped like a fish
a house
a door knob
a part in a film

B Listen again and tick the phrases you hear.

> **KEY PHRASES**
>
> Did you [hear this story/see the news] about … ?
> I [heard this story/read this article] about …
> Apparently what happened was …
> According to [the report/the guy on the news] …
> Anyway, so he …
> I don't remember all the details, but …
> The [weird/strange/interesting thing] was …

C Think about a recent news story. Make notes listing the events in the story and think about which key phrases you can use.

D Work in groups and tell each other your stories. Ask follow-up questions and take notes. Which story was the most interesting?

writeback a short summary

4 A Read the article and write down the one thing that the man traded that is mentioned in the article but not in the recording.

Man trades paper clip for house

A Canadian man has made headlines by trading a paper clip for a house. Bored blogger Kyle Macdonald started by exchanging small objects – a pen, a door knob, a neon sign – but step by step the 26-year-old built up to items of larger and larger value, and after one year his journey from paper clip owner to homeowner was over.

B Read the article again and do the tasks.

1 Circle three different ways that Kyle Macdonald is referred to in the story apart from *he* or *his*.
2 Underline two places where the writer uses two different words for the same thing.
3 Put a box round two places where a word is repeated. What effect does this have?

C The article is exactly 60 words. Imagine your editor tells you to cut it to exactly 45 words. Which words could you omit without losing important details (hyphenated words count as one word)?

D Write an article of exactly 60 words about one of the stories your group told in Exercise 3D. You may need to invent some details.

E Student A: read your article aloud. Other students: is it a summary of the story you told in Exercise 3D? If so, is it accurate?

TELEVISION

1 A Find fifteen kinds of TV programme in the wordsnake.

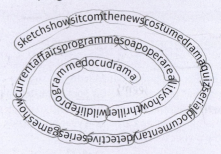

sketchshowsitcomthenewscostumedramaquizseriditysho wthrillerwildlifeprogrammedocudramadetectiveseriesgameshowcurrentaffairsprogrammesoapoperareality

B Work in pairs. Which type of programme would you choose if you wanted to:

• laugh?
• learn something?
• just relax and watch real people?
• catch up on the news?
• test your knowledge?

QUANTIFIERS

2 A Work in pairs and underline the correct alternative. The sentences are about two people.

1 *Both/Few* of us enjoy spending time in airports.
2 *None/Neither* of us plays a musical instrument.
3 We remember *a large amount of/quite a few of* our dreams.
4 Both of us take *a few/a little* sugar in our coffee.
5 We both got *hardly any/very few* sleep last night.
6 *Neither/Both* of us is allergic to anything.
7 We like *all/every* type of music.
8 We would like to live in *other/another* country.
9 We spend *several/a great deal of* hours in the gym every week.
10 We both like having *few/a few* minutes' sleep in the afternoon.

B Which sentences are true for you and your partner? Change any that are not true.

A: Do you enjoy spending time in airports?
B: No.
A: Me neither. OK, so neither of us enjoys spending time in airports.

REPORTED SPEECH

3 A Rewrite the sentences in reported speech.

1 Last week, an interviewer asked me, 'What's your biggest weakness?'
2 The other day, a complete stranger walked up to me and asked, 'What have you been doing lately?'
3 Once, I was trying on trousers and the shop assistant asked, 'Would you like to try a bigger size?'
4 Every day, my flatmate says, 'Could you do the dishes?' and then says, 'I'll do them next time.'
5 At the end of a first date, the girl asked me, 'So when do you want to get married?'
6 At 3a.m., my phone rang, and the caller asked, 'Are you sleeping?'

B Which question would make you feel the most uncomfortable?

REPORTING VERBS

4 A Complete the questions with the correct form of a verb in the box. Add any necessary words.

| ~~help~~ quit lend make |
| do pay be (x2) |

1 When was the last time you offered _to help_ someone?
2 Do you find it easy to admit _____ a mistake?
3 Would you ever agree _____ a friend a large amount of money?
4 Have you ever refused _____ a bill?
5 Would you always apologise _____ late?
6 Have you ever threatened _____ your job?
7 Have you ever been accused _____ too serious?
8 Do you often promise _____ something and then simply forget?

B Work in pairs and discuss the questions above.

ADDING EMPHASIS

5 A Find and correct the mistakes. There is one extra word in each sentence.

1 My hometown is such a so boring place.
2 I so do think that some people are very generous.
3 It's totally very ridiculous that people have such short holidays.
4 Why on the earth am I learning English?
5 Really, there's that's no way I would ever borrow money from a friend.
6 My teacher was the one who she had the most influence on me when I was young.
7 Sometimes learning English is so such difficult that I want to give up.
8 I like cooking, but the surprising thing that is that I never do it.

B Work in pairs and take turns. Student A: read one of your sentences from Exercise 5A. Student B: continue the conversation using some of these follow-up questions.

How do you mean?

In what way?

Why (not)?

For example?

What makes you say that?

IT'S A TOUGH CALL p92

FAIR SHARE p95

HAVE YOU GOT A MINUTE? p98

THE HUMAN ANIMAL p100

SPEAKING 8.1 Talk about difficult decisions you've made 8.2 Talk about values and behaviour 8.3 Deal with awkward situations 8.4 Give advice on how to behave in your culture

LISTENING 8.2 Listen to an experiment about fairness 8.4 Watch a BBC documentary about body language

READING 8.1 Read three articles about life-changing decisions

WRITING 8.2 Write an informal article; Use linkers of purpose 8.4 Write about behaviour in your culture

BBC INTERVIEWS

What kind of behaviour gets on your nerves?

READING

1 A Work in pairs. Look at the photos and read the headlines. What do you think happened in each situation? Write two predictions about each one.

B Read the articles and check your ideas.

C Look at statements 1–8 below. Who do you think said each one?

1 I'm looking for something to support my family. *Delroy Simmonds*

2 Her face wasn't covered so I recognised her immediately.

3 She said, 'I have a lot of money in that couch and I really need it.'

4 I'm incredibly grateful, and my three other kids are too.

5 It was hard for him. I think that's why he came in with his brother.

6 Look, there's something in here.

7 You shouldn't have done that.

8 We laid it all out and we were screaming.

D Work in pairs and discuss. Who had the most difficult decision: the three roommates, Simmonds or McQuinn's father? Do you think you would have behaved in the same way?

---

2 Man misses job interview to save baby from train

An unemployed Brooklyn man missed a job interview for the best of reasons: He was saving the life of a nine-month-old boy who was blown into the path of an oncoming subway train by a gust of high wind. Like a superhero without a cape, Delroy Simmonds jumped onto the tracks and lifted the bleeding child – still strapped into his stroller – to the safety of the platform as the train bore down on them. 'If he hadn't jumped down there, the baby wouldn't be alive,' said a worker at the station. 'Everybody thinks I'm some sort of superhero,' the father of two said. 'I'm just a normal person. Anybody would have done the same.' A friend of Simmonds thought differently. 'If that had happened to me, I might not have jumped.'

The out-of-work Brooklyn native was on his way to apply for a maintenance position at a warehouse. 'A strong gust of wind blew,' he recalled. 'There was a woman with four kids. One was in a stroller. The wind blew the baby onto the tracks.' He had no time to assess the situation. 'The train was coming around the corner as I lifted the baby from the tracks. I really wasn't thinking.'

---

1 New York roommates find $40,000 in sofa

Three roommates who bought a used couch for $20 found $40,000 in cash stashed inside and returned the money to the 91-year-old widow who had hidden it there.

Cally Guasti said that she and her friends had bought the beat-up couch and a chair for $55 at a Salvation Army thrift store. They noticed the arm cushions were weirdly lumpy. Then roommate Reese Werkhoven opened a zipper on one arm and found an envelope. It contained $4,000 in bubble-wrapped bills. Guasti, Werkhoven and roommate Lara Russo opened the other arm zipper and started mining the treasure stashed inside. They counted it up: $40,800.

Later on, Guasti found a deposit slip with a woman's name on it, and then phoned her. They drove to the home of the woman, who cried in gratitude when they gave her the cash she had hidden away.

Guasti said the three had considered the option of keeping the money, but decided they couldn't do that. It went against their principles. 'At the end of the day, it wasn't ours,' Guasti said. 'I think if any of us had used it, it would have felt really wrong.'

---

3 FATHER TURNS IN BANK-ROBBING DAUGHTER

An Adelaide man made the hardest choice of his life this weekend: he turned his own daughter into police after recognising her photo from a police report about a recent string of bank robberies. Neighbour Bill Baugely says the heartbroken dad was trying to protect his daughter. 'It's a really tough situation,' Baugely said, 'But I would have done the same thing.'

Twenty-seven-year-old Anne McQuinn was allegedly seen at the St George Bank in King William Street, at the Suncorp Bank in Grenfell Street, and at a bank in nearby Elizabeth in the past few months. Sergeant Tom Landers of the Adelaide police said, 'The father came into the station with the woman's uncle. They'd seen the photos on TV and the internet, and were sure it was McQuinn.'

Police say the father didn't want to put off the decision once he saw it was his daughter and came in immediately. 'The surveillance photos were clear,' said police. 'He really had no doubt it was her.'

The father said most of his friends were supportive, but not everyone. Local resident Gerry Comber said, 'OK, the guy wants to do the right thing, but who turns in their own daughter?'

VOCABULARY

COLLOCATIONS: DECISIONS

2 A Find verbs in the articles to complete the word webs.

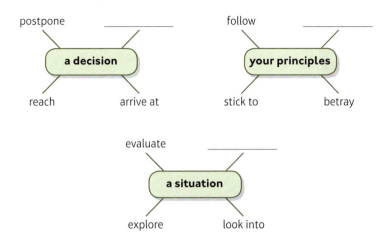

postpone _____   follow _____

a decision   **your principles**

reach   arrive at   stick to   betray

evaluate _____

a situation

explore   look into

B Each word web has two pairs of words with similar meanings. Draw a line to connect each pair.

C Match two collocations from Exercise 2B to each definition.

1 choose to do one thing or another   *arrive at a decision,*
2 delay deciding
3 be faithful to what you believe is right
4 do something that you don't believe is right
5 look at a situation in detail
6 judge a situation

3 A Read the extracts from a web forum below. Complete the texts with the correct form of the verbs from Exercise 2A. More than one answer is possible.

> ☆ At the store my food came to $10. I gave the cashier $20 but she gave me $100 in change. Obviously, she thought she'd given me a $10 note. I ¹_____ the situation – I needed money badly, it was her mistake. Should I ²_____ my principles and keep the money although I knew she might have to pay the missing cash back herself? In the end, I ³_____ a decision ...

> ☆ The night before my final school exams, a classmate sent me an email with the exam answers in an attachment. What should I do? Ignore the email or ⁴_____ the situation by asking him why he'd sent it and who else he'd sent it to? I really wanted to ⁵_____ my principles and do the exam without cheating. I ⁶_____ the decision by going to bed. In the morning, it was clear to me what to do ...

B Work in pairs and discuss.

1 What do you think each person did? Do you think that was a good decision?
2 Can you remember a time when you took a long time to reach a decision or where you decided to stick to your principles?

GRAMMAR

PAST AND MIXED CONDITIONALS

4 A Look at the sentences and underline all the verbs.

1 I think if any of us had used it, it would have felt really wrong.
2 If that had happened to me, I might not have jumped.
3 I would have done the same thing.
4 If he hadn't jumped down there, the baby wouldn't be alive.

B Work in pairs and answer the questions about sentences 1–4 above.

1 Do they refer to real or hypothetical situations?
2 Does each sentence refer to the past, or to the past and present?
3 Sentence 3 has only one (result) clause. Why is it unnecessary to have a conditional clause? In the second text find another example of a result clause on its own.

C Complete the rules with the words in the box.

modal (x2)   past perfect   *have*
infinitive   past participle

> **RULES**
>
> **1** In the conditional clause use: the <u>past perfect</u> to talk about the hypothetical past.
> **2** In the result clause use:
> a) <u>modal</u> + <u>have</u> + <u>past participle</u> to talk about the past.
> b) <u>modal</u> + <u>infinitive</u> to talk about the present.

5 ▶ 8.1   **CONNECTED SPEECH: weak forms** Listen and match the words in bold in sentences 1–4 with the weak forms a)–d). Then listen again and repeat.

1 I **would have** done the same.
2 I **might have** behaved differently.
3 I **wouldn't have** been so brave.
4 I **couldn't have** done what he did.

a) /ˈmaɪtəv/
b) /ˈkʊdəntəv/
c) /ˈwʊdəntəv/
d) /ˈwʊdəv/

▷ page 132 **LANGUAGEBANK**

6 Read the situations 1–3 and complete the sentences a) and b) with the correct form of the verbs in brackets.

1 A hiker saved two strangers lost on a snowy mountain by sharing his food and water with them and risking his own life.

a) If they _____ (be) more prepared when they set out that morning, he _____ (not need) to risk his own life.

b) They _____ (be) dead now if he _____ (leave) them there.

2 A 39-year-old man saved a woman by pulling her out of her burning car, which exploded moments later.

a) They both _____ (could die) if it _____ (take) any longer to pull her out.

b) Most of the other people there _____ (not do) that.

3 A woman found a winning lottery ticket and used the money to buy a house. Later she had to return the money to the original owner of the ticket, who still had the receipt proving he had bought it.

a) I _____ (feel) pretty bad if I _____ (do) what that woman did, and if I'd been caught.

b) If the man _____ (not save) the receipt, he _____ (might never recover) the money.

SPEAKING

7 A Think of decisions you've made: good and bad, easy and hard, major and minor. Look at the topics for ideas, and make notes about two situations.

> a subject you chose to study at school

> a job you accepted or turned down

> a trip you took, or almost took

> an activity you took part in or avoided

> a relationship you got into, or out of

> a school or university you chose to attend

B Work with other students and take turns. Ask and answer questions 1–5 about each situation. Who had the most difficult decision?

1 Where did it happen?
2 What happened leading up to the situation?
3 How did you feel, and what did you do?
4 What else could you have done?
5 Would you do the same again?

VOCABULARY *PLUS*

COMPOUND ADJECTIVES

8 A Work in pairs and discuss. How could you reword these phrases without using the compound adjectives?

1 the 91-year-old widow
2 $4,000 in bubble-wrapped bills
3 bank-robbing daughter

B Work in pairs and find a compound adjective above which is formed with:

1 a past participle
2 a present participle (verb + -ing)
3 a number and measure of age/time

speakout TIP

Compound adjectives are made up of two or more words that form a single idea. They often have hyphens. With phrases expressing quantity, do not use a plural: *nine-month-old baby* NOT ~~nine-months-old baby~~.

C Complete the sentences using a compound adjective formed from the underlined words.

1 The baby is three days old. She's a …
2 I like clothes that people make by hand. I like …
3 That wall is 15 metres high. It's a …
4 That moment changed my life. It was a …
5 The TV series has run for a long time. It's a …
6 The course is five years long. It's a …
7 Elaine Jones has very good qualifications. She's very …
8 Research is an activity that consumes a lot of time. It's a …

9 A Rewrite the sentences using a compound adjective that expresses the meaning in brackets.

1 A _____ child shouldn't be left alone at home. (one who is twelve years old)
2 All outdoor cafés should be _____. (you can't smoke there)
3 A _____ holiday is too long. (it lasts two months)
4 It's hard for me to remember names, especially _____ names. (ones that sound odd)
5 Auto manufacturers should spend more money developing a _____ car. (solar energy powers it)
6 I would never live at the top of a _____ building. (it's twenty storeys)

B Tick (✓) the statements you agree with, and put a cross (✗) if you disagree. Then discuss with a partner.

▷ page 140 **VOCABULARY**BANK

FAIR SHARE

 G -ing form and infinitive
P connected speech: intrusive /w/
V values

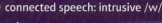 **8.2**

The Ultimatum Game

You have been given £10.
You have to offer some of
this money to your partner.
If your partner accepts your offer,
you split the money as agreed.
If your partner rejects the offer,
neither of you keep anything.
You must decide how much
money to offer to your partner.

THE SHARING EXPERIMENT

The Dictator Game

You have been given £10.
You have to offer some of
this money to your partner.
Your partner has no choice
and has to accept your offer.
You must decide how much
money to offer to your partner.

SPEAKING

1 A Work in pairs and discuss. Read the instructions above for The Sharing Experiment, two games that test people's behaviour. What do you think the games show about people?

B Work alone. Imagine you are playing the games. Write an amount from £0–£10.

1 The Ultimatum Game:
   I would keep £_____ and offer my partner £_____. The lowest I would accept from my partner is £_____.

2 The Dictator Game:
   I would keep £_____ and offer my partner £_____.

C Compare your ideas with other students and discuss the questions.

1 How different are your results?
2 What did the two games show about your personality?
3 Do you think you would behave differently in a real-life situation than you did in the game?

VOCABULARY

VALUES

2 A Work in pairs. Match 1–6 with a)–f) to make sentences.

1 I think it shows that you have a sense of **fairness**, *d*
2 It brings out **aggression** in people. In fact,
3 I enjoyed being in **control**
4 Here there's no **equality** because
5 I imagine some people give more than they have to
6 There's no **justice** in this game,

a) just as there's none in real life. I felt cheated and hard done by.
b) and that's why I kept all the money for myself. I'm surprised at my own **greed.**
c) one person has less **power**.
d) especially if you split it 50-50 even though you don't have to.
e) and that sort of **generosity** always surprises me.
f) I think someone might try to hurt the other person.

B Write the words in bold in Exercise 2A next to their meanings.

1 being kind and willing to give
2 threatening behaviour
3 a situation where people have the same rights
4 the ability to make someone do something (2 words)
5 being reasonable in judgement (2 words)
6 strong desire for more money, food or other things

C Discuss in pairs. Does each sentence in Exercise 2A refer to the Ultimatum Game, the Dictator Game or both?

LISTENING

3 A ▶ 8.2 Listen to two people, Heather and Dominic, play the Ultimatum Game and answer the questions.

1 How much did Dominic offer Heather?
2 Did she accept?
3 What reasons does Dominic give for his decision?
4 What does Heather say about the decision?
5 What was the lowest amount Heather would have accepted?

B Discuss in pairs. Did anything surprise you about the outcome of the game? How do you think Heather and Dominic will behave in the Dictator Game?

C ▶ 8.3 Listen to them play the Dictator Game and answer the questions.

1 How much did Dominic offer Heather?
2 What reasons does he give for his decision?
3 What does Heather say about the decision?

D Work in groups and discuss.

1 How different were Dominic and Heather's results from yours in Exercise 1B?
2 How much do you identify with the reasons Dominic gave for his decisions in either game?
3 How much do you identify with Heather's reaction? Were your reactions very different?

GRAMMAR

-ING FORM AND INFINITIVE

4 A Check what you know. Complete the article using the correct form of the verb in brackets. Use the -ing form, the infinitive or the infinitive + to.

AN EXPERT COMMENTS ON

▶ **The Ultimatum Game**

Research shows that people tend [1] __to respond__ (respond) differently depending on their cultural context and other factors. In Japan, players offered twice as much as those in Peru. But don't make the mistake of [2] _____ (think) that Japanese are more generous than Peruvians. Perhaps [3] _____ (be) generous in the game means you want people [4] _____ (think) you are in real life. The game gives you the chance [5] _____ (act) unselfishly or not; some people are playing [6] _____ (impress) people. If it's important to someone [7] _____ (see) as fair, it's easy [8] _____ (act) that way in the game because it's just a game.

The Dictator Game is very interesting because no one would imagine a genuine dictator really [9] _____ (share) money. True, some players would [10] _____ (keep) everything, but most people let their partner [11] _____ (have) a share of the money. Interestingly, most five-year-olds will [12] _____ (share) at least half of the money – they're not interested in [13] _____ (have) the most. My opinion is that deep down most human beings would rather [14] _____ (cooperate) and avoid [15] _____ (exploit) others, in the game and in real life.

B Work in pairs and discuss. What surprised you the most? Do you agree with the last sentence?

C Work in pairs. Look at the verb forms 1–15 in the article and complete the table.

	-ing form, infinitive or infinitive + to	example
after a preposition		
to express purpose		
after *let someone* or *make someone*		
as part of a semi-fixed phrase, e.g. *It's important/easy* and *the chance*		
as a subject or object (or part of one of these)		
after modal verbs		
after certain verbs, e.g. *enjoy, avoid, imagine*		
after certain verbs, e.g. *want, would like, tend*	infinitive + to	1
after *had better, would rather*		

▷ page 132 **LANGUAGEBANK**

[handwritten: vowel [ˈváuəl] 母音 cosonant [ˈkánsənənt] 子音]

5 A ▶ 8.4 Work in pairs. Complete each sentence with an alternative that means the same as the modal verb in brackets. Then listen and check.

1 I don't want _to have to_ refuse. (must)

2 I hate having to argue to get my way. (must)

3 I don't seem to be able to stand up for myself. (can)

4 I enjoy being able to offer people help. (can)

B CONNECTED SPEECH: intrusive /w/
Work in pairs. In sentences 1–4, circle *to* where it is pronounced /tə/ and draw a box around it where it is pronounced /tu:w/.

C Listen again and check. What is the rule? Then listen and repeat.

6 A Cross out the incorrect forms in the sentences.

1 I would rather *being/to be/be* a victim of unfairness than an unfair person.

2 It's good that some parents make their children *working/to work/work* from an early age.

3 Everyone is capable of *cheating/to cheat/cheat* another person, given the right circumstances.

4 Beware of anyone who says they can't stand *losing/to lose/lose,* as they'll do anything to win.

5 A child should *being/to be/be* taught when and how to be generous …

6 … but not just *earning/to earn/earn* the praise of others.

7 It's better *giving/to give/give* than *receiving/to receive/receive.*

8 *Being/To be/Be* good is easy; what is difficult is *being/to be/be* just. (Victor Hugo)

B Look at the sentences above. Tick (✓) two that you agree with, and put a cross (✗) next to two you disagree with.

C Work in groups and compare your ideas. Who in your group agreed with you the most?

speakout TIP

Record patterns after verbs and phrases, e.g. *would rather (do),* and write an example: *I'd rather stay at home.* How might you record these phrases: *look forward to …, had better …* ?

WRITING

AN INFORMAL ARTICLE; LEARN TO USE LINKERS OF PURPOSE

7 A Read the article and choose the best title.

a) Learn to be aggressive
b) Life isn't fair
c) Change the things you can

Do you hate it when people treat you unfairly? If you get a lower grade than you deserve, or you miss out on a promotion, do you lie awake all night fuming? Well, here are some things you can do about it to help you get past all that negativity.

First of all, it's important to remember that **for** a positive outcome, you need to maintain a positive attitude. It's much more difficult to change something if you're feeling angry or upset. If you know you're in the right, develop a can-do attitude **so as to** bring some positive energy to the situation.

Second, you have to get yourself to think rationally **so that** it's your head not your heart that dictates what you do. Don't get emotional **because** that'll only result in you making the situation worse; I've often made that mistake and lived to regret it. If you want to stand up for yourself or for someone else, you need to stay calm. That's how I managed to get a promotion recently after a long fight for justice.

Finally, you need to recognise the difference between things you can do something about, and things you can't. For example, once someone bumped into my car and drove away, and I couldn't really do anything about it; I had to accept the situation **in order to** move on. If on the other hand you see someone being unkind to someone else, you can say something to the person **to** change their behaviour as long as you do it clearly, firmly and unemotionally. They may not respond exactly as you'd like, but you'll have a better chance of influencing them.

With these ideas in mind, you can become much better at dealing with unfairness, and you might even have a positive influence on situations as well as people.

B Underline the correct alternative and give a reason.

1 The article is probably for a _student magazine/ serious newspaper_.
2 The aim of the article is to _describe/give advice_.
3 The topic sentence is at the _beginning/end_ of each main paragraph.

C Work in pairs and read the guidelines. Are they true (T) or false (F)? Find examples in the article.

In an informal article you should:

1 give personal examples.
2 use the pronouns _I_ and _you_.
3 avoid contracted forms.
4 use conversational language.
5 use linkers to help structure the article.
6 use questions to the reader.
7 avoid multi-word verbs.
8 use the passive where possible.

8 A Work in pairs. Look at the linkers of purpose in bold in the article and answer the questions.

1 Which linkers are followed by:
   a) an infinitive?
   b) a subject + verb?
   c) a noun?
2 Which two linkers can also be used in more formal situations?
3 How do you change the following underlined linkers to make the sentences negative?

Count to ten in order to lose your temper.
Control your emotions so as to act with aggression.

B Rewrite the sentences replacing the underlined linkers with the ones in brackets.

1 A good leader treats everyone equally in order to make everyone feel valued. (so that)
2 When I'm upset I usually phone my sister to chat. (for)
3 It's important to check everyone in a team reaches a decision together, because if you don't, someone will be left behind. (so as not to)
4 In a good relationship, it's important to sit down together from time to time so that you make sure everything is OK. (to)
5 Never make a decision late at night. Sleep on it to let your brain continue working overnight and you'll wake up knowing what to do. (because)
6 In a family, it's good to have a list of tasks for each person, because then no one is given the feeling they are doing more than their fair share. (in order not to)

9 A Work in pairs and brainstorm a list of main ideas for an article about one or two of the following topics:

- how to control your temper
- how to make decisions
- how to work as a team or a family
- how to have a good marriage or relationship
- how to do something that you know a lot about
- how to be a good leader or teacher

B Choose the topic you like and discuss ideas for opening/closing paragraphs. Then write the article (250–300 words).

F handling an awkward situation
P sentence stress and intonation
V behaviour

A

VOCABULARY

BEHAVIOUR

1 A Look at the pairs of adjectives. Are they similar (S) or different (D) in meaning? Use a dictionary to check.

D 1 supportive – unhelpful
S 2 diplomatic – tactful
D 3 sensitive – sensible
D 4 confrontational – collaborative
D 5 aggressive – assertive *push too much*
6 direct – focused *not acceptable*
stand your ground

B Which adjectives in Exercise 1A become opposites by adding/removing a prefix/suffix?

supportive – **un***supportive*

C Work in pairs. Which adjectives above describe your manner when: *give*

sensitive • you break bad news to someone? *sensitive, tactful*
• a friend is down or in trouble? *supportive, diplomat* *sad*
• making a complaint? *direct, assertive (insist)*
• you work on a project with someone? *collaborative focused*
• you are driving or cycling? *focused*
• trying to sort out a problem between two friends? *diploma tic*

I think I'm tactful but also quite direct if I have to break bad news to someone.

▷ page 140 **VOCABULARYBANK**

FUNCTION

HANDLING AN AWKWARD SITUATION

2 A Work in pairs. Look at situations 1–3 and photos A–C. What would be the best way to handle each situation?

1 Your colleague has loud, personal conversations on the phone when you're trying to work.
2 A flatmate of yours keeps borrowing money and never pays you back.
3 You're the manager of an elegant restaurant and a waitress has come in with purple hair.

B Work in pairs. Read the tips and discuss.

🔍 |Search

Tips for talking things through

Sometimes we have to raise topics with someone which we find embarrassing or awkward. Following these five tips will help smooth the process and minimise hurt feelings.

1 Say clearly why you want to talk to them at the start.
2 Give the message clearly. Be specific.
3 Don't tell them what other people say or think.
4 Give them space to say what they think and feel.
5 Suggest a solution (if they don't).

---

3 A ▶ 8.5 Listen to the conversation. Are the statements true (T) or false (F)? Correct the false statements.

F 1 Liz owes Jim a small amount of money.
F 2 She wants to pay him back immediately.
T 3 She doesn't always keep her promises.
F 4 Jim wants her to pay a set amount of money each week. *fix*
T

B Listen again. Tick the tips in Exercise 2B that the man follows.

4 A Complete phrases 1–5. Then look at the audio script on pages 150–151 and check.

Preparing the listener *meaning*
There's something I've been [1]_____ to talk to you about. *soften*

Giving the message
It's [2] *just* that …
I hope you don't [3] *take* this the wrong way, but …
I don't want you to get the wrong idea, but …

Getting the other person's point of view
Do you know [4] *what* I mean?
Do you see where I'm coming from?
How does that [5]_____? *sound*

B ▶ 8.6 **SENTENCE STRESS AND INTONATION**
Listen and underline the stresses in the phrases. Does the voice rise or fall at the end of each phrase? Why?

1 There's something I've been meaning to talk to you about. *finish*
2 I hope you don't take this the wrong way, but … *continue*
3 I don't want you to get the wrong idea, but … *continue*

C Listen again and repeat.

▷ page 132 **LANGUAGEBANK**

B

C

LEARN TO

SOFTEN A MESSAGE

6 A Work in pairs. Read the sentences below. When speaking, how could you soften the messages? What extra words or sounds could you add?

1 It's not that. I hope you don't take this the wrong way, but it's just that this isn't the first time I've lent you money and you haven't paid it back. I know it's not a lot, just small amounts each time, but it adds up quickly. I don't know. Do you know what I mean?

2 Actually, you've said that once before. I don't want you to get the wrong idea, but it never happened. And it makes things awkward. It makes me feel annoyed. Do you see where I'm coming from?

B ▶ 8.7 Listen to the sentences and add the extra words or sounds you hear.

speakout TIP

Fillers can help you sound less confrontational and allow thinking time. Some fillers (e.g. *um, er, well, you know, I mean, kind of*), are used instead of a pause. Modifiers (e.g. *just, a bit, slightly, quite*) often go before an adjective and soften a strong message (e.g. *I'm just a bit concerned = I'm VERY concerned*).

5 Work in pairs and role-play the situation. Use the flow chart to help.

Student A

there / something / I / mean / talk / you / about.

Student B

Yeah. What / up?

Well, look / don't / get / wrong idea, but …

But what?

It / just / I / very busy / you / always / phone.

Oh, right.

It / quite / annoying. / know / I / mean?

sorry / I / not / thinking.

I / suggestion. / Why / you / not / ask friends / call your mobile / instead of / land line?

You / mean / I / use / phone / different room?

That / right. / How / sound?

seem / reasonable. / really / sorry.

No problem. / Forget.

SPEAKING

7 A Work in pairs. For each situation below, write the first two sentences of the conversation.

1 You've been driving your colleague to work for over a month. He/She has never offered you money for petrol.

2 Your neighbour in a block of flats leaves bags of rubbish in the hall for days. He/She eventually takes them out but there's always a bad smell in the hall as a result.

3 Your friend has long conversations on her mobile when you're out together.

4 A friend often gives you a lift on his/her motorbike but his/her driving is scary.

B Role-play one of the situations.

C Work with another student and role-play a different situation.

8 Work with other students. Decide on the three most annoying things people do a) in your place of study or workplace b) at home.

DVD PREVIEW

1 A Work in pairs. Which gestures do you know? Show your partner.

1 shrug your shoulders
2 cross your fingers
3 tap the side of your head
4 give the thumbs up sign
5 hold your hands out, palms up
6 nod
7 shake your head
8 rub your thumb and first two fingers together

B What do these gestures mean in your country? Do people there use any other gestures?

2 Read the programme information and correct the sentences.

1 Desmond Morris observed human behaviour ~~even~~ *in a way that a bird watchers might.* ~~though he's a bird-watcher.~~

2 He created a classification system for words *He classified human behaviour* people use with animals.

3 His project took him over sixty ~~years~~ *countries* and he travelled to many ~~countries~~ to complete it. *for years*

4 The programme looks at ~~sign~~ language. *gestures.*

◁)) The Human Animal

BBC

Desmond Morris is widely known for his study of human behaviour, customs and <u>rituals</u>, a 'man-watcher' in the same way as some people are bird-watchers. Originally a zoologist, Morris decided to observe and classify human <u>behaviour in much the same way</u> as he would observe animals – in his words 'to do for actions what dictionary makers had done for words.' His project of cataloguing human gesticulation and movement took him to <u>over 60 countries</u> and engrossed him for many years. In this programme in the series, Morris focuses on fascinating customs connected with greeting and on the meaning of different gestures.

DVD VIEW

3 A Before watching, discuss:

1 How many ways of shaking hands do you know?
2 How do you say 'You're crazy!' with your hands?

B Watch the DVD. Does Morris mention or show any of the things you talked about in Exercise 3A? Which handshake and 'You're crazy!' sign did you find the most interesting?

C Match the types of gesture to the countries. Then watch the DVD again and check.

Shaking hands:

1 Masai elders   **a)** shake and kiss hands
2 Mali, West Africa **b)** continue until a deal is struck
3 Morocco   **c)** briefly touch the forearm
4 Kurdish farmers **d)** give a quick palm touch

Saying 'You're crazy!':

1 Rome   **a)** twist finger round and round
2 England **b)** circle finger anticlockwise
3 Japan   **c)** put fingers together and tap forehead
        d) tap side of head with finger

D Watch the DVD again and underline the correct alternative.

1 I *drew/directed* his attention to the fact that over the other side of the road there were two men who were *gesturing/gesticulating* in a particular way. *point out*

2 … a major new project, one that was to *keep my interest/engross me* for many years to come …

3 I began making huge charts naming every facial *gesture/expression*, every gesticulation, every movement, every *position/posture*.

4 Even the simplest human action such as the handshake has countless *differences/variations*.

5 The essential feature of handshaking is that it's an *equal/egalitarian* act.

6 They're all *exactly right/fine-tuned to* the precise *context/situation* in which they occur. *meaning of background*

speakout advice for a visitor

4 A ▶ 8.8 Listen to some advice for visitors to the USA. Is there anything that surprised you?

B Listen again and tick the key phrases that you hear.

> **KEYPHRASES**
>
> When people meet, they tend to …
> ✓ It's considered [good/bad] manners to …
> ✓ If you're not used to it, it can seem strange at first.
> It's not uncommon for people to …
> ✓ Having said that, don't be surprised if …
> ✓ It's [unacceptable/perfectly acceptable] to …

C Work in pairs or groups. Choose a country both of you know and prepare advice for visitors.

- Choose from the topics below and make notes on Do's and Don'ts for visitors.
- For each point, say why it is important and what can go wrong if a person doesn't know about the particular behaviour.

> Going out with friends – who pays?
>
> Time keeping
>
> Personal space, eye contact, posture, voice
>
> Using names (first? last? title, e.g. *Mr*?)
>
> Greetings
>
> Paying/tipping in a restaurant
>
> Special gestures
>
> Saying goodbye
>
> Going to someone's house for a meal

D Present your information to other students. When you listen to other students, make notes of anything you didn't know before.

writeback cross-cultural article

5 A Read the short article giving advice on an aspect of behaviour in Britain. Which topics in Exercise 4C does it mention?

B Which things are the same as in your country?

Body language in Britain:
Keep your distance

British people are friendly, but there are some important things every visitor should know when spending time with them.

When you meet someone for the first time, it's normal to shake hands firmly, regardless of gender, both in formal and semi-formal situations. On subsequent meetings, this is not usually expected unless you haven't seen someone for a while. While the habit of exchanging kisses is a growing trend amongst younger people, it should not be initiated by visitors and should generally be restricted to family members and to people you have already met and like.

In terms of personal space, British people feel uncomfortable if you stand too close, so try to keep some distance. Also it's important to make eye contact when talking to Brits, but don't overdo it, or you'll come across as rude or impolite. Gestures such as hugging and backslapping are not recommended. On the whole, British people tend to be less demonstrative than some other nationalities. They do not raise their voices or use gestures a lot to emphasise a point and shouting is never acceptable.

If you keep these points in mind, you'll have a much more comfortable, enjoyable visit to Britain.

C Write a short article (150–200 words) giving advice to a foreign student or business person coming to your country. Choose one or two topics from Exercise 4C to focus on.

D Read other students' articles. What information do you find that you didn't know before?

Ⓥ COLLOCATIONS

1 Underline the correct alternative in each sentence.

1 I had no time to *evaluate/stick to* the situation and had to act quickly – it was too dangerous to *postpone/reach* the decision till later.

2 I always try to *betray/stick to* my principles and never *go against/arrive at* them.

3 You should *explore/follow* the situation thoroughly and not be afraid of *doing/putting off* the decision.

4 We would like to take more time to *betray/assess* the situation before we *arrive at/follow* a final decision.

Ⓖ PAST AND MIXED CONDITIONALS

2 A Underline the correct alternative in each sentence.

1 If I hadn't started studying English,
   a) I *might study/might have studied* another language.
   b) I *wouldn't go/wouldn't have gone* to university.
   c) I *wouldn't be/wasn't* able to watch films in English.

2 If I'd had the chance to live in a different country,
   a) I *wouldn't take/would have taken* it.
   b) I *would find/would have found* it very hard to make a decision about where.
   c) I *would choose/would have chosen* to live in Spain.

3 If computers hadn't been invented,
   a) the world *would be/had been* a less open place.
   b) people would *spend/have spent* more time together now.
   c) my parents would *end up/have ended up* in different jobs.

B For each sentence, circle the ending a), b) or c) that is most true for you.

C Work in pairs and compare your ideas.

Ⓥ VALUES

3 A Add the vowels to complete the questions about values.

1 Is it possible to have f_a_irn_e_ss without _e_qu_a_lity? How about when a disadvantaged person is given special treatment?

2 If kids play team sports, are they more likely to learn cooperation or _a_ggres_i_o_n?

3 How can g_e_n_e_r_o_si_ty be used as a way of gaining c_o_ntr_o_l over people or a situation?

4 If you were a judge with total p_o_w_e_r, would you be able to practise perfect j_u_st_i_c_e, and never show favour towards anyone – even family and friends?

5 You can press a button and eliminate either gr_ee_d or ignorance from the face of the earth. Which one would it be?

B Work in pairs and ask and answer the questions.

Ⓖ -ING FORM AND INFINITIVE

4 A Complete the sentences with the correct form of the words in brackets.

1 The most difficult thing about my day is _____ to and from work. (travel)

2 I've always been able _____ new words just by _____ them. (learn, hear)

3 It's not very good for a person _____ alone when they're depressed. (be)

4 I never have time _____ the things I really want to do. (do)

5 _____ a bike is one of my favourite ways of relaxing. (ride)

6 I study English for an hour a day but I keep _____ the same mistakes! (make)

7 I enjoy _____ films in English. (able / watch)

8 _____ a uniform is the worst part of my job. (have / wear)

B Tick any sentences you agree with. Make the others true for you.

C Work in pairs and take turns. Student A: read one of your sentences. Student B: ask follow-up questions.

A: The worst part of my job is …
B: Oh, why is that?

Ⓕ HANDLING AN AWKWARD SITUATION

5 A Correct the mistake and add the missing word in each sentence.

1 Excuse me, Wendy. Do ^*you* / have a *moment* ~~monument~~?

2 There's nothing I've meaning to talk to you about.

3 Look, I want you to get the right idea, but …

4 It that just I've noticed that …

5 I feel brighter if …

6 How you fill about that?

B Work in pairs. Choose one of the situations below and practise the conversation. Student A: use all of the sentences from Exercise 5A in order. Then choose another situation and exchange roles with Student B.

- telling a colleague that their clothing isn't appropriate for the workplace
- telling a friend that they always forget your birthday and it bothers you
- telling a student they didn't pass an important exam

Excuse me, Juan. Do you have a moment? There's something I've been meaning to talk to you about …

9)) trouble

WITNESS p104

SCAM p107

IT'S AN EMERGENCY! p110

SURVIVAL p112

SPEAKING 9.1 Discuss how good a witness you are 9.2 Speculate about scams
9.3 Talk about emergency situations 9.4 Agree priorities

LISTENING 9.2 Listen to people talk about getting tricked 9.3 Listen to someone report
an incident 9.4 Watch a BBC programme about a sea rescue

READING 9.1 Read an article about memory 9.2 Read an infographic about scams;
Read an advice leaflet about avoiding trouble on holiday

WRITING 9.2 Write a 'how to' leaflet; Learn to avoid repetition 9.4 Write a story about
a lucky escape

BBC INTERVIEWS

)) Do you have any
phobias?

9.1))) WITNESS

- **G** *-ing* form and infinitive
- **P** connected speech: elision
- **V** crime; dependent prepositions

VOCABULARY

CRIME

1 A Work in pairs and discuss. What crimes are the most common in your city/town?

B Work in pairs and complete the newspaper extracts with the crimes in the box.

kidnapping   hacking   stalking   vandalism
identity theft   bribery   counterfeiting   mugging
arson   shoplifting   ++? fake"

1 A teenager has been accused of __arson__ after he was seen setting fire to an empty factory.

2 He was jailed for five years for __hacking__ into government computer systems.

3 There has been a reduction in __shoplifting__ in stores after the introduction of more security guards.

4 A man has been found guilty of __stalking__ film star Halle Berry. He followed her everywhere.

5 There have been several cases of __kidnapping__ of foreign journalists. In the latest case, a demand was made for $500,000.

6 __Bribery__ is a problem, with officials accepting money from companies that want to do business in the country.

7 There were no witnesses to the act of __vandalism__ in which a statue was damaged.

8 Police arrested three people for __counterfeiting__ dollars. More than a million fake $50 bills were found.

9 Banks revealed that cases of __identity theft__ have doubled. Customers are warned to keep PIN numbers more secure.

10 The increase in CCTV cameras has cut cases of late-night __mugging__ in town centres.

C Complete the table for the words in Exercise 1B. Use your dictionary to help if necessary. Add any other crime vocabulary you know.

crime	person	verb
arson	*arsonist*	*to commit arson*
hacking		

D Work with other students and discuss.

1 Which ones do you think are the most serious crimes and which are more minor offences?

2 Are any of the crimes serious problems in your country?

3 Do you know anyone who has had experience of any of these crimes?

Memories **on trial**

Even in these days of DNA tests and other forensic techniques, witness testimony still plays an important part in court cases. But how reliable are our memories? BBC *Focus* magazine's Andy Ridgway finds we know less than we think …

READING

2 A Work in pairs and discuss. Do you have a good memory? What do you remember easily? What do you have difficulty remembering?

B Read the article and find two examples of false memories.

C Read the article again. Are statements 1–6 true (T) or false (F)? Underline any words/phrases that help you decide.

1 In court, evidence from a witness is not important if there are other kinds of evidence.

2 Forty percent of people in one study were able to give a full description of the film of the bus exploding in Tavistock Square.

3 A poor memory doesn't usually matter in day-to-day life, according to the article.

4 In 1998, in the USA, almost all major criminal cases depended entirely on witness evidence.

5 The rumour about the white van was started by one witness.

6 One in five witnesses makes a mistake in ID parades.

D Look at the article again. What do the six highlighted words refer to? Draw an arrow backwards or forwards to the word/phrase.

Most of us have some recollection of the 2005 terrorist attacks in London. It could well be a mental image of …

E Work in pairs and discuss. Who/What does the author blame for false convictions? Would you make a good witness?

> In ID parades, forty percent of witnesses identified the police's suspect.
> In forty percent of cases no identification was made.
> In twenty percent of cases they pointed to a volunteer.

Most of us have some recollection of the 2005 terrorist attacks in London. It could well be a mental image of a red double-decker bus in Tavistock Square with its roof ripped off by the force of the explosion. That's not surprising given the number of photographs of the damaged bus that were carried in newspapers in the days after the attack.

But what about CCTV footage? Do you remember seeing a video of the bus exploding? What can you see in that video?

Well, the truth is, you shouldn't be able to see anything in your mind's eye because such CCTV footage simply doesn't exist. But don't worry. If it only took a suggestion that you may have seen a video of the explosion to create an image in your mind, you're not alone. In fact, in a study carried out by Dr James Ost at the University of Portsmouth, forty percent of people claimed to have seen this nonexistent footage. Some even went on to describe what happened in vivid detail.

Many of us think we have a good memory. After all, it's got us through the occasional exam. But what Ost's study clearly demonstrates is just how easily influenced our memories are. 'Facts' from the past can become confused in our minds. And it can simply be the fact that we've been asked about something, such as a nonexistent video clip, that can alter our memory.

In many cases, an unreliable memory is not a problem. It just means we forget to send a birthday card on time or a story we tell at a party is not one hundred percent accurate. But sometimes the contents of our memories can have huge consequences – putting people behind bars or even, in the USA, on Death Row.

In 1998, an American study calculated that in ninety-five percent of felony cases – the more serious crimes – witness evidence (in other words, people's memories) was the only evidence heard in court. In the UK, despite DNA and other forensic evidence being used more regularly, witness memories are still a vital part of court proceedings.

Even before a case gets to court, a few false memories can get an investigation off to a bad start. In the sniper attacks that took place in the Washington DC area in 2002, witnesses reported seeing a white van or truck fleeing several of the crime scenes. A white vehicle may have been seen near one of the first shootings and the media began repeating this. When they were caught, the sniper suspects were actually driving a blue car. It seems many witness memories had been altered by the media reports. ■

GRAMMAR

-ING FORM AND INFINITIVE

3 A Underline the correct alternative in sentences 1–3. Then check in the article.

1 Do you remember *to see/seeing* a video of the bus exploding?

2 Some even went on *to describe/describing* what happened in vivid detail.

3 It just means we forget *to send/sending* a birthday card on time.

B Work in pairs and check what you know. What is the difference in meaning between the pairs of phrases in bold?

1 a) I **remembered to set** the alarm before I left.
   b) I **remember thinking** the building was quiet.

2 a) I **forgot to buy** tickets for the Adele concert.
   b) I'll never **forget seeing** Adele in concert.

3 a) Henri **stopped to drink** some coffee.
   b) Then he **stopped driving** as he still felt tired.

4 a) After lengthy training, Billy **went on to become** a famous dancer.
   b) Billy **went on practising** every day even when he was famous.

5 a) He **tried to recall** her name, but couldn't.
   b) He **tried going** through the alphabet to remember it.

6 a) We **regret to inform** you that the concert has been cancelled.
   b) And I **regret spending** so much on the ticket!

C Match rules 1–12 below with meanings a) or b). Use the examples in Exercise 3B to help.

RULES		
1 remember doing	a)	do something that is one's responsibility
2 remember to do	b)	have a memory of something
3 forget doing	a)	not do something that is one's responsibility
4 forget to do	b)	not have a memory of something
5 stop doing	a)	finish an action
6 stop to do	b)	finish an action in order to do something else
7 go on doing	a)	do something after finishing something else
8 go on to do	b)	continue an action
9 try doing	a)	experiment with an activity
10 try to do	b)	make an effort to do something difficult
11 regret doing	a)	be sorry about something you are about to do
12 regret to do	b)	be sorry about something you did in the past

4 ▶ **9.1** **CONNECTED SPEECH: elision** Listen and write the sentences. Cross out letters at word endings that are not pronounced. Then listen and repeat.

I remembered to lock up.

▷ page 134 **LANGUAGEBANK**

5 A Complete the questions with the correct form of the verbs in the box.

get   study   buy   write   hide   take   help   become   witness
think   inform   do

1 If someone stole your wallet, would you run after them and try _to get_ it back?

2 Have you ever forgotten _____ a ticket for a train journey, then got caught?

3 If you were in a hurry and you saw an accident but there were lots of people around, would you stop _____?

4 Is there an event in your country you'll never forget _____, because it was so significant?

5 Is there anything thing you regret not _____ when you were a child?

6 Do you ever stay awake at night because you can't stop _____ about a problem?

7 Do you always remember _____ breaks when you're studying hard?

8 Has anyone you knew as a child gone on _____ famous?

9 Have you ever tried _____ on your hand as a way of reminding yourself to do something?

10 You open a letter that says, 'I regret _____ you that your application has been refused.' What's it referring to?

11 How long do you think you'll go on _____ English?

12 Do you sometimes remember _____ something 'in a safe place' but find you've forgotten where you put it?

B Work in pairs and ask and answer the questions.

SPEAKING

6 A Work alone. How would you have acted if you'd witnessed a crime? Read situations 1–4 and make notes on what you would have done. Use questions a)–c) to help you.

1 You caught a pickpocket trying to take your mobile and he threatened to hurt you if you called the police.

2 You saw a friend shoplifting in a department store.

3 You noticed a colleague stealing office supplies from your place of work.

4 You witnessed your neighbour's teenage children committing an act of vandalism, e.g. spraying graffiti on the wall of their school.

a) Would you have intervened or try to stop the person?

b) Would you have reported the person to the authorities?

c) If you'd been questioned by the authorities, would you have told the truth?

B Work in groups and compare your ideas.

VOCABULARY *PLUS*
DEPENDENT PREPOSITIONS

7 A Work in pairs. Complete the headlines with a preposition and the correct form of the verbs in brackets.

1 FAKE POLICE OFFICER CHARGED _____ £600 NECKLACE (steal)

2 Woman accuses con artist _____ bag and PIN (take)

3 Gang arrested _____ one car nine times (sell)

B Write the headlines in full. Which are active and which passive?

1 A fake police officer has been charged with stealing a £600 necklace. passive

C Complete the headlines using a dependent preposition and the correct form of the verbs in brackets. Then check with a partner or in a dictionary.

1 Hacker suspected _____ government computers (access)

2 Student apologises _____ in exam (cheat)

3 President blames 'greedy' banks _____ crisis (cause)

4 Local girl dreams _____ top talent (become)

5 Agency criticised _____ size-zero models (employ)

6 Train company bans teenager _____ for one year (travel)

7 Mother thanks toddler _____ her life (save)

8 Animal rights activists rescue lobster _____ (be eat)

9 Jury clears actress _____ husband number three (murder)

10 Dolphin saves swimmer _____ (drown)

8 A Work in pairs. Choose two of the headlines above and write a news article in three sentences.

B Work in groups and take turns. Student A: read out your article. Other students: close your book and say the appropriate headline.

▷ page 141 **VOCABULARYBANK**

G past modals of deduction
P connected speech: past modals
V synonyms

9.2

VOCABULARY

SYNONYMS

1 A Read the dictionary extract. Think of an example of a scam.

> **S** **scam** /skæm/ *n* **[C]** *informal* a clever but dishonest way to get money

From Longman Active Study Dictionary.

B Work in pairs. Read the infographic and answer the questions.

1 What are your answers to the first two questions in the text?
2 Which of the five scams can be done by one person?

C Match meanings 1–6 with two of the underlined verbs or verb phrases in the infographic. Write the verb phrases in the infinitive.

1 act as if you're someone else   *pretend to be,*
2 trick someone
3 cause somebody to <u>not</u> notice something
4 take something quickly
5 believe a trick
6 exchange one thing for another

speakout TIP

Use synonyms to improve your speaking and writing. You can a) notice synonyms when you read b) record them in your notebook c) look up synonyms in a thesaurus or on the internet d) use synonyms when writing to avoid repetition.

Rewrite the following, using synonyms for *nice*: *Yesterday was very nice. I had a nice meal at a nice restaurant with some nice people.*

LISTENING

2 A ▶ 9.2   Listen to the conversations. Which two scams from the infographic happened to the people?

B Work in pairs and try to complete the statements. Then listen again and check your ideas.

1 The thieves distracted Lise by …
2 She trusted the man because …
3 She thought she was talking to the bank on the phone because …
4 The thieves got her PIN code by …
5 The man in the jewellery shop was posing as …
6 He accused the woman of …
7 He left the shop with …
8 Dan thought that the man was going to …

3 Work in pairs and discuss the questions.

1 What should/shouldn't the people have done in each situation?
2 Why do you think people fall for scams?
3 Have you read or heard about any other scams (over the phone, internet or face-to-face)?

Scam-proof yourself

How easily do you think you could <u>be taken in</u> by a professional con artist? Is it easy for a well-dressed but ill-intentioned stranger to <u>deceive</u> you and walk away with your money, credit cards or phone? Once you understand the basic principles of street scams, you'll never <u>fall for</u> a scam again.

1) The Shoulder Surf

You're standing at the ATM and some nice person asks if that's your 20 euros on the ground. An innocent question, or a trick to <u>distract</u> you so they can <u>snatch</u> your card out of the slot?

2) The Fake Police Officer

If a man walked into a shop where you worked and <u>pretended to be</u> a police officer, would he <u>fool</u> you?

3) Escalator Jam

As you reach the bottom of the escalator, suddenly there's a jam of people and you get bumped into. You drop your mobile, but a kind woman picks it up and gives it back to you. Are you sure she hasn't <u>switched</u> it for an identical (but broken) one?

4) The Tourist Photo

'Can you take our photo?' It's just one of many ways to <u>divert your attention</u> so the hustlers can easily <u>grab</u> your wallet or mobile or <u>swap</u> it for an identical one.

5) The Squirt

A stranger bumps into you and gets ketchup all over your jacket! How nice that some people are helping you wipe it off … or are they just thieves <u>posing as</u> helpful passersby?

GRAMMAR

PAST MODALS OF DEDUCTION

4 A Match sentences 1–7 with meanings a)–c).

1 It can't have been the young couple because I was looking at them all the time.
2 So it must have been stolen when I was taking the photo.
3 He must have taken my bag when I wasn't looking.
4 He could have hidden it in his case.
5 The woman must have been working with the guy.
6 She couldn't have been a real customer.
7 But she might have had fake money.

a) I'm almost certain this happened.
b) I feel it's possible this happened.
c) I'm almost certain this didn't happen.

B Complete the rules. Use the sentences in Exercise 4A to help.

> **RULES**
>
> 1 To speculate or make a deduction about something that happened in the past, use the modals:
> *must* /_____/_____/_____/_____ + *have* + _____.
> 2 To emphasise that an activity was in progress, use modal + *have* + _____ + _____.
> 3 In the passive, use modal + *have* + _____ + _____.

5 A ▶ 9.3 **CONNECTED SPEECH: past modals** Listen to the pronunciation of the past modals in connected speech. Then listen again and repeat.

must have	could have	might have	can't have	couldn't have
/mʌstəv/	/kʊdəv/	/maɪtəv/	/kɑːntəv/	/kʊdəntəv/

B ▶ 9.4 Listen to the phrases and repeat.

must have, must have been, It must have been great!

▷ page 134 **LANGUAGE**BANK

6 A Complete the accounts of two scams. Use modals of deduction and the verbs in brackets.

> I was taking out money at an ATM. Just as my card came out, a guy behind me said I'd dropped some money. Sure enough, there was a twenty-euro note on the floor. I bent down, picked it up and my card was gone … and so was the man! He ¹_____ (drop) the twenty-euro note and pretended it was mine, or the note ²_____ (fall) out of my wallet and he simply took advantage of the situation. He ³_____ (pull) my card out of the ATM when I bent down.

> An estate agent was showing me a flat when she got a phone call from another customer who wanted to put down a deposit on that same flat. So I gave the agent my deposit, signed the contract, and was given the key. When I went back later to move in, the key didn't work … and the agent didn't answer her phone number! The woman ⁴_____ (be) an estate agent. She ⁵_____ (be) an imposter and the other customer ⁶_____ (work) with her.

B Discuss in pairs. Which scam in Exercise 6A would be most likely to fool you?

SPEAKING

7 A Work in pairs. Student A: turn to page 146. Student B: imagine the following situation happened to you. Add some details about the place, time, the amount of money spent on the gifts and your feelings. Prepare to tell Student A.

> It was [name of a festival] and everyone was buying presents. I was in a shopping mall and I'd bought some games and a camera for people in my family. In the middle of the mall there was a big sign saying 'Free Gift Wrapping', so I left the presents with a woman there and collected them half an hour later. On the morning of [name of festival], the kids opened their presents and inside the boxes there were just oranges and straw.

B Tell Student A the situation and discuss these questions.

1 Who swapped the presents?
2 How did they trick people into giving them the presents?
3 Why didn't people notice that the presents felt different?
4 How do you think the scam was done?

C Now listen to Student A's situation and discuss his/her questions.

D Turn to page 144 to see if your ideas were right.

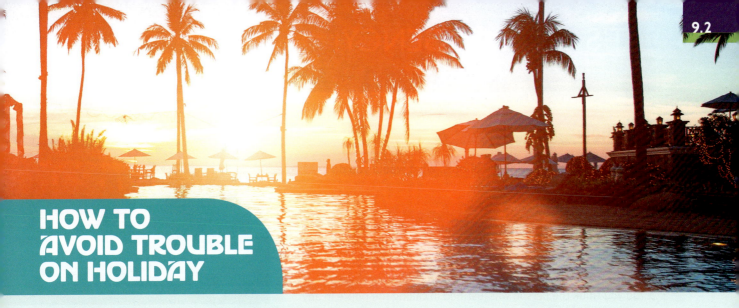

HOW TO AVOID TROUBLE ON HOLIDAY

Taxis

Be careful when taking taxis, especially at the airport. As an unsuspecting tourist, you may find yourself charged up to three times the normal fare or in a taxi with a driver who claims to have no change.

- Never **take** a taxi without a company name on its side.
- Always **ask** the approximate fare before getting in.
- **Phone** for a taxi ahead of time rather than catching one in the street.
- Make sure you **carry** plenty of change with you.

Money

Be careful around any major tourist sites. Pickpockets often work in gangs and will come up behind you while you're walking and unzip your backpack or may 'accidentally' bump into you and steal your money or mobile before passing these on immediately to a partner. Also, take care when using an ATM. A tiny hidden camera may have been installed to steal your card number and PIN.

- **Keep** your credit cards and larger sums of money in a money belt under your clothes.
- Be sure to **keep** any money that you think you'll use that day loose in your pocket, so that you don't need to pull out large notes.
- Be particularly careful to **cover** the keypad when you enter your PIN into an ATM machine.
- **Use** ATMs inside a bank where they are less likely to have been interfered with.

Tours

If someone offers a 'budget' tour, you may find that the price is cheap but you'll spend more time at shopping places not on your itinerary than the places you intended to visit. This is because your 'guide' is being paid by the shopkeepers for taking you there.

- **Book** tours only with reputable companies.
- Try to **check** with other visitors or with your hotel before booking a tour.
- Take time to **look** on the internet for reviews and recommendations.

WRITING

A 'HOW TO' LEAFLET; LEARN TO AVOID REPETITION

8 A Work in pairs. What advice would you give a visitor to a city about how to avoid getting into trouble?

B Read the extract from a 'how to' leaflet for tourists. Which ideas are different from the ones you discussed?

C Complete the guidelines for writing a 'how to' leaflet with the words in the box.

> bullet points   title   fonts   sections   contracted   subheading   underlining

1 Give the leaflet an overall _____ .
2 Divide the leaflet into different _____ , each with its own short _____ .
3 Use different _____ or _____ so that it is easier for the reader to see the main points before they start reading.
4 Use _____ when you are writing a list.
5 To make your leaflet more direct and informal, use 'you' and _____ forms.

9 A Look at the verbs in bold in the leaflet and:

1 put a box around two adverbs used before the verbs.
2 underline five verb phrases used before the verbs.
3 circle the remaining four imperatives.

B Complete the rules and examples with words from the leaflet.

To avoid repetition when giving a list of advice:
1 use the adverbs ___always___ and _____ .
2 use a range of synonyms (words/phrases) in the imperative:
a) Make _____ you
b) Be _____ to
c) Be particularly _____ to
d) Try _____
e) Take _____ to

10 Write a 'how to' leaflet (200–250 words) on one of the following topics. Use a variety of ways to give advice and avoid repetition.

- advice for people travelling solo
- advice for internet banking
- advice for passing exams
- advice for joining a particular social networking site
- advice for (your own idea)

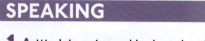

F reporting an incident
P sentence stress
V incidents

SPEAKING

1 A Work in pairs and look at the photos. What would you do if you witnessed these situations?

B Work in pairs and discuss.

1 List three situations in which you think you should phone the emergency services.

2 Read the reasons for calling the emergency services below. Which reason do you think is the most ridiculous?

3 Do you think the person was justified in calling the police in any of the situations?

Police are becoming concerned because a significant percentage of calls to the emergency services are about everyday inconveniences and problems or are simply ridiculous. Some of the silliest calls include:

- I need help with my maths homework.
- I'm having a bad dream. In fact this is part of it.
- My husband's snoring and I can't sleep.
- There's a squirrel on my porch and it's acting suspiciously.
- The weather report was wrong. And now I'm stuck in the snow.
- I'm stuck in traffic and need to get to the toilet.
- My boyfriend promised to marry me and now he won't.
- I'm locked in a house. Not my house – I'm a burglar.

VOCABULARY

INCIDENTS

2 A Complete sentences 1–10 with the correct form of a verb phrase in the box.

| fall off   get stuck   knock over   break down   lock out |
| run over   get knocked out   be on fire   steal   rob |

1 'My card has _____ in the machine.'

2 'The house _____ – there's smoke coming from the windows.'

3 'We crashed into a lamp post and _____ it _____.'

4 'My car has _____ on the motorway.'

5 'My wallet has _____.'

6 'A workman on my roof has just _____ the ladder.'

7 'I've _____ myself _____ of my house.'

8 'I fell down but I don't remember anything after that. I think I _____.'

9 'Someone's just _____ my cat and I think they've killed it.'

10 'I've just _____! Someone's taken my bag from the changing room.'

B Work in pairs. Look at the sentences above and discuss.

1 Who might the person be phoning in each case?

2 What two questions might the other person ask the caller?

3 Which situations would you find the easiest to deal with?

1 In number one, they might be phoning the security department in a bank.

▷ page 141 **VOCABULARYBANK**

FUNCTION

REPORTING AN INCIDENT

3 A ▶ **9.5** Listen to the phone conversation. What happened to the man?

B Listen again and complete the report form.

INCIDENT REPORT 2047561A

Name: _____

Date and time of incident: _____

Location of incident: _____

Description of incident (what exactly happened?): _____

_____

Description of stolen or damaged property (serial number, bank card type, value of property, colour, make, model of car, etc.): _____

_____

Description of suspect or offender (age, sex, ethnicity, build, clothing, distinguishing marks or features, etc.):

_____

Witnesses: _____

Contact details: _____

_____

4 A ▶ 9.6 Complete the phrases. Then listen and check.

1 _____ I realised what _____ _____, he had run on.

2 It was _____ about thirty seconds _____ _____ I realised my wallet _____ _____.

3 But did it _____ your _____ that it wasn't just an accident?

4 It never _____ to me _____ he'd done it on purpose.

5 My mind just went _____.

6 He looked _____ _____ he was just out jogging.

7 It _____ _____ so quickly.

8 He just _____ _____ a normal guy.

9 He _____ me a bit _____ that actor.

10 I didn't _____ what he said. It was too quick.

B Work in pairs. Which phrases above a) describe impressions of a person b) refer to time?

C SENTENCE STRESS Underline the main stressed syllables in sentences 1–10 in Exercise 4A. Listen and check. Then listen and repeat.

Before I realised what had happened, he had run on.

▷ page 134 **LANGUAGE**BANK

5 Work in pairs and role-play the conversation between a police officer and a caller whose bag has been stolen from a shop changing room. Use the flow chart to help.

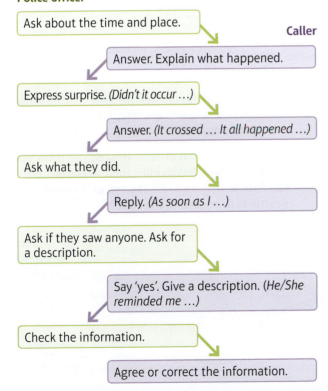

Police officer

Ask about the time and place.

Caller

Answer. Explain what happened.

Express surprise. *(Didn't it occur …)*

Answer. *(It crossed … It all happened …)*

Ask what they did.

Reply. *(As soon as I …)*

Ask if they saw anyone. Ask for a description.

Say 'yes'. Give a description. *(He/She reminded me …)*

Check the information.

Agree or correct the information.

6 Work in pairs.

Student A: choose a situation from Exercise 2A and phone the police to report what happened.

Student B: you are the police officer. Use the report form in Exercise 3B to ask questions.

LEARN TO

REPHRASE

7 A Look at the extract. Underline two places where the police officer (A) rephrases something to help the caller (B) understand.

A: Could you tell me exactly when the incident happened?

B: Just now. About an hour ago.

A: Could you be more precise?

B: Excuse me?

A: Could you give me the exact time?

B: I think at 2.50 or 2.55.

A: And where did it happen?

B: Park Avenue.

A: Can you pinpoint the exact location?

B: Pinpoint?

A: Tell me exactly where.

B Match the meaning of the words in bold in 1–5 with phrases a)–e) below.

1 I'll need **to take a statement**.

2 And he **hit into** me **hard** …

3 … **a sweater**, grey colour, **with a – you know – something you put over your head**.

4 … some sort of dark **trousers, for running or for the gym**.

5 And were there any other people **in the vicinity**?

a) in the surrounding area – nearby

b) tracksuit bottoms

c) a hood … a hoodie

d) to write down some details

e) collided with

C ▶ 9.7 Listen and check your answers.

speak**out** TIP

Using familiar words to explain unfamiliar vocabulary not only helps communication but can also be an opportunity to learn more sophisticated vocabulary.

SPEAKING

8 A Work in pairs. There was a burglary in your house last night. Student A: turn to page 146. Student B: turn to page 144.

B Work in pairs. Student B: ask Student A how the burglar got into the house. Draw a line showing his route. Help Student A with difficult vocabulary.

A: The burglar first climbed the … thing for rainwater … going down …

B: It's like a pipe, right? Which one?

A: Yes, like a pipe. The one on the left.

C Change roles. Student A: ask Student B how the burglar got out of the house. Draw a line showing his route. Help Student B with difficult vocabulary.

DVD PREVIEW

1 A Work in pairs and discuss.

1 What are different ways that people react in a disaster situation? Think about a building on fire, a sinking ship or a plane making a crash landing.

2 What do you think survival in a disaster depends on?

3 Which factors are connected to the character of the survivor?

B Read the programme information. What factors for survival does it mention? What do you think it means by 'how your brain reacts'?

Horizon: How to survive a disaster

BBC

When disaster strikes, who lives and who dies is not purely a matter of luck. In every disaster, from those people face once in a lifetime, to those they face every day, there are things that can be done to increase the chances of getting out alive. Some of these things have to do with planning ahead, some have to do with how your brain reacts, and some are simply down to luck. In this programme, we look at the sinking of the car ferry *Estonia* in 1994 through the experience of Paul Barney, a passenger on the *Estonia*, and examine why it is that he ended up among the survivors.

DVD VIEW

2 A Watch the DVD. Why did Paul Barney survive while others didn't?

B Are the statements true (T) or false (F)? Watch the DVD again and check your ideas.

1 Paul Barney slept in the cafeteria below the waterline.

2 He said he wasn't scared on board the ship, but was in the life raft.

3 One hundred and thirty-seven people died on the *Estonia*.

4 His tunnel vision caused him to focus on saving himself.

5 Professor Silke said that tunnel vision is not always a good thing.

6 Paul doesn't understand why some people didn't try to escape.

7 Most people keep a clear head in a disaster.

C Work in pairs. Complete the extracts by writing three words in each gap. Then watch the DVD again to check.

1 … I say to them really that there was no time _____, there was literally no time.

2 It was a very scary place to be because you never knew whether the next wave was going to _____ from the life raft.

3 I'm purely thinking of what's going to _____.

4 … our brain is focusing on whatever the threat or danger is, and it's focusing on that to the exclusion _____.

5 One of the things I remember clearly is the water actually coming into the cafeteria and seeing lots of people around just _____ spot.

D Work in pairs and discuss. How do you think you would react in a disaster like this? Would you be like Paul or would you be like one of the people he describes as 'rooted to the spot'?

speakout agreeing priorities

3 A ▶ **9.8** Listen to people deciding on things to take on a life raft. Which items below do they talk about? Why do they decide to take/reject each one?

- blankets
- tinned food
- torch (with generator)
- lighter
- dried fruit
- plastic raincoat
- first aid kit
- hand mirror
- fishing kit (line, hook)
- sun cream
- survival manual
- drinking cup

B Look at the key phrases. Listen again and tick the phrases you hear.

> **KEYPHRASES**
>
> It depends on [what/whether] …, doesn't it?
> It's important to … isn't it?
> It's (not) a top priority to be able to …
> What would we do with a … ?
> I'd say that … is/are [essential/vital/crucial]
> … to keep you [warm/dry/alive],
> … to [prevent/keep/protect] you from [the sun/dehydrating/getting …]
> [It/That] hadn't occurred to me.
> We need to prioritise them.
> I can't see the point of [taking, choosing] …

C Work alone and choose six items from the list in Exercise 3A. Make notes on why they are important and why other items are not as important.

D Work in groups and take turns. Try to persuade the other students that your choices are important then decide on six items as a group.

writeback an escape story

4 A A website has asked readers to write a story about a lucky escape prompted by a string of words. Work in pairs and discuss. What story can you imagine for the word string below?

> August   camping   forest   dry   tent
> sleep   smoke   fire   trapped   soup
> escape

B Read the story. What happened and how did the man get out of the situation without being hurt?

It was mid-August, and some friends and I went camping in a forest about an hour's drive from where we were living. It had been a very dry summer and we should have thought about the dangers of fire, but we didn't. We pitched our tents, made a campfire and cooked a nice soup for dinner. After a while we were all quite tired, so we went to sleep.

About an hour later I woke up to the smell of smoke. I realised straightaway that there was a fire, and that it was right in front of the tent – in fact some dry leaves next to the campfire had caught fire, and the front of the tent was starting to burn. I was trapped inside.

Luckily, one of my friends who was in another tent woke up too, and he poured the leftover soup on the burning tent. That made it possible for me to escape, and I crawled out as fast as I could. We put out the campfire but I couldn't go back to sleep. I think I was in shock – it was a very lucky escape.

C Choose another word string. Write your story (150–250 words) using three paragraphs.

> spring   countryside   lost   dark   fence
> garden   dog   sandwich   run   jump   escape

> sea   cool   friends   swim   snorkel   hours
> tired   cold   stiff   drowning   save   escape

D Read other students' stories. Which one do you think was the most unusual escape?

V CRIME

1 A Make a list of as many crimes as you can remember.

B Work in pairs and think of:

1 two crimes that involve damage to property.

2 three crimes that involve people and can happen on the street.

3 three crimes that involve technical expertise on computers or other machines.

4 a crime involving money that could be committed by a company.

5 a crime that involves theft but not usually in a street.

C Work in pairs and discuss. Which crimes are most often in the news in your town/city/country?

G -ING FORM AND INFINITIVE

2 A Underline the correct alternatives in the article.

→ OK, you've just been mugged. Your first impulse may be to go on ¹doing/to do whatever you were doing, but don't. First, stop ²checking/to check that you're fine. Some victims who have been struck actually forget ³being/to be hit and only discover injuries later. Try ⁴finding/to find a safe place, maybe a café with people (you may need to borrow a phone). You're probably in shock – give yourself time to stop ⁵shaking/to shake and take slow, deep breaths to calm yourself. If this doesn't work, try ⁶drinking/to drink some cool water – avoid coffee. Remember ⁷phoning/to phone someone you know and tell them where you are and what happened. If you remember ⁸seeing/to see what the mugger looked like, write down the details. If you forget ⁹doing/to do this you may find that you can't recall much detail later when you talk to the police, and you'll regret not ¹⁰doing/to do this.

B Work in pairs and discuss. Which ideas do you agree with?

V SYNONYMS

3 A Rewrite the sentences with a synonym for the words/phrases in bold.

1 Does listening to music when you study **divert your attention**?

2 Can you **snatch** fifteen minutes' sleep in the middle of the day?

3 Would you find it easier **to pretend to be** someone older or younger?

4 If you exaggerate your internet profile, are you **fooling** people unacceptably?

5 Have you ever **been taken in by** a lie someone told you?

6 Imagine you could **swap** identities with someone for just one day. Who would it be?

B Work in pairs and take turns. Ask and answer the questions.

G PAST MODALS OF DEDUCTION

4 A Work in pairs and read the situations. For each one, rewrite the options using a modal of deduction.

1 A man checked his post box every day but it was always empty. Meanwhile his friends sent him dozens of letters a week.

a) I'm sure the man moved recently. *The man must have moved recently.*

b) Maybe his friends sent mail to the old address.

c) I'm certain the postman didn't deliver the letters.

2 A pianist performed a concert in a concert hall. She played perfectly but at the end no one clapped.

a) She was probably practising in an empty concert hall.

b) I'm certain she was deaf.

c) They definitely didn't like the music.

B Look at the extra information below and make a final guess to explain each situation. Then turn to page 146 and check your ideas.

1 The friends wrote the correct address on the letters. The postman always put the letters in the post box. There wasn't a hole in the bottom of the post box.

2 The concert hall was full. No one had hearing problems – everyone heard the performance and liked it.

F REPORTING AN INCIDENT

5 A Complete the sentences with the correct form of a word in the box. One of the words is not used.

occur if go not catch remind become like cross realise happen (x2)

1 It *occurred* to me that he/she shouldn't have …

2 He/She _____ me of …

3 It was only later that I _____ …

4 My mind _____ blank.

5 Before I realised what had _____, she/he'd …

6 I _____ _____ the number plate.

7 It all _____ so fast.

8 It _____ my mind that …

9 He/She looked as _____ …

10 He/She seemed _____ …

B Work in pairs. Choose one of the following incidents to report to the police and decide which sentences from Exercise 5A you could use.

• someone shoplifting in a department store

• someone looking at confidential information on someone else's computer

• someone hanging around an ATM with two friends sitting in a car nearby

C Work in pairs and take turns. Role-play the phone call. Student A: you are the police officer. Student B: you have seen the incident.

10 culture

MOVING EXPERIENCES p116

POPULAR CULTURE p119

ON YOUR LEFT … p122

BBC

THE PEOPLE'S PALACE p124

BBC

INTERVIEWS

◉❱ What area of the Arts do you enjoy?

10.1))) MOVING EXPERIENCES

G relative clauses
P intonation: relative clauses
V adjectives to describe films

Bill Mury

VOCABULARY

ADJECTIVES TO DESCRIBE FILMS

1 A Work in pairs and discuss. Do you like the types of films shown in the photos? What types of films do you like?

B Work in pairs and check what you know. Cover Exercise 1C and complete the descriptions with a suitable adjective.

j **1** The documentary really made me think and raised lots of questions. It was … *wildlife documentary*

a **2** I got lost sometimes – you had to pay attention to keep up with the plot and the action because it was so …

b **3** The relationship between the two people was sensitively handled and almost made me cry. It was very …

f **4** Some scenes were scary and made my skin crawl. It was …

c h **5** I was on the edge of my seat and couldn't look away for a single moment. It was really …

i **6** The acting and direction were all exceptional, it'll win all the awards this year. It was absolutely …

g **7** I shouldn't be surprised if people start protests against this documentary. It's extremely …

d **8** There was a lot of violence and blood. For me it was just too …

e **9** We couldn't stop laughing, it was …

C Complete sentences 1–9 above with the words/ phrases a)–j). One item has two answers.

a) fast-paced
b) touching *(= poignant)*
c) gripping
d) gory *involving violence and blood*
e) hysterical
f) creepy
g) controversial
h) full of suspense
i) outstanding
j) thought-provoking

hysteria ur **D** Check what you remember. Which adjectives in the box are synonyms or near-synonyms for the adjectives in Exercise 1C?

extremly funny

| hilarious moving offensive superb dramatic |
| stunning poignant intense |

b sadness

2 A Work in groups. List the names of ten to fifteen films you all know.

B Take turns. Student A: describe one of the films using at least three of the adjectives from Exercise 1C. The other students: ask a *yes/no* question each and *then* guess the film.

A: It's fast-paced and the special effects are brilliant and some of it is gory.
B: Is it a thriller?
A: Yes.
C: Does it star … ?

LISTENING

3 A ▶ 10.1 Listen to someone talk about a film he never gets bored with watching. What is the film and what is the main reason he likes it?

B Listen again and make notes on the following:

1 why it's family-friendly
2 a memorable thing about the 'baddy'
3 where the film got its title
4 what the woman thinks about the film
5 examples of gripping moments
6 something unusual about the stunts
7 something the two people say about the heroine
8 the woman's preference in films

C Work in pairs and discuss. If you haven't seen the film, would you like to watch it based on this description? Is it true that there aren't many action films which include comedy?

4 A Work alone. Choose a film you never get bored with and make notes about:

• the actors.
• the setting. *place time*
• the plot. *story*
• why you like it.

B Work in pairs. Tell each other about your film.

C Work with other students. Take turns telling each other about your choice. Which film you heard about would you most like to see?

GRAMMAR

RELATIVE CLAUSES

5 A Check what you know. Complete the online forum messages with *who, which, whose, where* or *when*.

What film do you never get bored with?

The *Shawshank Redemption* is a prison movie ¹ which *[that]* goes beyond the violence seen in most such films. The story centres on the life-changing relationship between a new prisoner, Andy (Tim Robbins), ² who is imprisoned for murder, and Red (Morgan Freeman), a long-time prisoner ³ who *[that]* he makes friends with. You really care about these two characters, ⁴ whose unlikely friendship blossoms over the course of the film. I must have seen it twenty times and it's the one movie ⁵ which I never get bored with, especially Robbins' and Freeman's performances, for ⁶ who, surprisingly, neither won a major award. ✗ which.

that

My all-time favourite is *Groundhog Day*, in ⁷ which . Bill Murray relives one day over and over again. He plays Phil, a TV weatherman visiting a small U.S. town, ⁸ where he reports on a local annual festival. Phil detests the assignment and the local people, ⁹ who makes his situation even worse when he gets stuck with both. The story is endlessly inventive, by turns hilarious and poignant. It is especially touching in the moment ¹⁰ when Phil realises he loves Rita (Andie Macdowell) but can't win her, ¹¹ when *which* is a turning point in his transformation into a decent human being. He actually ends up loving the town ¹² where inhabitants he initially despised. A classic! whose

NO. 1, 5, 3.

B Work in pairs. Add *that* next to any relative pronouns which it could replace. Put brackets around relative pronouns that could be omitted.

C Complete the rules. Use the forum messages in Exercise 5A to help.

RULES

1 Defining relative clauses give *essential/extra* information about a person, thing, place or time. Non-defining relative clauses give *essential/extra* information.
2 The relative pronoun *that* can replace *who* or *which* in *defining/non-defining* clauses only.
3 The relative pronoun can be omitted when it is the *subject/object* of the verb in the relative clause.
4 Prepositions can come (a) at the *beginning/end* of a clause or (b) *before/after* the relative pronoun. *(a)/(b)* is more formal.
5 *What/Which* introducing a relative clause can be used to refer to the whole of a previous clause.
6 Commas are used before and after *defining/non-defining* clauses.

6 A Complete the forum message with commas.

It's a film which appeals to the teenage market and centres on the relationship between Bella who has just arrived in town and her mysterious classmate Edward whose family seems to have a strange secret. When Bella discovers Edward's true identity which happens about a third of the way through the film she has a big decision to make, a decision which will change her entire life.

B ▶ **10.2** **INTONATION: relative clauses** Listen to the intonation in the non-defining clauses. Are they higher or lower than the rest of the sentence?

C Listen again and say the recording at the same time, copying the intonation.

▷ page 136 **LANGUAGEBANK**

7 Combine the extracts from reviews using a relative clause.

1 The main role is played by Chiwetel Ejiofor. His portrayal of Solomon Northup earned him several awards.
2 Megastar Chris Hemsworth gives an emotional performance in his latest film. His career got its biggest boost from his role in *Thor*.
3 *Invictus* is a story about leadership and forgiveness at a critical period. Nelson Mandela had just become president of South Africa.
4 The film *Star Trek* was based on a popular TV series. William Shatner played the role of Captain Kirk in the series.
5 The film was Daniel Craig's third outing as James Bond. It was directed by Sam Mendes.
6 Adrian Brody shot to fame after starring in *The Pianist*. He won the Best Actor Oscar for this.
7 *Lost in Translation* takes place in a Tokyo hotel. The two main characters meet and form an unusual bond there.
8 *The Hurt Locker* is a war film directed by Kathryn Bigelow. The choice of Jordan as the filming location was important for her.

SPEAKING

8 A Complete the sentences below so that they are true for you.

I loathe films where …
I like the work of the director … , whose …
My favourite actress is … , who …
My favourite actor is … , who …
The film I most liked recently is …
I like it in films when …

B Work in pairs and take turns. Talk about your ideas and ask follow-up questions. Find out what you have in common.

MIDNIGHT IN PARIS

Midnight in Paris is set in Paris in the present and in different periods in the past. It stars Owen Wilson as Gil, a Hollywood screenwriter, and Rachel McAdams as Inez, his beautiful fiancée.

As the film opens, Gil is on holiday in Paris with Inez and her wealthy parents. He is supposed to be in love with his girlfriend but his love affair really seems to be with Paris in the springtime. One evening while wandering around the city, he gets lost and as the clock strikes midnight an old Peugeot car pulls up. Inside the car are a group of party-goers who are dressed in 1920s clothes and who invite him to join them. They go to a party where Gil realises he has been transported to the 1920s, a period which he loves. We see him meeting some of his intellectual and artistic heroes from that time and falling in love with Adriana, Picasso's mistress. Meanwhile, in the present, Gil's bride-to-be and her parents become more and more annoyed and suspicious about his nightly disappearances. Eventually Gil realises Inez is not right for him and breaks up with her. He decides to stay and live in his beloved Paris.

Skilfully directed by Woody Allen, the film cuts between the glitter of Paris in the twenties and the present-day city. The script is alternately gripping, shocking and hilarious and the camerawork is stunning. As Gil, Owen Wilson is appealing in his enthusiasm and love of Paris in the past. However, for me, it is the character of Adriana, convincingly acted by Marion Cotillard, who is the most fascinating of all.

With its charm, sparkling wit and engaging leaps forwards and backwards in time, *Midnight in Paris* is a light, delightful film which I'd thoroughly recommend.

(Handwritten margin notes: actor's names; setting; plot summary; reviewer's opinion; recommendation)

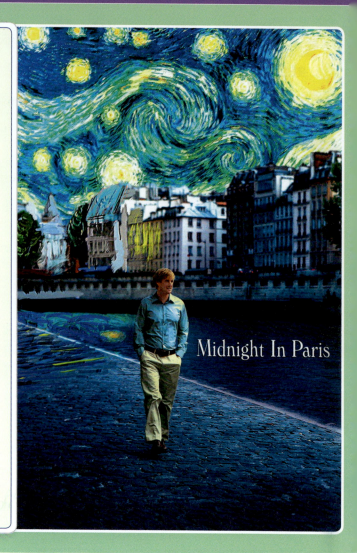

Midnight In Paris

WRITING

A REVIEW; LEARN TO USE ADVERB + PAST PARTICIPLE COMBINATIONS

9 A Work in pairs and discuss the questions.

1 Where do you usually read film reviews (e.g. on the internet, in magazines)?

2 What is the <u>main</u> purpose of a film review?
- to make people want to see the film
- to help people decide if they want to see a film
- to give factual information about the film

3 Which of the topics in the box do you usually find in a film review?

> plot summary   description of the film's ending
> actors' names   recommendation
> ticket prices   setting of the film   *place, time*
> reviewer's opinion of different elements

B Read the film review above. Would you like to see the film? Why/Why not?

C Read the review again and write the topic of each paragraph. Use the topics in the box to help.

10 A Underline two adverb + past participle combinations in paragraph 3 of the review.

B Write three adverbs from the box next to each participle to complete the phrases. Some can be used more than once.

> *believe* *誤得很*
> convincingly   harshly   skilfully   widely
> sensitively   overwhelmingly   highly
> poignantly   heavily   *too much.*

1 skilfully / over- / sensitively directed by …
2 convincingly / sensitively / poignantly acted by …
3 highly / over- / widely praised by …
4 harshly / heavily / widely criticised by …

11 A Make notes about a film you have seen recently or a film you never get bored with. Use the topic areas from Exercise 9C.

B Write a first draft of your review (120–180 words). Use adjectives and at least two adverb + past participle combinations.

C Exchange with another student and read each other's review. Is it interesting and clear? Suggest two or three improvements.

D Write a final version of the review.

POPULAR CULTURE

G participle clauses
P word stress; connected speech
V the Arts; two-part phrases

((**10.2**

READING

1 A Work in pairs and look at the photos. What do you think is the most difficult part of each performer's job?

B Work in pairs and discuss these questions from a magazine article. Make notes on your answers.

1 How do actors cry on demand?
2 Do big stars have to audition for film roles?
3 How do singers keep their voices steady when they're dancing?
4 Why is rock music played so loud at concerts?
5 Who decides whether something is 'art' or not?
6 Why do works of art get stolen if they can't be sold without attracting attention?
7 What's the secret to making an audience laugh?
8 How does a comedian deal with hecklers?

dislike
which

C Work in pairs. Student A: turn to page 145. Student B: quickly read the text on this page. Which four questions above does it answer?

D Read the text again. Write a maximum of five key words for each answer to help you remember the information.

E Work in pairs. Cover the text and look at your notes from Exercise 1D. Tell your partner about the answers.

POPULAR CULTURE Q&A

Want to know the best-kept secrets of popular culture?
Read our Top Questions & Answers to find out.

Q: 7

A: Every stand-up comedian knows that making people laugh with prepared material, on stage, is very different from making your friends or colleagues laugh in an informal setting. You need to focus on technique, such as which words to stress, when to pause, how to use facial expressions and body movements, as well as sensing how to work each individual audience. Interestingly, shows with paying audiences are better than freebies. Having paid to be entertained, people are often more ready and willing to laugh.

Q: 4

A: Rock music is characterised by a strong bass line and hard, driving rhythm and percussion parts, which are greatly enhanced by amplification. At some point in the evolution of rock, audiences became almost addicted to the sensations of the music they loved 'vibrating' inside them at concerts. The listeners go beyond hearing the music and feel it through their whole body, feel its vibrations, provided it is loud enough. Heavy metal music played softly sounds stupid and can only be played as it was intended to be: very, very loudly.

Q: 6

A: Criminals steal paintings only when they already have a buyer. Sometimes, a wealthy private collector actually requests a particular piece to be stolen – essentially orders it – for part of their private collection. The collector knows that it can never be shown publicly but that's not why they want the piece in the first place. Valuable works of art are a favourite commodity for criminal organisations, who will use them in place of cash for making deals with each other. They are also useful for money launderers, as works of art are easier to transport and harder to trace than cash, as well as easily traded on the black market.

Q: 2

A: A big star auditioning for a part is almost unheard of. Actors such as Tom Hanks go straight from film to film, so directors and producers have access to a whole portfolio of their work. The closest such actors ever get to anything resembling an audition is when they're invited to chat about the project informally, which gives the director and producer a chance to evaluate the actor without it feeling like a test. The stars don't usually even have to read part of the script. More often, it's actually a matter of the actor choosing whether to work with the director!

GRAMMAR

PARTICIPLE CLAUSES

2 A Read the article below. In what situations do celebrities use fake names? What is the joke in each chosen name?

Do stars use their real names when travelling?

In short, no. In fact, stars [1]**registered at hotels under their real name** are a rarity – their day can be ruined by paparazzi [2]**trying to take their pictures** and members of the public [3]**taking selfies**. So if you're going to change your name, why not have fun doing it? Names [4]**involving wordplay** are common: Britney Spears uses Ms Alotta Warmheart among other names, and Brad Pitt and Jennifer Aniston, [5]**married in 2000 but divorced five years later**, used to call themselves Mr and Mrs Ross Vegas. And the fun doesn't end there – the name [6]**used by George Clooney** when he was travelling caused him great amusement: Arnold Schwarzenegger. 'It was funny, the hotel staff had to call me Mr Schwarzenegger, when they knew of course, I wasn't him,' said Clooney.

B Work in pairs and look at the participle clauses in bold in the article. Then answer the questions.

1 Which participle clauses in bold replace relative clauses?   *all of them*

2 What is the full relative clause in each case?

3 Which two verb forms can a participle clause begin with?   *present participle / past participle*

C Compare the sentences below and underline the participle clauses. Then complete the rule.

1 a) Names which involve wordplay are common.
   b) Names involving wordplay are common.

2 a) The people who worked in the hotel thought the name was funny.
   b) The people working in the hotel thought the name was funny.

3 a) The hotel, which was built in the 1980s and which is often used by film stars, is famous.
   b) The hotel, built in the 1980s and regularly used by film stars, is famous.

RULES

1 When a relative clause has an active verb in the present simple or past simple, the participle clause uses a _present_ participle.

2 When a relative clause has a passive verb in the present simple or past simple, the participle clause uses a _past_ participle.

PP

speakout TIP

Using participle clauses can improve the level of your writing and speaking. Try to improve this sentence by using a participle clause: *I couldn't concentrate on the concert because there were so many people who took photos.*

▷ page 136 **LANGUAGEBANK**

---

3 A Rewrite the sentences using a participle clause.

1 People who take photos should ask their subjects' permission first.   *after* ... *taking*

2 Films that are based on books are disappointing.

3 It's great to see rock stars in their sixties who still play concerts.   *playing*

4 Architecture which was designed in the 1960s is generally quite ugly and ought to be pulled down.

5 Photos of people who are posing for the camera don't work as well as spontaneous pictures.

6 Film and TV stars who appear at the theatre attract huge audiences.   *appearing*

7 Jokes which involve racial stereotypes are not funny.   *involving*

8 Photographers who used software to enhance their photos were justifiably banned from entering a national competition last month.   *using* ... *improve*

B Work in pairs and discuss. Do you agree with the statements in Exercise 3A? Give examples.

VOCABULARY

THE ARTS

4 A Which of the forum comments are generally positive (✓), negative (✗) or mixed (–)?

❝ I'd read a lot about this new singer in the music press. She's certainly **creating a stir** with her **ground-breaking** mix of rap and folk. Ever since she got those **rave reviews** in the press, each performance has been a **sell-out** and it's impossible to get tickets. Everyone says it's the **must-see** performance of the year. Is she really that good? ❞

❝ Well, after all the **hype** surrounding her concerts, I went to see her on Friday, expecting something really sensational … but the concert was a real **letdown**! It was a complete **flop** because we couldn't hear her properly. ❞

❝ Yeah, I was at that gig and the technical side was pretty bad but her album is amazing, really innovative. I've never heard anything quite like it before. I just hope she doesn't go **mainstream** and boring like all the other **alternative** artists. ❞

B Work in pairs. What do you think the words and phrases in bold above mean? Use the context, grammar and your knowledge of similar words to help. Then check in a dictionary.

C ▶ 10.3 **WORD STRESS** Work in pairs and say the words and phrases in bold. Which syllable(s) is/are stressed? Listen to the words in context and check.

D Think of a performance you have seen or heard. Write a forum entry about it using at least four of the words which are new to you.

E Read other students' forum entries. Find a performance you would like to see or hear.

▷ page 142 **VOCABULARYBANK**

SPEAKING

5 A Choose three of the questions below to answer. Write the name of the thing/person and two or three words to explain why you liked it/him/her.

1 What's the best gig/concert or dance performance you've ever been to?
2 What's the best music album ever made?
3 Who's the funniest comedian you know?
4 What's the most moving, scary or exciting film you've ever seen?
5 What's the most memorable exhibition you've ever been to?
6 What's the best photo you've ever taken?
7 Who's the painter or other type of artist you most like? What's your favourite work of his/hers?
8 What's the most unforgettable show or play you've ever seen?

B Work in pairs and take turns. Talk about your experiences and feelings.

C Work in groups and take turns. Recommend something you've recently been to/seen/heard.

VOCABULARY *PLUS*

TWO-PART PHRASES

6 A Work in pairs and look at the two-part phrases in sentences 1 and 2. What do you think they mean?

1 There are some basic **dos and don'ts** when taking a good photo.
2 I've worked in the film business **off and on** for most of my life.

B Check your ideas with the dictionary entries.

> **D** **dos and don'ts** things that you should and should not do: *the dos and don'ts of having a pet*

> **O** **off and on/on and off** for short periods of time but not regularly: *I worked as a secretary off and on for three years.*

From Longman Active Study Dictionary.

7 A Match a word from A with one from B to make a two-part phrase.

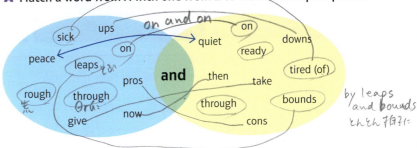

sick and tired of ～にうんざりする

sick   ups   on and on   on   downs
quiet   ready
peace   on
leaps   tired (of)
and   then   take
rough   pros   through   bounds
through   by leaps and bounds
give   now   cons   どんどん すごい勢いで

B ▶ **10.4** **CONNECTED SPEECH** Listen and check. Then listen and repeat, paying attention to the linking, the weak form of *and* /ən/ and the dropping of /d/ in connected speech.

ups and downs

8 A Work in pairs. Student A: turn to page 145. Student B: turn to page 143. Read the definitions and then complete five of the sentences below.

1 I hate having music on in the background. I prefer some _____ and _____.
2 I used to go to rock concerts a lot but nowadays I only go _____ and _____.
3 I'm a reggae fan _____ and _____.
4 I'm _____ and _____ of having to listen to people's favourite music on the train. I wish they'd turn their MP3 players down.
5 Any skill such as playing the piano improves in _____ and _____ if you practise enough.
6 Every relationship has its _____ and _____ so it's not surprising that most bands break up after a few years.
7 I don't like jazz. Some of the pieces go _____ and _____ for far too long.
8 It's OK for my neighbours to play music I don't like. You have to have a bit of _____ and _____. I'm sure they don't like my music!
9 There are _____ and _____ to listening to a live recording as opposed to a studio album.
10 Some of the music videos made by ordinary people on *YouTube* are a bit _____ and _____ but that's OK.

B Work in pairs and take turns. Help your partner to complete the sentences and understand the two-part phrases.

C Change five of the sentences so that they are true for you. Then compare with a partner. How many do you agree on?

▷ page 142 **VOCABULARYBANK**

10.3)) ON YOUR LEFT …

F giving a tour
P intonation in comments
V dimensions

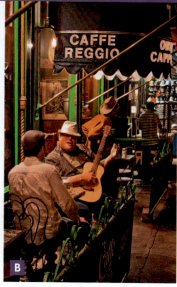

A

B

C

D

Greenwich Village, New York, USA

SPEAKING

1 Work in pairs and discuss the questions.

1 Have you ever shown anyone around your town/city?

2 What places of interest in your town/city you would take a visitor to? Why?

FUNCTION

GIVING A TOUR

2 A Work in pairs. Look at the photos of Greenwich Village and Oxford and discuss. What do you know about each place? Which would you most like to visit?

B ▶ 10.5 Listen to two people showing visitors around Greenwich Village and Oxford. Number the photos in the order you hear them.

C Listen again and write one fact you hear about each place.

1 The Blue Note Jazz Club
2 The Café Reggio
3 Greenwich Village in general
4 Washington Square Park
5 The Bodleian Library
6 The Oxford colleges
7 The Bridge of Sighs
8 New College
9 The 'Schools'
10 Christ Church College

3 A Work in pairs and complete the phrases. Sometimes there is more than one possible answer.

Leading the way

Let's ¹ *head* over to Washington Square Park and then ² *circle* back.

Why don't we ³ *retrace* _____ our steps and go back to the Café Reggio?

Giving facts

It was ⁴ *modelled* _____ on the Arc de Triomphe.

It was built to ⁵ *celebrate* _____ the hundredth anniversary of the inauguration of George Washington as president.

In front of us is the Bodleian, ⁶ _____ after the ⁷ _____ – Thomas Bodley.   *named*   *founder*

Commenting on facts

⁸ *As* I'm sure you ⁹ *know*, Greenwich Village has always been a centre of artistic life – very bohemian.

¹⁰ *Interestingly*, the oldest college was actually only founded a hundred or so years earlier!

¹¹ *Apparently*, the biggest room can seat somewhere in the region of 500 students although I haven't seen it myself.

We can actually go inside if we're quick. It's well ¹² *worth* a visit.

B Compare your answers with the audio script on page 153.

C ▶ 10.6 **INTONATION IN COMMENTS** Listen to the intonation in the phrases. Then listen again and repeat.

Interestingly, the statue disappeared at the time of his death.

The story goes, he threw it in the lake.

Apparently, it was made of gold.

Surprisingly, no one has ever tried to find it.

▷ page 136 **LANGUAGEBANK**

E F

Oxford, England

4 A Complete A's part in the extracts from a tour of Paris.

A: ¹Let's / head / over / the cathedral, Notre Dame.

B: On the island? Do we have time to go inside?

A: ²Yes, / well worth / visit it.

B: … So that's the Arc de Triomphe?

A: ³Yes, / model / a famous Roman arch.

B: And why was it built?

A: ⁴celebrate / one / Napoleon's great victories.

A: ⁵… So here we are / the Eiffel Tower / named / its designer, Gustave Eiffel.

B: Wow! It's impressive.

A: ⁶Yeah / apparently / can sway six to seven centimetres in the wind!

B Work in pairs and take turns. Practise the conversations using the prompts above.

VOCABULARY

DIMENSIONS

5 Complete the tourist's questions with the noun or verb form of the adjectives in brackets.

1 What is the _hight_ of the tower? (high)
2 So the road goes the _length_ of the town? (long)
3 When did they _broad_ _widen_ the entrance? (wide)
4 What is the _thickness_ of the wall here? (thick)
5 The road _narrows_ here. Why's that? (narrow)
6 What's the _breadth_ of the river and _depth_ of the water here? (broad, deep)
7 Why don't they _enlarge_ the map? It's so small. (large)
8 It's nine o'clock and it's still light. When do the days _shorten_ here? (short)

broad breadth broaden / wide width widen
adj. n. ✓ adj. n. ✓
s bredd3

LEARN TO

EXPRESS ESTIMATES

6 A Look at the extracts and underline five phrases for expressing estimates (when we don't know the exact number).

1 **A:** How many colleges are there?
   B: Just under forty. Well, thirty-eight to be exact.

2 **A:** How 'new' is new?
   B: Roughly 1370.
   A: You're kidding!
   B: No, really! Interestingly, the oldest college was actually only founded a hundred or so years earlier!

3 Apparently, the biggest room can seat somewhere in the region of five hundred students.

4 **A:** How many students are there at the university in total?
   B: To be honest, it depends. In term time, you'd probably get upwards of twenty thousand.

B Which phrases in Exercise 6A could be replaced by 1) *fewer than*, 2) *more than* or 3) *about/around/ approximately*?

C ▶ 10.7 Listen and tick the exact number.

1 **a)** 1,400   **b)** 1,518
2 **a)** 30   **b)** 38
3 **a)** 1,180   **b)** 1,220
4 **a)** 712   **b)** 746
5 **a)** 2.13   **b)** 1.10
6 **a)** 318   **b)** 371

D Work in pairs and take turns to estimate:

- the number of students in your school/employees in your workplace.
- the age of the building you're in.
- the population of your town/city.
- the distance from your home to where you are now.
- the cost of dinner in a good restaurant in your town/city.
- the number of contacts on your mobile phone.
- the number of English words you know.

SPEAKING

7 A Work in pairs. Design a one-hour walking or cycling tour of a town/city you know for a visitor. Make notes on:

- four or five places to see.
- a fact or personal opinion about each place.
- some approximate numbers associated with the place (how many people visit it; how much it costs; how old/long/high, etc. it is).

B Work with a new partner and take turns. Role-play the tour. Student A: lead the way. Student B: ask questions.

DVD PREVIEW

1 A Look at the photos of a new library and discuss the questions in pairs.

1 Which words/phrases in the box would you use to describe the building?

> crazy   makes a bold statement   unique   fresh
> pleasing on the eye   modern   too busy   delicate
> too elaborate   beautiful   amazing   unsightly

2 How is it different from what you expect a library to look like?

3 What facilities would you expect to be included in a 21st-century library?

B Read the programme information and look at the photos. Which of the following do you think you will see in the DVD?

1 The reporter interviews local people, the designer of the building and celebrities.

2 The designer explains why she used rings as part of the design.

3 The local people feel mostly positive about the new library.

▶)) The Culture Show: BBC The People's Palace

At a time when many libraries across Britain face budget cuts and closure, Birmingham is opening the biggest public library in Europe. Is this a new breed of super library for the future?

This programme explores the cutting-edge building to discover what a 21st-century library looks like, what goes into its design, and how local people – the taxpayers – feel about it. Perhaps most importantly, we find out what role the library has in the internet age.

DVD VIEW

2 A Watch the DVD and check your answers to Exercise 1B.

B Work in pairs and answer the questions. Then watch the DVD again and check.

1 Why and how is Birmingham regenerating its city centre?

2 How does the designer describe the city of Birmingham? What characteristics did she try to reflect in the library's design?

3 Why did she call it a 'People's Palace'?

4 What is there inside the library besides shelves of books?

5 What is the 'façade bench' and what can you do there?

6 What do people say they like once they're inside the library?

C Watch the DVD again and underline the correct alternative.

1 We started with this idea, that's the *tradition/ heritage* of the proud industrial city, with the steel industry.

2 I think any *funding/investment* of money put into libraries at the moment is fantastic.

3 And in a time of economic *austerity/strictness*, what a bold step to take. Wonderful stuff!

4 There's a lot of people, students, they want to be *independent/individual* but be part of a bigger collective.

5 It's brilliant, yeah, I really like it, it's very *user-friendly/easy-to-use*.

6 I love this *in particular/especially*. I love this outside *bit/section* with the balcony.

3 Work in pairs and discuss whether you agree/ disagree with the statements.

1 Local governments shouldn't spend taxpayer's money on expensive architecture.

2 Libraries still have an important role in the internet age.

3 For a society to be healthy, it needs public spaces like libraries, parks and theatres.

speakout a town project

4 A ▶ **10.8** Listen to three people discussing a new public space or artistic project for their town. Which project does each person, Tim, Nigel and Sarah, like from the list below? Why?

- an outdoor sculpture (modern or traditional)
- a concert space
- a theatre workshop space for young people
- a state-of-the-art multiplex cinema
- a botanical garden
- a skateboarding park

B Listen again and tick the key phrases you hear.

> **KEYPHRASES**
>
> I'm really in favour of the …
> I think that it would be [beneficial for the community/popular/ …].
> The only thing that would concern me though is that …
> I'd rather have something that would [appeal to all ages/make a statement/…]
> We have to consider [costs/maintenance/ …]
> Can you see the [older/younger] generation [using/liking] it?

5 A Work in pairs. You are responsible for choosing an artistic project for your town/city. Choose two items from the list in Exercise 4A. The items must:

- have artistic and/or architectural merit.
- represent the town/city in some way.
- convey a positive image.

B Work with other students. Discuss your ideas and decide on one project.

C Present your decision to the class.

writeback a work of art

6 A Work in pairs. Read about the competition and tell your partner what you would choose and why.

> We want you to write about a favourite work of art or building. It could be a statue or sculpture, a fountain or bridge, a painting or even a favourite room. Send us your description in 150–250 words, and we'll put the five best entries on our website.

B Read the description and tick (✓) the topics in the box that the writer mentions.

> setting   when it was made   material   colour
> size   who made it   why he/she likes it

My favourite building is in fact a bridge, the Millau Viaduct in southern France. It's an awe-inspiring structure, as much a work of art as it is a bridge. It towers over the valley that it crosses, but is so graceful that it seems to me more an integral part of the natural environment than the architectural and engineering achievement that it is.

It was designed by a French engineer and a British architect who conceived it as a series of towers, which look like the masts of a ship, from which cables are suspended, the cables that support the road surface that runs 2500 metres across the valley. The highest tower is the tallest structure in France, taller than the Eiffel Tower, and I think the tallest bridge in the world.

This 21st-century masterpiece is breathtaking to behold, and it gives me a sense of calm every time I look at it. No one should miss it if they are visiting this part of France.

C Write your competition entry. Use the box in Exercise 6B for ideas of what to include.

D Read your classmates' competition entries. Which one makes you most want to visit the place they write about?

V ADJECTIVES

1 A Work in pairs. Make a list of as many adjectives for describing films as you can remember.

B Complete comments 1–4 with a suitable adjective.

1 The ending was sensitively handled and made me cry! Very _____!

2 The script was basically one joke after another. Absolutely _____!

3 It kept my attention for two hours. Utterly _____!

4 My friends and I are still arguing about it. Quite _____!

C Work in pairs. Write four review comments similar to the ones above. Use a suitable adjective for describing films in each review.

G RELATIVE CLAUSES

2 A Underline the correct alternative.

I'd like to find …

1 a person *who/for whom/whose* main interests include **doing sports**.

2 a place *that/which/where* I can **speak English with native speakers**.

3 someone *that/whose/whom* knows **a famous person**.

4 a shop *where/which/that* I can buy **reasonably priced clothes**.

5 a person for *whose/that/whom* **money** is not important.

6 three **interesting places in this town/city** *which/to which/ where* I've never been to.

B Change the words in bold in four of the sentences above so that they are about things/people you'd like to find.

C Ask other students questions about your sentences in Exercise 2B.

A: Do you know anyone whose main interests include going to the cinema?
B: Yes – me.
A: Right. Who's your favourite actor?
B: At the moment, Christian Bale.

G PARTICIPLE CLAUSES

3 A Complete the quiz with the present or past participles of the verbs in brackets.

Trivia quiz

1 It's an arts building _____ (stand) in Sydney Harbour and _____ (make) of white tiles to look like sails.

2 It's a company _____ (start) by Steve Jobs, Steve Wozniak and Ronald Wayne, best _____ (know) for its iPod and iPhone products.

3 It's a game _____ (play) by two players, _____ (involve) a small rubber ball and racquets and _____ (take) place in a four-walled court indoors.

4 He was a great leader, born in Corsica, _____ (crown) Emperor of France in 1804 and _____ (defeat) at Waterloo in 1815.

5 It's a statuette _____ (award) to people in the film world every year by the American Academy of Motion Picture Arts and Sciences.

6 They're a group of people _____ (live) in cold, snowy parts of the USA and Canada, and _____ (use) blocks of ice to build their houses, _____ (call) igloos.

7 It's a Japanese dish _____ (consist) of raw fish and rice _____ (roll) up in seaweed.

8 It's a play _____ (write) by Shakespeare and _____ (feature) a Danish prince.

B Work in pairs and do the quiz.

C Check your answers on page 143.

V THE ARTS

4 The words in bold are in the wrong sentences. Put them in the correct sentences.

1 The musical was a complete **sell-out** and had to close early.

2 Does the Picasso exhibition deserve all those **hype** reviews?

3 The new sculpture is **alternative**. Everyone's arguing about it.

4 He's famous for his **mainstream** work in photography, never done before.

5 You can't get tickets for the show. It's a complete **rave**.

6 I thought the new album was a real **must-see**, very poor.

7 That new comedian is certainly creating a lot of **flop**. Everyone's talking about him.

8 This Virtual Worlds Exhibition is a **letdown** event. Don't miss it!

9 I don't listen to **ground-breaking** pop music much. It all sounds the same.

10 During **creating a stir** Fashion Week you can see some shockingly original clothes.

F GIVING A TOUR

5 A Complete descriptions 1–3 below with the words in the box. Where are the places?

| ~~was~~ | story | worth | it | you |
| honour | named | rebuilt | | |

was

1 It built in the 17th century by Shah Jahan in of his wife. As may know, it's made of white marble and is well a visit.

2 It was after its designer and was built in 1889. The goes that many Parisians hated it because it was too modern.

3 Parts of it were many times. Believe or not, millions of Chinese died in its construction.

B Write two sentences about a tourist site you know.

C Read out your sentences. The other students guess the place.

IRREGULAR VERBS

Verb	Past simple	Past participle
be	was	been
beat	beat	beaten
become	became	become
begin	began	begun
bend	bent	bent
bet	bet	bet
bite	bit	bitten
bleed	bled	bled
blow	blew	blown
break	broke	broken
bring	brought	brought
broadcast	broadcast	broadcast
build	built	built
burn	burned/burnt	burned/burnt
burst	burst	burst
buy	bought	bought
catch	caught	caught
choose	chose	chosen
come	came	come
cost	cost	cost
cut	cut	cut
deal	dealt	dealt
dig	dig	dug
do	did	done
draw	drew	drawn
dream	dreamed/dreamt	dreamed/dreamt
drink	drank	drunk
drive	drove	driven
eat	ate	eaten
fall	fell	fallen
feel	felt	felt
feed	fed	fed
fight	fought	fought
find	found	found
fly	flew	flown
forbid	forbade	forbidden
forget	forgot	forgotten
forgive	forgave	forgiven
freeze	froze	frozen
get	got	got
give	gave	given
go	went	gone
grow	grew	grown
hang	hung	hung
have	had	had
hear	heard	heard
hide	hid	hidden
hit	hit	hit
hold	held	held
hurt	hurt	hurt
keep	kept	kept
know	knew	known
lay	laid	laid
lead	led	led
leap	leapt	leapt
lean	leaned/leant	leaned/leant
learn	learned/learnt	learned/learnt

Verb	Past simple	Past participle
leave	left	left
lend	lent	lent
let	let	let
lie	lay	lain
light	lit	lit
lose	lost	lost
make	made	made
mean	meant	meant
meet	met	met
mistake	mistook	mistaken
pay	paid	paid
put	put	put
read	read	read
ride	rode	ridden
ring	rang	rung
rise	rose	risen
run	ran	run
say	said	said
see	saw	seen
sell	sold	sold
send	sent	sent
set	set	set
shake	shook	shaken
shine	shone	shone
shoot	shot	shot
show	showed	shown
shrink	shrank	shrunk
shut	shut	shut
sing	sang	sung
sink	sank	sunk
sit	sat	sat
sleep	slept	slept
slide	slid	slid
smell	smelled/smelt	smelled/smelt
speak	spoke	spoken
spell	spelt	spelt
spend	spent	spent
spill	spilled/spilt	spilled/spilt
split	split	split
spread	spread	spread
stand	stood	stood
steal	stole	stolen
stick	stuck	stuck
sting	stung	stung
swim	swam	swum
take	took	taken
teach	taught	taught
tear	tore	torn
tell	told	told
think	thought	thought
throw	threw	thrown
understand	understood	understood
wake	woke	woken
wear	wore	worn
win	won	won
write	wrote	written

GRAMMAR

6.1 modal verbs and related phrases

(handwritten: へるべきだったのに 実際はしなかった)

(handwritten: HW 27/2)

	present	past
obligation (strong) *(強制)*	have to go must go make someone go	had to go – made someone go
obligation (mild)	should go ought to go [ɔːt] *(handwritten: [ɔːt])* am supposed to go	should have gone ought to have gone was supposed to go
lack of obligation	don't have to go	didn't have to go
prohibition (strong) *(禁止)*	mustn't go can't go am not allowed to go	– couldn't go wasn't allowed to go
prohibition (mild)	shouldn't go oughtn't to go am not supposed to go	shouldn't have gone oughtn't to have gone wasn't supposed to go
permission *(許可)*	can go am allowed to go may go let someone go	could go was allowed to go might go let someone go
ability	can/can't go am/am not able to go manage/ don't manage to go	could/couldn't go was/wasn't able to go managed/ didn't manage to go

(handwritten left margin: Question ·Ought I to do? ✗Do I ought to?)

(handwritten: (やっかいなことを) 何とかうまくやっていく)

(handwritten: へるべきではなかったのに 実際はしてしまった)

obligation
Must can express that the obligation is internal, not (only) because of a rule.
*I **must** finish this report – I don't want to annoy the boss.*
Use *make someone do something* when someone forces another person to do something.
*My mum **makes** me study for two hours every night.*
Use *be supposed to* especially when the obligation is broken.
*I'm not **supposed** to eat chocolate but…*

lack of obligation/prohibition
Note the difference between *don't have to* and *mustn't*:
*You **don't have to** arrive before 5p.m.* (it's **not necessary**)
*You **mustn't** arrive before 5p.m.* (you're not allowed to)

permission
Use *let + someone* or *allow someone to* to say that someone gave permission to someone.
*Do you think she'll **let** me take a day off?*
*My company **allows us** to work from home one day a week.* *(handwritten: [au])*

ability
For ability on a single occasion in the past, use *was/were able to* or *managed to* (not *could*).
*He **was able to** find his way out of the forest and get help.*
NOT *He could find his way …*
Use *manage to* for something that is/was difficult to do.
*He **managed to** run the race in under three hours.*

(handwritten: (やっかいなことを)何とかうまくやっていく)

6.2 future perfect and continuous

future continuous
Use *will + be + -ing* form for:
- something that will be in progress at or around a specific future time. 
  *I'll **be driving** home when you call, so just leave a message.*

(diagram: now — driving — you call)

- something that will happen in the normal course of events, not as part of a particular intention or plan.
  *I expect I'll **be talking** to Ian tomorrow, so I could ask him then.*

Note: We can use this meaning to introduce requests in a neutral way.
*A: **Will you be passing** the postbox?*
B: Yes.
A: In that case, could you post this for me?

(handwritten: Q. Do you think.)

future perfect
Use *will + have + past participle* to talk about something that will finish before a specific time in the future, often with the preposition *by*, meaning *at the latest*.
*I'll **have finished** this report by the end of the week.*

(diagram: now — ? ? ? ? — the end of the week — finish the report)

It's possible to use other modals, adverbs and phrases with both forms.
*I **might have finished**/I **definitely won't have finished**/
I'd **like to have finished** by then.*
*This time next week I **could be relaxing**/I'll **probably be relaxing**/I'd **like to be relaxing** on a beach.*

6.3 persuading *(説得する)*

Use the following phrases to persuade someone by giving a strong opinion:

Surely Clearly Anyone can see that	parents need to take more responsibility for their kids' education.

Use negative questions when you want to persuade someone by inviting them to agree with you.

Don't you agree/think (that) Isn't it true/obvious that	texting is harmful for children's writing?
Shouldn't people Doesn't she want to	spend more time at home?

PRACTICE

6.1

A Underline the correct alternatives in the blog.

HW 22/2

HOME » TRAVEL

Traveller's journal – Changing times

… it was the 1980s and travel there was very restricted back then. Of course you [1]*had to/must* get a visa to enter the country as well as a permit to travel to most cities. Or at least you [2]*should/were supposed* to get a permit; I didn't always get one, and once without a permit I [3]*could/managed to* go to a town that foreigners technically [4]*couldn't/didn't have to* go to. The police called me in and [5]*made/let* me answer questions. I spoke the language a little so I was [6]*able to/allowed to* communicate with them. Once they were convinced that I wasn't a spy, they [7]*allowed/let* me go and I was [8]*allowed to/able* stay there as long as I wanted. Of course, it's changed so much now. You still [9]*must/have to* get a visa to enter, but you [10]*mustn't/don't have to* get a permit to go anywhere within the country. As was always the case, if you [11]*are able/can* speak the language, it's a really enriching experience, and I think everyone [12]*ought to/is supposed to* try to spend at least a few weeks travelling there.

B Rewrite the sentences. Use the word in brackets so that the meaning stays the same.

1 I fell asleep. It was difficult. (manage)
   I _managed to fall asleep_ .
2 We stayed for dinner. There was no choice. (to)
   We _had to stay for dinner_ .
3 He gave me permission to listen to my MP3 player. (let)
   He _let me to listen to my MP3 player_
4 It was too dark to see anything. (not able)
   He _wasn't able to see anything_ *because of* darkness
5 It's a good idea for her to leave before dark. (ought)
   She _ought to leave before dark_ .
6 The rule was to pay before going in. We didn't pay at all. (suppose)
   We _were supposed to pay before going in_
7 The maximum age to enter this disco is eighteen. (not allow) *aren't*
   Adults _weren't allowed to enter this disco_
8 I had to change my passport photo. (make)
   They _made me ~~to~~ change my passport photo._

6.2

A Complete the sentences with the future perfect or the future continuous form of the verb in brackets.

1 The film starts at eight, and it's about two hours long.
   At nine, I'll _be watching_ the film. (watch)
   By eleven, the film _will have finised_ (finish)
2 Her plane lands at 11.45p.m.
   At midnight she _probably will be waiting_ for her luggage. (probably/wait)
   By the time we wake up tomorrow, she _will have arrived_ in Madrid. (arrive)
3 The world hotdog-eating champion can eat more than six hotdogs a minute.
   In ten minutes from now, he _will have eaten_ over sixty hotdogs. (eat)
   Tonight in his sleep, he _will be dreaming_ about hotdogs! (dream)
4 Give me a day to think about it.
   By this time tomorrow, I'll _have decided_ (decide)
   This time next week, I'll _be wishing_ I had decided differently. (wish)

B Find and correct the mistakes in A's part of the conversations.

27/02 HW

Conversation 1 *see – be seeing*
✗ A: [1]Will you ~~seeing~~ Frank today?
   B: Yes, do you want me to give him a message?
   A: [2]Yes, could you tell him I won't *probably* have finished the report ~~until~~ tomorrow. *by*   · *positive. I'll probably*

Conversation 2
   A: [3]Just think – this time tomorrow you'll ~~finish~~ all your exams. *have finished*
   B: I know. That's what keeps me going.
   A: [4]And you *you'll* be celebrating with your friends.

Conversation 3
   A: [5]Will you ~~use~~ your computer at lunchtime today? *be using* I've got a problem with mine.
   B: No, I'm going out and I won't be back till four if you want to use it till then.
   A: [6]I might still *be* using it when you get back. The technicians might not have fixed mine by then.

6.3

A Use the prompts to complete the sentences. Use negative questions where appropriate.

A: [1]Do / agree / people / should / able / start a family when they're teenagers?
   Don't you agree that people should be able to start …
B: What, even at 16 or 17?
A: Yes. [2]Clear / they at the peak of their physical health.
B: [3]But / is / it / obvious / most / 17-year-olds aren't even mature enough to be responsible for themselves?

A: Yeah, [4]but does / depend / the individual? Some 18-year-olds might make good parents.
B: [5]But / sure / they / need / time to sort out their own lives first.
A: [6]But / is / it / fact / that in some cultures 18 is a normal age to have a family?
B: Yes, [7]but / anyone / see / that what works in one culture won't necessarily work in every culture.
A: Hmm. Maybe you're right.

GRAMMAR

7.1   quantifiers

	100%	a large amount	a small amount	0%
uncountable or plural nouns	all, any	a lot of, lots of, plenty of, most	some, hardly any	no, not any
uncountable nouns		much, a large amount of, a great deal of	a little, little	
plural nouns	both (= all of two)	many, a large number of, quite a few	several, a small number of, a few, few	
singular nouns	each, every, any			no, not any, neither (= none of two)

no, not any @ uncountable / plural / singular.

a few/a little = some or a small amount
*There's still **a little** butter left.*

few/little = not many/much or not as many/much as wanted or expected
*Very **few** people came to the meeting.*

any = It doesn't matter which/who
*I like **any** brand(s) of chocolate.*
Any is stressed.

Use *both* + plural verb, *neither* + singular verb.
***Both** of us run a business but **neither** of us is good with numbers.*

Another + singular nouns and numbers = something is additional to the existing number.
*Could I have **another** piece of cake, please.*
*We've got **another** three meetings today.*

Use the pronoun *none* for a short answer.
*How much sugar have we got? **None**.*

7.2   reported speech

In reported speech, the original verb form often goes back further into the past. Pronouns, time references, etc. also change.

direct speech	reported speech
present simple/continuous *'I want to be a chef.'* *'We're working.'*	past simple/continuous *He said he wanted to be a chef.* *She told me they were working.*
past simple/present perfect *'Ben phoned me last week.'* *'I've read your book.'*	past perfect *She told me Ben had phoned her the week before.* *He said he'd read my book.*
will/would/can/could/should *'We'll help you tomorrow.'* *'You can stay with me.'*	would/could/should *He said they'd help me the next day.* *She said I could stay with her.*

It is not necessary to change the verb form when reporting something that is still true now or was said very recently.
'It's going to rain.' Sam's just said it's going to rain.

reported questions
Use normal statement word order without *do/does/did* or a question mark.
*'What does Ian think?' She asked me **what Ian thought**.*
NOT ~~She asked me what did Ian think.~~
With *yes/no* questions, use *if* or *whether*.
*'Are you OK?' She asked **if** I was OK.*
Also use *wanted to know, enquired* and *wondered*.
*They **wanted to know** what time the train left.*

reported requests
Use verb + object + infinitive with *to*.
*'Could you sing?' He asked us **to sing**.*

time phrases and place references
Time phrases and place references usually change.
now → then/at that time
yesterday → the day before/previous day
tomorrow → the following/next day
a week ago → the week before
here → there

7.3   adding emphasis

auxiliary verbs	
add or stress auxiliaries	I **do** hate it when people smoke indoors. It **is** annoying.

intensifiers	
really, so + any adjective or adverb	It's **so** outrageous. You play **really well**.
absolutely, completely, totally + extreme adjectives	It's **completely** ridiculous.
such (a/an) + (adjective) + noun	It'll be **such an** amazing day. It was **such** terrible weather.

emphasising phrases	
pronoun/noun + *be* + *the one who*	**You're the one who** chose it.
the + adjective + *thing* + *be*	**The best thing was** the music.

informal phrases	
There's no way (that) …	**There's no way** Tom stole the money.
What/Who/Where/Why/How on earth … ?	**Why on earth** didn't you say? **Where on earth** did you buy that?

PRACTICE

8/3 HW

7.1

A Underline the correct alternative.

What does your ringtone say about you?

Almost everyone now has a mobile phone and ¹*a great deal/a large number/the most* of us have our own ringtone. Is it *only* so that we can distinguish our own phone from others or is it because ²*each/a large number of/both* time our phone rings we want to be able to say, 'Listen to that. That's me!'? Maybe ³*either/both/each* reasons are true. Here is a quick guide to ⁴*some/few/a little* typical ringtones and what they say about their users.

If your ringtone is ⁵*either/both/neither* a hip hop tune or a current hit, then you are young at heart but not particularly original.

⁶*Any/All/Either* classic rock tune means you're probably over thirty but you know you're still cool.

⁷*Not much/A few/Very few* people think annoying animal noises are as funny as the phones' owners obviously do. So ⁸*no/none/neither* points for maturity there.

You download a new one every month? You must be a teenager or you have ⁹*plenty of/a large number of/hardly any* time and money.

You never change it? Either you're too lazy or you don't know how. ¹⁰*Neither/Both/Any* is an acceptable reason!

specific quantity

annoying (adj) making you feel slightly angry

B Complete sentences 1–10 with a quantifier from the box.

| quite a few | a few | very few | a little | very little |
| other | another | any (x2) | either |

not many

1 Everyone wanted to get home and so there were ___very few___ questions at the end of the lecture.

2 I'm afraid I've spilt ___a little___ wine on the carpet.

3 ___A few___ of the students (four of us to be exact) have signed your petition.

4 I've watched ___quite a few___ basketball games, probably twenty or thirty, but I've never seen such an exciting match.

5 Carla couldn't afford a taxi because she had ___very little___ money left.

6 You can click on ___either___ 'save' or 'save as' and then give the document a name.

7 Are you having ___any___ other problems with the photocopier?

8 I like ___any___ music by Jade. She's great.

9 One car isn't enough. We need ___another___ car.

10 I don't care what ___other___ people think.

7.2

A Read the questions then complete the reported speech below.

1 Where <u>have</u> you <u>been</u> all day?

2 What <u>were</u> you <u>watching</u> on TV last night?

3 <u>Have</u> you <u>washed</u> your hands for dinner?

4 <u>Have</u> you <u>got</u> any homework for tomorrow?

5 Are you going to help me with the housework this weekend?

My mother used to ask me questions at the strangest times:

- When I came home from school she wanted to know ¹ ___where I...___ *had been all day*

- The morning after we'd spent the evening watching TV together, she asked me ² *what I had been watching on TV the previous night*

- At 10 in the morning, she used to ask ³ *if I had washed my hands for dinner*

- In the middle of the summer holiday, she asked me ⁴ *If I had gotten any homework for the following day*

- When she knew I was going on a weekend camping trip with friends, she asked ⁵ _____. *if I was going to help her with the housework that week.*

B Find and correct ten mistakes with reported speech in the story.

WEDNESDAY, FEBRUARY 23

My first (and most embarrassing) job interview
I was eighteen when I went for my first job interview, at a photo laboratory. The manager asked me take a seat and then asked what's my name and I was so nervous that I told him I don't understand the question. Then he wanted to know do I have any plant experience; I told that I had done some work in my grandmother's garden. He laughed and said that by 'plant' he had meant 'factory', not trees and flowers. I felt terribly embarrassed and simply told him that I have never worked in a factory. He had my file of photos and he asked that I talked about them. I was so nervous that I dropped them all on the floor! Then he asked me if I have had any referees; I thought he meant the kind of referees they have in a football match, so I told him that I didn't play team sports but that I had been doing long-distance running for years. I was sure that I'd messed up the interview, but then he enquired when I can start! He wanted me that I start the following Monday!

Posted by Online Blog at 8:54PM

7.3

A Make the soap opera script more dramatic by using the words in brackets. Make any other changes necessary.

A: What's the matter? You look terrible. (on earth)

B: I've just seen Marco with Claudia. I'm furious, I can hardly speak. (so)

A: That's crazy. I'm sure there's a mistake. Why don't you call him? (totally)

B: I'm not going to phone him. (there's no way)

A: But Marco's a great guy and you're good together. (such, so)

B: Well, you can be sure that Claudia's going to regret it. (really)

A: I hope you're not going to do anything stupid. (do)

B: You told me to fight for him. I'm just following your advice. (the one)

GRAMMAR

8.1 past and mixed conditionals

hypothetical past conditional (third conditional)

conditional clause	result clause
If + past perfect 過去完了	would/might/could + have + past participle 因主/分詞
If + past perfect continuous	

Use this to talk about a hypothetical situation and result in the past. The situation cannot be changed.

If Leon **had known** about the problem, he **would have helped.**

If you **hadn't overslept**, we **wouldn't have been** late.

For a longer action, use the past perfect continuous.

If I **hadn't been sitting** there, we **wouldn't have met.**

It is common to use only one clause of the full conditional.

Why didn't you tell me you wanted some grapes? I **could have bought** you some.

I'm surprised Paul didn't tell her what he thought. I **would have said** something.

A: **Would you have done** it?   B: Yes, if I**'d noticed** in time.

mixed conditional

conditional clause	result clause
If + past perfect	would/might/could + infinitive

Use this to talk about a hypothetical condition in the past with a result in the present.

If she **hadn't missed** her plane, she**'d be** in Mexico now.

If I**'d been** successful in the exam, I **might have** a better job now.

clause order

It is possible to change the order of the clauses. Note the non-use of the comma.

You **would have known** about the meeting if you**'d checked** your emails.

You **wouldn't need** a visa to work in Australia if you**'d been born** there.

8.2 -ing form and infinitive

Use an infinitive + to:	Examples
after these verbs: afford, agree, arrange, decide, expect, hope, intend, learn, manage, need, offer, plan, pretend, promise, refuse, seem, tend, threaten, want	We hope to start the meeting at 9. They promised to be here early.
after these verbs with an object: ask, advise, expect, help*, invite, persuade, remind, require, teach, want	Will wants me to go to the party with him.
After semi-fixed phrases: be good/lucky/happy/necessary/the first, have the chance/opportunity/time, somewhere/something/nowhere/nothing	She was lucky to get the job. There's nowhere to go and nothing to do.
to express purpose	I'm going there to see Tom.

-ing form	Examples
as a subject or object, i.e. as a noun.	Doing is better than thinking.
after prepositions (often part of a fixed phrase): look forward to, be used to, be accustomed to, be keen on, instead of	I'm not used to getting up early. I'm looking forward to sleeping late this weekend.
after these verbs: avoid, come, consider, discuss, deny, enjoy, go, hate, involve, keep, like, love, mind, miss, practise, suggest	Dave came fishing with me. I keep getting headaches. What do you suggest doing?
after certain phrases: can't bear/stand, it's not worth, it's no use, have trouble	We're having trouble finding a hotel.

Use an infinitive:	Examples
after modal verbs	They might be late.
after had better, would rather	You'd better take an umbrella – it looks like rain.
after these verbs with an object: let, make, help*	Our supervisor let us go early today.

*help can be used either with or without to.
Can you help me **(to) lift** this?

8.3 handling an awkward situation

preparing the listener

There's something	I've been meaning to talk to you about. I'd like to talk to you about.

giving the message

I hope you don't take this the wrong way, but …
I don't want you to get the wrong idea, but …
It's just that, (you know you borrowed/you said you'd … etc.)

suggesting a solution

I have a suggestion/an idea.
I'd feel better if …

getting the other person's point of view

Do you see where I'm coming from?
How does that sound?
How would you feel about that?
Do you know what I mean?

PRACTICE

8.1

A Choose the correct sentence ending.

1 If the builders had begun the job two weeks ago,
   a) they might have finished it by now.
   b) they might finish it by now.

2 If Chun had started the race better,
   a) she could win the gold medal.
   b) she could have won the gold medal.

3 We wouldn't be lost
   a) if you hadn't given me the wrong directions.
   b) if you gave me the wrong directions.

4 If Marco hadn't ignored my advice,
   a) he wouldn't be in this mess now.
   b) he couldn't have been in this mess now.

5 I would have noticed the hole in the ground
   a) if I hadn't thought about something else.
   b) if I hadn't been thinking about something else.

B Join the sentences using a past or mixed conditional form and the words in brackets. In some cases both forms are possible.

1 Beth didn't study. She didn't pass the exam. (could)
   If Beth had studied, she could have passed the exam.

2 You didn't invite me to the party. That's why I didn't come. (would)

3 Ludmila lost all her money on the stock market. That's why she's not rich now. (would)

4 Greg wasn't travelling fast. That's probably why he didn't hit the motorcyclist. (might)

5 They stopped the fire. That's probably why it didn't destroy most of the building. (could)

6 The plant died because you didn't water it. (would not)

7 Mei-li was able to afford a new car because she had just won some money. (could not)

8 We were working together in Tokyo and now we're married. (would not)

8.2

A Find and correct the mistakes in the sentences. Do not change the underlined phrase.

1 It's no use to explain – you never listen anyway.
   It's no use explaining – you never listen anyway.

2 There's no point in go to bed now – we have to get up in an hour. *going*

3 Do you expect that I know all the answers? *for me to know*

4 Listen to your MP3 player during class is rude. *Listening*

5 My parents never let me to stay out past 8 o'clock.

6 We all look forward to see you in person. *seeing*

7 You'd better to get ready – the taxi's arriving in ten minutes.

8 The trip was a good opportunity practising speaking English. *to practise*

9 They're used to speak English with each other even though they're both Japanese. *speaking*

10 I phoned the station for asking about departure times. *to ask*

B Use the correct form of the verbs in the box to rewrite the sentences so that they mean the same.

avoid / consider / expect / keep / manage / remind / teach

1 Why don't you become a doctor?
   Have _____.

2 I've passed my driving test – after three tries!
   I've _____.

3 I can type without looking. I learnt that from my mother.
   My mother _____.

4 We didn't talk to each other all through the party.
   We _____.

5 Jorge thinks that he'll finish the painting by the end of the week.
   Jorge _____.

6 My computer freezes whenever I hit the delete button.
   My computer _____.

7 Don't let me forget to lock the door, Jan.
   Could you _____?

8.3

A Complete the conversation with phrases a)–f). There is one phrase you do not need.

A: Max, ¹ _____C_____.
B: Sure, go ahead.
A: Look, ² _____ …
B: That sounds bad …
A: ³ _____b_____ you know how you always open the window when you come into the office? Well, it's often too cold for me.
B: Oh, right. I find it too stuffy.
A: It's a bit annoying because you don't ever ask us. ⁴ _____?
B: Fair enough. Look, I'll make sure I check first. ⁵ _____a_____?
A: Good. I'd really appreciate that.

a) How does that sound
b) It's just that
c) there's something I've been meaning to talk to you about
d) I'm sure we can sort it out 解決する
e) Do you see where I'm coming from
f) I don't want you to get the wrong idea, but

GRAMMAR

9.1 -ing form and infinitive

	+ infinitive with to	+ -ing form
remember forget	for things you plan, want or have the responsibility to do *He remembered to turn off the lights.*	have a memory of an earlier action *I'll never forget visiting Paris.*
try	attempt to do something difficult *Angus tried to change his ticket but it was impossible.*	experiment to see if something will work *Try clicking on OK in the box.*
stop	stop one action in order to do another (infinitive of purpose) *We stopped to have some lunch.*	finish an action or activity *My father stopped driving when he was eighty.*
go on	for a change of activity *She started by defining obesity and went on to talk about its causes.*	continue *Joe went on working although he wasn't well.*
regret	be sorry about something you are about to say *BA regrets to announce a delay of flight BA5276.*	be sorry about something you did before *We regretted going to the party. It was awful.*

Verbs followed by the -ing form or infinitive with to with no difference in meaning

These include: *like, love, hate, prefer, can't stand, can't bear, start, begin*
I hate writing/to write by hand.
I much prefer using/to use a computer.

In American English, the infinitive with *to* is often preferred. In British English, this is often used to talk about choices and habits.

I like to go to the dentist twice a year.
I hate to interrupt, but we have to go.

If the verb after *prefer* is in the negative, use the infinitive with *to*.

I prefer not to write by hand.

When we use the verbs *begin, continue* and *start* in continuous forms we usually use the infinitive with *to*.

They're beginning to annoy me.
NOT *They're beginning annoying me.*

9.2 past modals of deduction

Use modal verb + *have* + past participle to make deductions or guesses about past actions or states.
You could have left it in the café.

Use modal verb + *have* + been + -ing form to make deductions about continuous actions or states.
She must have been feeling ill.

Use modal verb + *have* + been + past participle for deductions using the passive.
It can't have been stolen from your bag.

must have	you are almost certain that something is true, based on the evidence	*I must have deleted the email. I can't find it anywhere.*
might/ could/ may have	you think it is possible that something is true, based on the evidence	*The plane could have been delayed by the weather. There's a bad storm at sea.*
couldn't/ can't have	you are almost certain something is not true or is impossible, based on the evidence	*It can't have been the waitress. She wasn't in the room when the bag was stolen.*

Note: *have* + past participle (the perfect infinitive) is also used with other modals: *should have (been)* and *would have (been)*.

9.3 reporting an incident

referring to time

Before/As soon as/ When	I realised what had happened/ was happening …
It was only (a minute/much) later	(that) I realised/remembered …
It all happened	so quickly/fast/slowly.

describing impressions of a person or thing

He reminded me of	Tom Cruise.
He looked/seemed	as if he was a student. like a student. about 30/very strong.

other phrases for reporting

It never occurred to me It didn't cross my mind	(that) he was a thief.
My mind/I	went blank.
I didn't catch	the car number plate. what he said.

PRACTICE

9.1 **A** Match the sentence halves.

1 I tried drinking the medicine — *b* a) but I couldn't – it was too disgusting.
2 I tried to drink the medicine — *a* b) but it didn't help.
3 He stopped to smoke — *b* a) a cigarette before continuing.
4 He stopped smoking — *a* b) because he wanted to get fitter.
5 Julia remembers to text me — *a* a) whenever she needs a lift from the station.
6 Julia remembers texting me — *b* b) but I didn't get any messages from her.
7 Xavier went on to perform — *b* a) even though audiences became smaller and smaller.
8 Xavier went on performing — *a* b) in all of the best opera houses in the world.
9 We regret saying — *b* a) that the car won't be ready till Monday.
10 We regret to say — *a* b) that the Games would be a failure.

B Underline the correct alternative. Sometimes both are possible.

Most people prefer not ¹*getting/to get* involved in a crime investigation, according to Detective Jaime Lopez. 'I'll give you an example,' said Lopez. 'Last week we were just starting ²*investigating/to investigate* a car theft that had happened in broad daylight in the city centre, and we realised that our biggest challenge might be to find someone who remembered ³*seeing/to see* anything at all. We estimate that twenty or thirty people witnessed the crime but no one tried ⁴*intervening/to intervene* and most people went on ⁵*doing/to do* what they were doing. Interestingly, one tourist stopped ⁶*taking/to take* pictures of the theft in process but then continued sightseeing. He only came forward three days after the incident. "Sorry, I forgot ⁷*telling/to tell* you that I have some pictures of the crime," he said, but he didn't seem genuinely to regret ⁸*not coming forward/to not come forward* earlier. We tried ⁹*identifying/to identify* the thief from the tourist's photograph but it wasn't clear enough.' We asked Lopez how he can bear ¹⁰*doing/to do* such a frustrating job. 'I like ¹¹*helping/to help* people. I love this city. I never stop ¹²*being/to be* glad I live here.'

9.2 **A** Rewrite the underlined sentence with *must/might/may/could/can't/couldn't have.*

1 Perhaps Jenna phoned while we were out. Let me check on the answerphone.
   Jenna might have phoned while we were out.
2 Knock louder. You know he's a bit deaf. I'm sure he didn't hear you.
3 I locked the door. I'm certain. Maybe the thieves got in through the window.
4 I can't find the final version of the report in my computer. I realised it was impossible that I saved the document.
5 Ooh, that was a bad knock to your head. I'm certain it hurt a lot.
6 I don't know why Wanda was late for the meeting. Maybe her plane was delayed.
7 I'm sure I've made a mistake. The date looks wrong.
8 Paola should have won the race. It's impossible that she was trying hard enough.

B Complete the conversations with the correct form of a verb from the box and a modal of deduction.

look   tell   think   cost   work   switch off

1 A: Look at her necklace. Are those real diamonds?
   B: Yes. It _____ a fortune!
2 A: I tried phoning Mike four times but he didn't answer.
   B: He _____ his phone or maybe he left it at home.
3 A: Why was Danielle in the office at midnight?
   B: She _____ late. She had a big meeting the next day.
4 A: I'm sure Len told me you were a doctor.
   B: He _____ of my sister, Rachel, or maybe he confused me with someone else.
5 A: I've lost my boarding card. It's not in my bag!
   B: You _____ properly. I saw you put it there just now.
6 A: Do you think Yves knows he didn't get the promotion?
   B: I suppose he _____ by the boss but I doubt it.

9.3 **A** Correct each of B's sentences by adding a word from the box.

looked   realised   crossed   occurred   if   strange

A: Why didn't you phone us when you first saw the man behaving strangely?

B: ¹It never my mind until I saw the picture on *Crimebeat* on TV.

A: And when you saw *Crimebeat* … ?

B: ²It to me then that I should contact you.
A: We appreciate that. Tell me what happened.

B: ³I saw him near the factory. He looked as he was taking photos of the building.

A: Do you remember anything else?

B: ⁴When he saw me, he left quickly and he guilty.

A: Why didn't you call someone right away?

B: ⁵It was only later that I that there was something strange about how he left.

A: Maybe he'd finished?

B: ⁶I don't know. It just seemed quite but then I didn't think any more about it till I saw the programme.

GRAMMAR

10.1 relative clauses   *whom*

defining relative clauses

- give essential information about a noun.
  *That guy is the actor **who is going to play the president**.*
  Don't use commas before or after the clause.
- can use *that* instead of *who* or *which*.
  *Ken's just seen a woman ~~who~~ **that** he went to university with.*
- can omit the relative pronoun/adverb when it is the object of the relative clause.
  Ken's just seen a woman (who) he went to university with.
  He is the subject of the relative clause, *who* is the object, so we can omit *who*.

pronouns and adverbs in relative clauses

Use the relative pronouns *who/that* (people), *which/that* (things), *whose* (possession) and the relative adverbs *when* (time) and *where* (place).
*I remember the time **when** you were just a little girl.*
Whose can be used to refer to cities, countries and other nouns which suggest a group of people. It is rarely used with things.
*It's a city **whose** inhabitants always seem to be upbeat.*
Omit words which have been replaced by the relative pronoun.
NOT *She's someone **who** I know ~~her~~ well.*

non-defining relative clauses

- give additional, non-essential information.
  *That's Sam, **who is going to play the president**.*
- use commas to separate this clause from the rest of the sentence.
- cannot use *that* instead of *who* or *which*.
  *The film, **which** won the Oscar last year, was made in India.*
  NOT ~~The film, that won the Oscar last year, was made in India.~~
- cannot omit the relative pronouns/adverbs.
  *Gwen, **who** I'm going to see later, is my fiancé.*
  NOT ~~Gwen, I'm going to see later, is my fiancé.~~
- can use *which* to refer to the whole of a previous clause.
  *The plane was delayed, **which** meant we were late.*

prepositions in relative clauses

In informal spoken and written English prepositions usually come at the end of the relative clause.
*This is the book **which** she's famous **for**.*
In formal and in written English prepositions often come before the relative pronoun. Use *whom* for people.
*He is someone **with whom** I can work.*
Where can be replaced by *which … in*, or, in more formal English *in which*.
*The room **where** she slept/**which** she slept in/**in which** she slept is over there.*

10.2 participle clauses

- Use participle clauses (clauses that start with a present participle or a past participle) to vary your style or to include more information in a sentence.
- Use them as a shorter alternative to relative clauses. In this use they are also known as 'reduced relative clauses'. Form the participle clause by omitting the relative pronoun and any auxiliary verbs.
- Clauses beginning with a past participle have a passive meaning.
  *The children **caught in the rainstorm** came home soaked.*
  = The children who were caught …
  *The film, **directed by Miyakazi**, won an award for animation.*
  = which was directed by Miyakazi …

- Clauses beginning with a present participle have an active meaning.
  *The team **playing in red** is Chile.*
  = The team that is playing in red …
  *Do you know the man **standing in the corner**?*
  = the man who is standing …
- Clauses beginning with a present participle replace continuous and simple verbs in different tenses.
  *Give me a number **beginning** with three.*
  = Give me a number which begins with three.
  *Anyone **cheating** in the exam failed.*
  = Anyone who cheated in the exam failed.
  *The bus **leaving** tomorrow will stop at Lima.*
  = The bus which is leaving/leaves tomorrow …

10.3 giving a tour

commenting on facts
As you may know,/As I'm sure you know, …
The story goes that …
Apparently,/Supposedly,/Interestingly, …
Surprisingly,/Strangely,/Believe it or not, …
It's well worth (going/seeing/a visit)

leading the way		
Let's/We could	head over to	the park.
Shall we Why don't we	head back to retrace our steps to	the café?

giving facts		
It was	built	to celebrate … to commemorate … in honour of …
	founded by/ named after	(Thomas Bodley).
	modelled on/ modelled after	(the Arc de Triomphe).
	burnt down destroyed rebuilt restored	in the 15th century. in the 1990s.

PRACTICE

10.1 *4/24 HW → Note.*

A Combine the sentences using a relative clause. Omit the relative pronoun where possible. Sometimes there is more than one answer.

1 The man is marrying Suzanne. He's very lucky.
The man *who is very lucky is marrying Suzanne*

2 The house burnt down yesterday. I used to live in it.
The house *which I used to live in burnt down yesterday.*

3 Pablo Picasso spent his early childhood in Malaga. His father was also an artist.
Pablo Picasso *whose father was also an artist spent his —.*

4 That was the most important moment of my life. I realised I wanted to be an actor.
The moment *was the most important of my life, which*

5 The holiday was in Canada. I enjoyed it most.
The holiday _____.

6 Usain Bolt is a global superstar. He was the first man to win six gold Olympic medals in sprinting.
Usain Bolt, *who was the first man to win six gold Olympic*

7 I lived with a guy when I was a student. His hobby was fixing motorbikes.
When I was _____.

8 You should make a speech. This is that sort of occasion.
This is _____.

B *4/24 HW*

Add the missing prepositions (*for, from, in, on, to* or *with*). There is one extra preposition you do not need. *→ ✗ 2 from*

1 It was the house which I spent my childhood. *in*

2 It was a lesson which I'll always be grateful. *for*

3 She's definitely the woman whom he wants to spend the rest of his life. *with*

4 The cinema I most often go is the Odeon in the town centre. *to*

5 Funnily enough, it was the planning which we spent the most time. *on* / *to / for*

6 He was an athlete whom success came ~~from~~ as naturally as his speed. ?

7 He was a friend I could always depend. *on*

8 You're the person who we always turn when a speech is needed. *to / for*

turn to 租1
" to.

whom 人の目的語

10.2 *4/28 HW*

A Complete the sentences with the present or past participle form of the verb in brackets.

1 A beret is a type of flat hat often _____ on one side of the head. (wear)

2 The large number of people _____ outside meant the doctor would be working late that night. (wait)

3 Items permanently _____ from your inbox can usually be found again if you know where to look. (delete)

4 I knew two people _____ in the fire. (injure)

5 Babies _____ in a bilingual household have more flexible brains. (bring up)

6 The dance _____ place tomorrow is to celebrate the end of the exams. (take)

B *4/28 HW*

Combine the sentences using a participle clause and the correct punctuation. Sometimes there is more than one possibility.

1 The taxi almost drove over a man. He was lying in the street.

2 *Sunflowers* was painted by Van Gogh. It's one of the most popular paintings ever.

3 The army advanced towards the hill. It was led by Napoleon.

4 I don't know the people. They live next door to me.

5 I used to like block-busters. They involved lots of action.

6 The apartments overlook Central Park. They are the most expensive.

7 Some factories were forced to close during the recession. They still haven't reopened.

8 Many people think that the Taj Mahal is the most beautiful building in the world. It was built in the seventeenth century.

10.3

A Correct eight mistakes in A's part of the conversations.

1 A: So here we are at Margit Island, named from a nun whose father was once king.
 B: Wow! It's beautiful.
 A: Yeah, interesting at one time it was three islands and only used by people who had land here.

2 A: Supposingly these caves run for miles.
 B: What were they for?
 A: The story tells that when there was an invasion, the local people hid in these tunnels.

3 A: That's the Vajdahunyad Castle. It was modelled from a castle in Transylvania.
 B: And why was it built?
 A: It was built for the city's millennium exhibition in 1896, to memorise the one-thousand-year anniversary of the founding of the state.

4 A: Let's retrace our feet to Castle Hill.
 B: Great. We hardly spent any time there this morning.
 A: Exactly, and the museum is well worse a visit.

VOCABULARY BANK

Lesson 6.1
WORD-BUILDING: PREFIXES

1 A Find a prefix in A which means:

1 very small   *micro*
2 very big   *mega*
3 many   *multi*
4 between   *trans*
5 two   *bi*
6 across   *inter*

A

bi multi
micro mega
trans inter

B

lingual chip
national media
late wave port
task phone cycle
scope val monthly
city view it
storey byte

view – storey ?

B Match a prefix in A with at least three endings in B.

C Complete the sentences with the correct form of a word formed from a prefix in A and an ending in B.

1 I left my car in one of those huge _____ car parks and now I can't find it.
2 It's a long opera but there are two *interval*. We can take a break and have a coffee then.
3 I've never really been to Hong Kong, only in the airport when I was in *transit* on my way to Beijing.
4 The crowd was so noisy, I had to use a *megaphone* to make my voice loud enough.
5 He didn't get the job because he was late for the *multi task*
6 No, it's too small. You can only see it under a *microscope*
7 Our newsletter only goes out *bi monthly*. It's January now, so the next one is in March.
8 People who grow up in a *multi lingual* environment end up understanding three or more languages.

Lesson 6.2 TIME IDIOMS

2 A Match the phrases and idioms in bold with pictures A–I.

1 Your food will be here **in no time**.   c   (D)
2 Sorry, I'll have to **cut this short**.   g (F)
3 He's **dragging his heels** over the decorating.   d (I)
4 I was **making up for lost time** – you see I overslept.   i (G)
5 I've told you **time after time** to take your shoes off!   f (H)
6 She got home **in the nick of time**.   h (B)
7 I'm just **killing an hour or two** before my interview.   a (A)
8 Please **take your time**.   e (C)
9 The train should be here **any time now**.   b (E)

B Match meanings a)–i) to the phrases and idioms.

a) to spend time doing something unimportant while you are waiting for something else to happen
b) very soon
c) very quickly
d) to delay doing something
e) to do something without hurrying
f) again and again
g) to stop doing something earlier than you had planned
h) at the last moment before it is too late to do something
i) to do something quickly because you started late or worked too slowly

Lesson 7.1 MULTI-WORD VERBS

1 A Look at the sentence pairs. How are the meanings of the multi-word verbs in bold different? *raise a child*

1 Did your parents **bring** you **up** as a Buddhist?
2 Oh, here's Edith now. Just don't **bring up** anything about her divorce. *talk about / mention*
3 Anna keeps **putting off** the meeting. I don't think we'll ever get a chance to discuss things.
4 Stop talking about your illnesses. You're **putting me off** my food! *食事が躊躇になる*
5 Why did they **turn** Neil **down** for the job?
6 Could you **turn** the cooker **down** – the sauce in the pan is going to burn.
7 My car's in the garage. It **broke down** on the way to work today.
8 Negotiations between the two corporations have **broken down**, but they may restart next month.
9 The company **took on** ten school-leavers last month. *卒業者*
10 After Brazil won the semi-finals, they **took on** the favourites, Spain.
11 He **pulled out** without looking and hit another car.
12 Both countries have **pulled out** of the talks, so there won't be any agreement.

B Complete the table with the multi-word verbs from Exercise 1A.

a	take on	hire (lent) / compete against
b	turn down	say no / lower the level
c	pull out	end one's involvement, or quit / drive onto a road from another road
d	put off	make sb dislike sth / postpone
e	bring up	raise / start to talk about
f	brake down	fail or end unsuccessfully / stop working, usually for a machine

Lesson 7.3 PARTS OF A NEWS WEBSITE

2 Match 1–10 to the parts of a news website.

1 breaking news
2 lead story
3 headlines
4 news feed
5 forum link
6 weather forecast
7 video link
8 menu bar
9 navigation buttons
10 popup ad

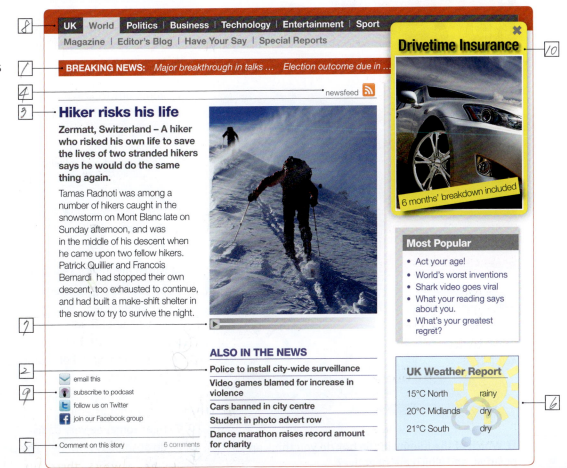

UK | World | Politics | Business | Technology | Entertainment | Sport
Magazine | Editor's Blog | Have Your Say | Special Reports

BREAKING NEWS: *Major breakthrough in talks … Election outcome due in …*

newsfeed

Hiker risks his life

Zermatt, Switzerland – A hiker who risked his own life to save the lives of two stranded hikers says he would do the same thing again.

Tamas Radnoti was among a number of hikers caught in the snowstorm on Mont Blanc late on Sunday afternoon, and was in the middle of his descent when he came upon two fellow hikers. Patrick Quillier and Francois Bernardi had stopped their own descent, too exhausted to continue, and had built a make-shift shelter in the snow to try to survive the night.

email this
subscribe to podcast
follow us on Twitter
join our Facebook group

Comment on this story — 6 comments

ALSO IN THE NEWS
Police to install city-wide surveillance
Video games blamed for increase in violence
Cars banned in city centre
Student in photo advert row
Dance marathon raises record amount for charity

Drivetime Insurance

6 months' breakdown included

Most Popular
- Act your age!
- World's worst inventions
- Shark video goes viral
- What your reading says about you.
- What's your greatest regret?

UK Weather Report
15°C North — rainy
20°C Midlands — dry
21°C South — dry

VOCABULARY BANK

1 A Look at the picture and complete the compound adjectives with words from the box.

brand	broad	brown
curly	dark	high
sun	tight	

B Which words or phrases can be turned into opposites by using the opposite of the first part?

curly-haired – straight-haired

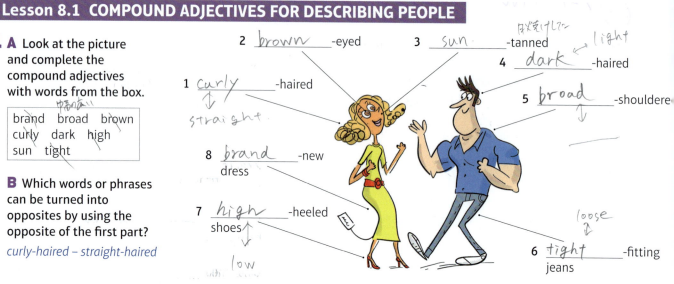

2 _brown_-eyed
3 _sun_-tanned
4 _dark_-haired _light_
5 _broad_-shouldere[d]
1 _curly_-haired _straight_
8 _brand_-new dress
7 _high_-heeled shoes _low_
6 _tight_-fitting jeans _loose_

5/4 HW

2 A Match pictures A–F with the idioms in the box. Two idioms are not in the pictures.

?

A talk behind sb's back ⊖	walk all over sb B	
E not lift a finger ⊖	be always there for sb ⊕	
⊕ go out of one's way to do sth	lock horns with sb C ⊖	
D (be) a shoulder to cry on ⊕	give sb a helping hand F ⊕	

n (negative)

A

B n

C n

D p (Positive)

E n

F p

B Which of the idioms in the box do you think are positive, and which are negative?

5 (be) a shoulder to cry on 7 walk all over sb
6 talk behind sb's back 8 not lift a finger

C Complete the sentences with the correct form of the idioms.

1 She loves to help out. She'll _____ anyone a _____ _____ if they need it.
2 He often sits and watches me clean and doesn't _____ _____ _____ to help.
3 When I'm really upset and need a _____ _____ _____ _____, I always turn to Martin.
4 I don't trust her, she's such a gossip. She's always _____ _____ my _____.
5 He argues about everything. In fact he'll _____ _____ _____ you on just about any topic.
6 She's the best friend I can imagine. She _____ _____ _____ for me, through good times and bad.
7 He's so kind and generous. He'll always _____ _____ his _____ to help you.
8 Don't just do everything he wants. He's very selfish. Don't let him _____ _____ _____ you.

D Match meanings 1–8 to the idioms in Exercise 2A.

1 be available whenever somebody needs you
2 do something to help even though it's not convenient for you
3 be in conflict with somebody
4 do something to help somebody
5 give somebody sympathy when they're upset
6 say something (usually bad) about somebody when they're not listening
7 treat someone very badly
8 do absolutely nothing to help

1. be always there for sb.
2. go out of one's way to do sth.
3. lock horns with sb.
4. give sb a helping hand

Lesson 9.1 DEPENDENT PREPOSITIONS

1 Complete the headlines with a dependent preposition.

1 Innocent man mistaken _____ gang leader

2 **Woman jailed for hiding robbers _____ police**

3 *Couple punished _____ balloon hoax*

4 **Mugger caught after boasting _____ crimes in local bar**

5 Jailed criminal prohibited _____ selling his story

6 **Politician condemned _____ involvement in banking scandal**

7 **Murderess given strong sentence for joking _____ crime**

8 **Local teacher fired for participating _____ protest march**

9 **College president conceals financial woes _____ board of trustees**

10 **Mother fined _____ leaving baby unattended in car**

Lesson 9.3 CARS AND ACCIDENTS

2 Match the car parts 1–12 to A–L in the picture.

1	boot _J_	7	tail light
2	bonnet	8	windscreen
3	number plate	9	tyre
4	indicator	10	windscreen wiper
5	wing	11	sun roof
6	wing mirror	12	steering wheel

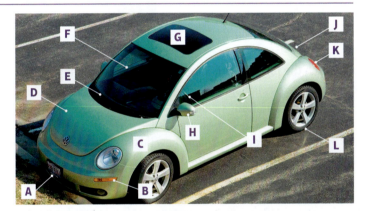

3 Complete the sentences with the verbs and verb phrases in the box in the past simple.

skid   collide with   pull out   overtake   drive the wrong way   swerve   exceed the speed limit   scratch

The car _____ on the ice.

She _____ to avoid hitting the dog.

She increased her speed and _____ the blue car.

He _____. He was going at 100 kph.

She _____ the side of the car by parking too near a wall.

He was driving too fast in a narrow street and _____ another car.

A car _____ in front of him and he almost crashed into it.

He _____ down the motorway.

VOCABULARY BANK

4/26 HW

Lesson 10.2 MUSIC

1 A Match the instruments 1–12 with the photos.

E 1 acoustic guitar
J 2 drums
I 3 bass guitar
L 4 violin/fiddle (informal)
C 5 cello
H 6 grand piano
A 7 trumpet
K 8 trombone
D 9 flute
B 10 clarinet
G 11 saxophone
A 12 harp

B Can you play any of the instruments above?
Which instrument would you most like to learn?

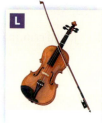

2 Match the phrases and idioms in bold with meanings a)–h).

C 1 There goes Jim again, saying how great he is, **blowing his own trumpet**.
d 2 Clara began **fiddling with** her necklace. I could see that she was worried. *nervous*
e 3 We need to **drum up** some new business or we'll have to close down.
a 4 I'm tired of **playing second fiddle**.
g 5 Interesting how Larry **changed his tune** after he found out it was his own assistant who stole the money.
e 6 I know, it looks like an expensive car but I got it **for a song**.
f 7 The boss wants to see me about my mistakes on the contract. It's time for me to go in and **face the music**.
b 8 Her name **rings a bell** – maybe I've met her before.

a) take a less important role
b) remind sb of sth, sound familiar
c) talk positively about oneself
d) touch or play with something in a restless or nervous way
e) get (support or attention) through making a lot of effort
f) accept responsibility for mistakes
g) suddenly take a different perspective
h) very cheaply

Lesson 10.2 TWO-PART PHRASES

3 A Complete the sentences with the words in the box.

| take | death | leave | later | swim | another | miss | nothing |

1 It's only a question of time, and **sooner or** _later_ you'll find a new job.
2 That's the highest salary we can pay you. We can't go higher, so **take it or** _leave_ it.
3 You've finished the training, and now you have to go out and do the job. It's **sink or** _swim_.
4 The shop is about twenty kilometres from here, **give or** _take_ a kilometre. 약간
5 It was **all or** _nothing_ – she either had to get in the car with him or lose him forever.
6 This is the biggest choice of my life – it's a **life or** _death_ decision.
7 Mark took a **hit or** _miss_ approach to finding a girlfriend. He simply asked every girl he saw out on a date.
8 I know, we're lost, but **one way or** _another_ we'll find our way back.

B Match meanings a)–h) with the two-part phrases in Exercise 3A.

2 a) the offer won't change
5 b) risking everything
4 c) to within (a small amount)
7 d) unplanned/disorganised
1 e) eventually =finally
8 f) somehow
3 g) fail or succeed
6 h) extremely important

COMMUNICATION BANK

Lesson 7.3

7 B Student A

The top five most dangerous animals

1 mosquito   2 Asian cobra   3 Australian box jellyfish
4 great white shark   5 African lion

Lesson 10.2

8 A Student B

T **through and through** completely: *a typical Englishman through and through*

O **on and on** used to say that someone continues to do something, or that something continues to happen: *He talked on and on about his job.*

R **rough and ready** (= not perfect, but good enough to use)

N **(every) now and then/now and again** sometimes: *He sees her every now and then at college.*

U **ups and downs** n [plural] the good and bad things that happen in life, business, etc: *Every marriage has its ups and downs.*

Lesson 10.5

3 C

1 Sydney Opera House
2 Apple Inc.
3 squash
4 Napoleon Bonaparte
5 Oscar
6 the Inuit
7 sushi (makizushi)
8 *Hamlet*

Lesson 6.2

7 C

Key
a) = 3 points
b) = 2 points
c) = 1 point

12–15: You are amazingly optimistic! On the one hand, your positive attitude can make people around you feel good. On the other hand, sometimes people may find your constant cheerfulness slightly irritating.

8–11: You are calm and level-headed and can always see both sides of a situation. This means you don't have great highs and lows but can also mean you miss out on some of the drama of life.

5–7: You're not always easy to be with, usually seeing the negative side of things. However, this can be extremely useful in some situations because you will tend to be more cautious and see what could go wrong with any plans or projects.

Lesson 6.3

7 B Student A

1 You are going to take part in a radio phone-in, and you are the DJ. Ask Student B to tell you about their situation. Ask for clarification to check you understand. Then invite Student C to give their opinion. Encourage B and C to exchange their points of view.

2 Now change roles. You are a caller. Give your opinion when the DJ asks you.

3 Now change roles. You are a different caller. Explain your situation to the DJ:
   A well-known social networking site has a minimum age of thirteen. Your daughter is thirteen next week and she says some of her friends' parents have allowed their children to join. You think she's too young.

COMMUNICATION BANK

Lesson 9.2

7 D

Free gift wrapping
Preparation:
1 The con artist team goes to a busy shopping mall during the festival season and sets up a tent with a sign saying 'Free gift wrapping'.
2 An attractive, friendly, female con artist stands behind the counter.
3 The other two con artists are inside the tent, out of sight. They have a scale for weighing things, oranges and packing material.

The scam:
1 When a customer brings an item for wrapping, the woman passes it into the tent.
2 The two con artists there open the package, remove the item and weigh it, then put the same weight in oranges into the box with packing material and wrap it attractively.
3 They pass it back to the female colleague, who gives it to the customer. The package feels like the original and won't be opened till later!

Hire car scam
Preparation:
1 The con artist team hires an expensive car, changes the number plates and removes any evidence that it's hired.
2 The team places an advert in a newspaper or online offering the car at a very low price.
3 The team finds an empty house, breaks in and puts some toys around the rooms and driveway. This address is given when people answer the advert.

The scam:
1 An attractive female con artist poses as a young mother and greets customers as they arrive. She explains to the customers why there are no car papers. Some of the customers will offer a cash deposit.
2 At the end of the afternoon, the team clears out of the house, returns the car to the hire agency and disappears.

Lesson 6.3

7 B Student B

1 You are going to take part in a radio phone-in, and you are a caller. Explain your situation to the DJ:
Your son, who is seventeen, has started going out with a young woman who he says is the love of his life. He wants to get a tattoo linking her name and his. You're strongly against the idea.

2 Now change roles. You are the DJ. Ask Student C to tell you about their situation. Ask for clarification to check you understand. Then invite Student A to give their opinion. Encourage A and C to exchange their points of view.

3 Now change roles. You are a different caller. Give your opinion when the DJ asks you.

Lesson 7.3

7 B Student B

The top five countries with the tallest people
1 the Netherlands   2 Sweden   3 Denmark
4 Norway   5 Estonia

Lesson 9.3

8 A Student B

Lesson 10.2

1 C Student A: read the text on this page. Which four questions below does it answer?

1 How do actors cry on demand?
2 Do big stars have to audition for film roles?
3 How do singers keep their voices steady when they're dancing?
4 Why is rock music played so loud at concerts?
5 Who decides whether something is 'art' or not?
6 Why do works of art get stolen if they can't be sold without attracting attention?
7 What's the secret to making an audience laugh?
8 How does a comedian deal with hecklers?

D Read the text again. Write a maximum of five key words for each answer to help you remember the information.

E Work in pairs. Cover the text and look at your notes from Exercise 1D. Tell your partner about the answers.

POPULAR CULTURE

**Want to know the best-kept secrets of popular culture?
Read our Top Questions & Answers to find out.**

Q: 3

A: Singers such as Beyoncé, whose stage show involves her dancing all over the stage, can't always deliver high-quality vocals live as it's physically extremely difficult to control the voice while jumping around. Because of this, many performers rely on a backing track to provide vocals during some songs, and whilst they may be singing live, the audience can't actually hear their voice. Some stationary performers use a backing track when they're concerned about difficult parts of the performance, for example hitting a very high note or even remembering the words to a song.

Q: 8

A: Every comedian has his or her own strategy for dealing with members of the audience interrupting their performance with rude comments. Strategies range from simply telling the heckler to be quiet ('Shut up!') to humiliating the heckler into silence by insulting them or someone with them such as their girlfriend. Armed with the microphone, the comedian has a great advantage over the heckler. Some comedians, known for their particularly aggressive way of handling hecklers, actually become more famous for this aspect of their act than their scripted sections.

Q: 1

A: There are certain ways of making it look like you're crying, such as putting glycerine in your eyes, sniffing a freshly cut onion or, on stage, concentrating on a bright point of light. Most actors use more internal techniques that exploit emotional memory. By recalling a time when they were sad or upset, an actor can often get the tears flowing. Or sometimes they'll build an association between an object – a prop they'll be handling during the scene – and that emotion, so that, when they touch the prop, they feel inclined to cry. Interestingly, most actors say it's easier to cry convincingly than to laugh convincingly.

Q: 5

A: This is an age-old question. The range of works and styles of painting regarded as art at different times is astonishing – from ancient Chinese ink paintings to Leonardo Da Vinci to Jackson Pollock. One argument goes that a painting is art if the painter says it is, and gives convincing reasons to support their position. Many artists would reject this idea; they don't care who regards their work as art. We'll probably never agree on who the most beautiful woman or best-looking man is, so we'll just have to enjoy exploring and sharing our notions of art and beauty without a definitive answer.

Lesson 10.2

8 A Student A

G give and take n [U] If there is give and take between two people, each person agrees to do some of the things that the other person wants: *In any relationship there has to be some give and take.*

B be sick and tired of sb/sth to be annoyed with a person or situation: *I'm sick and tired of waiting.*

P peace and quiet When everything is quiet and calm: *All I want is some peace and quiet.*

L leaps and bounds *He improved in leaps and bounds* (= very much, very quickly).

T the pros and cons (of sth) the advantages and disadvantages of something

Lesson 7.3

7 B Student C

The top five cities for art lovers

1 Berlin   2 Chicago   3 Florence
4 London   5 New York

COMMUNICATION BANK

Lesson 9.2

7 A Student A: imagine the following situation happened to you. Add some details about the place, time, the amount of money of the deposit, and your feelings. Prepare to tell Student B.

I went round to a house to look at a car. I'd seen the advert earlier. There were kids' toys in the driveway by the car. A young woman, the kids' mother I  guessed, showed me round the car – it was a fantastic bargain and I wanted to buy it. She couldn't show me the car papers because her husband had just taken them to pay the car tax. She told me that she'd got lots of other interested people coming round later so I gave her a deposit and she said I could pick up the car at six. At six o'clock, I found eight other people outside the house, no car and no one at home.

B Listen to Student B's situation and discuss his/her questions.

C Tell Student B the situation and discuss these questions.

1 Who was the woman?
2 How did she trick people into thinking she was a mother?
3 Who did the car belong to?
4 Who were the other eight people?
5 How do you think the scam was done?

D Turn to page 144 to see if your ideas were right.

Lesson 7.3

7 B Student D

The top five friendliest countries

1 Ireland 2 the USA 3 Malawi 4 Fiji 5 Thailand

Lesson 6.3

7 B Student C

1 You are going to take part in a radio phone-in, and you are a caller. Give your opinion when the DJ asks you.

2 Now change roles. You are a different caller. Explain your situation to the DJ:

Your eighteen-year-old son has just passed his driving test. He wants to borrow your car so that he can drive his friends around. He says that his other friends' parents let them borrow their cars. You think he's not ready yet.

3 Now change roles. You are the DJ. Ask Student A to tell you about their situation. Ask for clarification to check you understand. Then invite Student B to give their opinion. Encourage A and B to exchange their points of view.

Lesson 9.3

8 A Student A

Lesson 9.5

4 B

1 The man always checked the post box before the postman came. His wife took the letters out when they arrived.

2 A record company was making a recording of the performance and had asked the audience not to applaud, so that the recording would be clean.

AUDIO SCRIPTS

UNIT 6 Recording 3

OK … so … Dear the future me, I hope this letter has found its way to you/me. As I write this, I am sixteen in year eleven; and as I read it, I am twenty. Wow! I will have changed so much. I can only guess what I will be like at twenty. I envisage myself at Oxford Uni, sitting … oh, this is embarrasing … sitting under a tree by the river in the college grounds. I think I'll be wearing something floaty and a bit indie, but I bet when I get this, it'll be raining.

I know, I'm a romantic. I hope that hasn't changed. My plans for myself in the following years are to find a man, someone good-looking, romantic and intelligent who shares my interests. Either way, I hope I'll have someone. I don't remember this … and then I think I'll have three children with long, brown hair and green eyes.

Well, I'll stop now even though I want to write everything I can down, but I'm running out of time. I hope I'm happy, and I hope this letter makes me feel good about who I was, or am, as I write this. Keep smiling, and while I can't really say bye, but good luck for the future and keep dreaming. Don't change too much, and be happy with who you are – I like who I am now more than any other time.

Love, Laura.

UNIT 6 Recording 4

It all seems really shallow looking back and reading what I thought I'd be doing or hoped I'd be doing. I think my sixteen-year-old self might have been disappointed with where I am, but because I as my twenty-year-old self have sort of grown up and matured, I'm absolutely ecstatic with where I am, and it doesn't have to be this perfect sitting-by-a-lake kind of image.

Unit 6 Recording 6

P = Presenter   E = Ed   J = Julia   D = Dan
Z = Zara

P: And up next, it's time for 'Just tell me I'm wrong.' Today's topic: how young is too young or, perhaps more accurately, how old is old enough? We've received hundreds of calls, emails and text messages about the right age for a child to do all sorts of things like have a smartphone. In fact our first caller asks about just that. His name is Ed. Go ahead, Ed. You're on.
E: Hi. My situation is that my eight-year-old kept asking for a smartphone, and eventually we bought her one a few months ago. Then, last week, I got a bill for over £200! I knew something like this would happen.
P: So basically you think she's too young for a phone?
E: Yeah, yeah, that's right.
P: Surely it's up to the parents to set guidelines.
E: So what you're saying is I should give her some rules?

P: Exactly. Right from the beginning. OK, thanks, Ed. Next caller is Julia. What's your question, Julia?
J: My question is about social networking sites. I don't let my daughter use them. She's only ten and I'm worried about online bullying.
P: So in other words, you're worried about kids being horrible to other kids.
J: Yeah. You hear so much about it nowadays.
P: That's a very good point. Online bullying is a serious problem … but isn't it better to talk it over with her? I'm sure they have lessons at school about how to stay safe online. She has to learn some time.
J: So what you mean is I'm being overprotective?
P: To be honest, yes. And if you try and stop her, she'll only find a way to go onto a social networking site in secret. And if she ends up in a bullying situation and you haven't prepared her, that could be much worse.
J: Oh dear … I'm sure you're right but it's not easy being a parent nowadays.
P: I agree. Thanks for your question, Julia. Let's go to our next caller. Dan, you're on.
D: Hi, my question's also about technology.
P: It seems like that's everyone's main worry. Anyway, go ahead Dan.
D: Well, my son, Seth, he's twelve and, up till recently he was a normal twelve-year-old, you know, he used to go out with his friends, play football with me, you know … we had a great relationship.
P: So, Dan, basically I'm guessing he doesn't want to spend so much time with you now and you feel …
D: Oh no, it's not that. It's just that he spends all his time on the computer now.
P: Surely that's just normal nowadays.
D: It's hard to say. Sometimes at the weekend he spends all day in his bedroom on social networking sites or playing video games. I don't think it's right. I mean for one thing, he never gets any exercise.
P: Don't you think it's just a stage he's going through? I used to spend hours in my bedroom listening to music when I was that age.
D: So what you mean is I should just relax and let him get on with it?
P: Yeah, he'll grow out of it. And you can't force him to go and play football if he doesn't want to.
D: I guess not. Thanks.
P: OK, our next caller is Zara. You're on.
Z: Um, I was wondering how you would deal with a thirteen-year-old wanting to get pierced ears?
P: Thirteen years old? Doesn't she simply want to be like her friends? I imagine a lot of them have pierced ears.
Z: Well … that's it. I'm not talking about a she.
P: Oh, in other words you're upset because your thirteen-year-old son wants to get his ears pierced.
Z: That's right.
P: Ah … so it's because he's a boy rather than his age?
Z: I suppose so.
P: Well, does he have friends who've got …

UNIT 6 Recording 8

W = Woman   M = Man

W: I'm going to speak against the statement: 'Employers should give preference to younger applicants when hiring.' The first point I'd like to make is that selecting a person for a job on the basis of their age is unfair. It's as bad as choosing someone because of their gender or race or religion. People should be selected for a job because of their abilities and suitability and not because they are a certain age. For example, if a sixty-year-old person is able, physically and mentally, to do a job, they should be judged on the same basis as a thirty-year-old.
M: I would like to speak in favour of the statement. I would like to start off by saying that I fully support equal opportunities for people applying for a job. However, I would like to pick up on the point made by Sarah when she said 'if a person is able, physically and mentally, to do a job'. I think we need to be realistic here. As people age, this can affect their energy, their ability to react quickly and their memory. In some jobs it may be vital for people to have high levels of energy, for example in a creative industry such as advertising. Or people need to be able to react quickly, for instance if they're a lorry driver, or be able to concentrate for long periods of time if they're an airline pilot. It is simply a fact of life that, as we age, our mental and physical capabilities deteriorate and that, for certain jobs, younger people are better.

UNIT 7 Recording 2

P = Presenter   H = Hoaxer

P: Welcome to *Insight*, where the topic for the day is hoaxes, specifically photo hoaxes. It was extremely difficult get someone who produces hoax photos, a hoaxer, to agree to appear on the show, and it was only on condition that we promise to keep his identity secret. So, I'd like to welcome my guest to the show.
H: Thank you.
P: For starters, can you explain why you want to remain anonymous?
H: Two reasons really. I suppose, one is mystery. What I mean is a good hoax photo is more powerful if people don't know where it came from. If people knew I'd produced the photo, the effect would be lost.
P: Fair enough. And the other reason?
H: Well, it's a fact that hoaxers often use photographs taken by someone else, and often without permission, and the original photographer could sue us.
P: So basically, you're playing it safe then.
H: Yeah, you could put it that way.
P: OK. Now I asked you before the show if you'd ever earned money for your hoax work, and you said that you often work with the police and detectives. What exactly do you do for the police?

H: Well, when a politician, for example, appears in a published photograph in any … embarrassing situation, say accepting money … sometimes the police ask me to look at it. Then, if I decide if the photograph is a hoax, they see if they can find out who did it.

P: Right. OK, well, let's look at some photographs that we found on the internet – some hoaxes; some not. Talk us through the photographs if you would.

H: So, this photo of a bike in a tree looks like a hoax simply because it's such an unusual image. Also, it looks a bit like a composite photo …

P: What's a composite photo?

H: When you combine two or more photos, that's a composite. In this case, it would be very easy to put a picture of the two halves of the bike over a photo of a tree. In fact, this would be a very easy hoax photo to put together.

P: So what you're saying is, it isn't real.

H: No, it actually is real. I wasn't sure myself, but I found out it was near Seattle, Washington. So I asked a friend who lives there, and he told me he'd seen it with his own eyes a number of years before. Apparently, there are many different legends about how it got there.

P: Well, I thought that one was definitely a hoax. Let's look at the next one. This one could be real. A man hanging on the landing gear of a jet plane is such an extraordinary sight, maybe that's why it looks a bit fake.

H: Well, even if you'd never seen such a thing, common sense would tell you that a man couldn't survive even the landing. The wind would pull him off.

P: Then it IS a hoax photo.

H: Yes, a classic composite photo. Not badly put together, though.

P: Remarkable. Now this next one could be real, sharks swimming through a flooded suburb. I remember seeing this on the internet. After one of those big hurricanes.

H: Ha, you've probably seen lots of photos like this, and maybe this exact one.

P: Why? Why's it funny?

H: I'm ninety-nine percent sure this is a hoax simply because it's a cliché – yet another photo of sharks swimming where they shouldn't be! Look on the internet and you'll find plenty of hoax photos of sharks.

P: And that's it? Is there a technical reason why you know it's a hoax?

H: Well, yes. The water next to the fins isn't right. The surface of the water would break differently if there really were sharks there. Look closely.

P: I see. You know, it seems like a lot of work. Why do people do it? It can't be for the money.

H: I dunno. I can only speak for myself and to be honest I'm thrilled when people believe one of my photos.

P: Because they want to believe it?

H: Well, yes. Maybe we all like to believe something really unusual could be true.

UNIT 7 Recording 4

Conversation 1

A: Wow!
B: What's that?
A: It's this story. Listen to this. 'A woman used a wooden soup ladle to save her husband from attack by a tiger'.
B: What? A ladle?
A: Well, her husband was being attacked by a tiger.
B: Where was this?
A: In Malaysia. Apparently, her husband had just gone into the forest. She saw the tiger attack him and grabbed the first thing she could find, which was a wooden soup ladle. And she just charged at the animal yelling at the top of her voice and bashing its head.
B: And it didn't attack her?
A: No. The amazing thing is that the tiger ran off.
B: Wow, there's no way I'd do that!
A: Not even for me?
B: Not even for you! You're the one who's always telling me to stop.
A: Stop what?
B: Stop helping people so much.
A: I didn't mean to stop helping me!

Conversation 2

A: Hey, Mike. Did you buy a lottery ticket?
B: No, why?
A: Well, you want to be careful. It says here that some store clerks are taking the winnings. You know when customers take in a winning ticket and they have to check it in the store …
B: Yeah …
A: Well, these guys have been telling customers that they didn't win and then they take the winning tickets for themselves.
B: That's so wrong! Suppose it was, like, a big amount?
A: One of the tickets was for $1,000 and the …
B: That's totally outrageous!
A: Yeah. Exactly.
B: So, how did they find it out?
A: The police did some undercover investigations at convenience stores. And … yeah, one of them was for $1,000 and the …
B: Hey, maybe we won something …
A: In your dreams. You don't buy lottery tickets anyway.
B: That's true.
A: But it's weird that the customers didn't notice, isn't it? That's more surprising than the actual theft.
B: Yeah. I do think they should do something about it.
A: Who?
B: The lottery companies.
A: They are doing something about it. They're going to install machines so you can check your own numbers.
B: That is a good idea.

Conversation 3

A: That's extraordinary!
B: What is?
A: This story about the baby in China.
B: What happened?
A: It's about a baby and apparently it climbed out onto a window ledge on the second floor. Oh there's a video … And, oh look, you can see these people underneath just holding out their arms because they know it's going to fall. And there are some people putting cardboard down to try and break the fall. Wow!
B: Let me see. Wow! Look at that man! How on earth did he catch it?
A: 'Just human instinct,' that's what one man said.
B: What a catch! That's such an amazing thing!
A: It's lucky the men noticed the baby.
B: Yeah, I suppose they saw some movement.
A: Or maybe they heard something.
B: What's that? The woman's bringing something.
A: It's hard to say but it looks like a cushion.
B: Yeah, it could be a sofa cushion.
A: I guess they thought the baby might fall on it.
B: That must be the luckiest baby alive.
A: Absolutely incredible. Let me see again.

UNIT 7 Recording 8

M = Man   W = Woman

M: Did you hear this story in the news about this guy that swapped a paper clip for a house?
W: No.
M: It sounds a bit out there but apparently what happened was he started … he was at his desk looking for a job or phoning up about jobs …
W: Yeah.
M: … and, um, he saw a paper clip on his desk, and he thought, I wonder what I can do with this paper clip – whether I can swap it for something.
W: Oh.
M: Anyway, so he got onto the internet and he made this website – I think it's called the-red-paper-clip dot com.
W: Right.
M: And he put this, this on the internet, photographs it, puts it on, and sees if anyone wants to swap something with him.
W: And did, did anything happen?
M: Yeah, so first of all, I don't remember all the details but as I recall two Vancouver women, um, took up the first challenge and they swapped the paper clip with, I think it was a pen shaped like a fish they had found …
W: Random.
M: Yeah – they had found on a camping trip, yeah random. But he meets up with all these people he doesn't just send the things. And so then from that, I believe, this guy in Seattle wanted the pen and swapped

AUDIO SCRIPTS

it for a doorknob. And the door knob was swapped for something to do with camping, …

W: Oh, so he kept trading up each time.

M: Yeah, he kept trading, trading up so, and then that was swapped for a beer keg I think. Apparently what happened was all these people were … the same sort of thought patterns as him and they wanted to sort of meet up and it was about a social event as well.

W: Ah.

M: Anyway, the next thing he got was a snow globe and, according to the report, it said a film director wanted it and said he'd swap it for a part in his film. And then this town decided they had this house in this town, and that they would swap the house for a part in this film.

W: No! So he went all the way from the red paper clip to getting a house.

M: … a house. And my impression was that he, he was just crazy at the beginning but he, he ended up having this – I'm not sure how good the house was but, well, yeah.

W: Well, better than a paper clip.

M: I know basically that's what happened.

W: Wow!

UNIT 8 Recording 2

P = Presenter   D = Dominic   H = Heather

P: OK, Dominic and Heather we're going to play a game

D: Oh.

H: Ahem.

P: Its, it's an experiment. Um what I'm gonna do is – hang on I'm just gonna get it out of my pocket. I'm going to give you, Dominic, £10.

D: OK, can I keep it?

P: OK – for now. And you have to decide how much you're going to offer Heather.

D: OK.

P: And if Heather accepts then you divide the money as agreed. You get some and she gets some.

D: Right.

P: But, if Heather rejects your offer and she doesn't like the way you've split the £10 …

D: Mmm.

P: … then I get the £10 back and neither of you get anything.

H: Um.

D: Ah, OK.

H: OK.

P: Could you understand?

D: Yeah, I think so.

H: Yeah.

P: Are you sure?

H: Yeah.

D: Yeah – so I basically have to choose how much money I'm going to offer Heather.

P: Yeah.

H: And then …

D: And if she's happy with it …

H: I decide if I want it or not.

P: That's right, OK?

H: OK?

D: So …

P: Right there you go.

D: Thank you, that's for me. That's a lot of money, I would quite like all of it. Uh, do I just say it now, out loud?

P: Yeah.

D: OK, uh I'm going to offer you £5.

P: Um.

H: Go on then, I'll accept that.

D: Yeah.

H: Yeah, I will yeah.

D: Great so we get a five, fiver each.

P: You do indeed and I, and I lose £10.

D: Yeah, that was worth it.

P: OK, so I mean that's really interesting. Why, why Dominic did you decide on that split?

D: Um, I guess, if I offered any less I didn't think you'd take it.

H: No.

D: So I thought this way.

P: But why, why, why would you?

D: Um, because it's, it's not fair, you know cos this isn't any more my money than it is hers really, just cos it's a game, you've given it to me.

P: Interesting.

D: Um it, it was.

P: And why, why did you accept?

H: Um, because I felt that it was equal you know an, an equal split, um, I thought it was very kind and yeah generous to give me half.

D: Uh.

P: OK and um, OK then – here's an interesting question. Heather, in your mind what would have …

H: Um …

P: been the lowest amount?

D: Ahem.

H: It act-

P: that you would have accepted?

H: It actually would have been £5 because I think any lower than that and I'd have felt sort of you know.

D: Hard done by.

P: Very interesting.

H: Hard done by, yeah, is the word, yeah.

P: Thanks guys, cheers.

UNIT 8 Recording 3

P = Presenter   D = Dominic   H = Heather

P: OK guys, uh we're gonna play another game now.

D: Um.

P: It's called the Dictator game. And, uh, I think I'm gonna be very out of pocket by the end of the day.

D: More money?

P: Yeah. Another £10 note.

H: Oh, a ten.

P: And, I'm gonna give it to you again.

D: Thank you.

P: But this time – instead of making an offer which you can, you Heather can accept or reject …

H: OK.

P: You have to accept it.

D: Ah.

P: So Dominic …

D: OK.

H: OK.

D: I have the power.

P: It's your decision. You have the power. It's your decision.

D: Um, OK so I just say it out loud?

P: Yeah.

D: Uh, the offer I'm going to give you this time is £1 and that means £9 will be for me.

P: OK.

H: Well then I accept that cos I have no choice.

D: You have no choice.

P: You have no choice. But, but the question here is how do you feel, how do you feel about that?

H: Yeah I feel a bit hard done by, to be honest. I feel a bit cheated really, um.

P: His fairness, from last time has all disappeared.

H: Yeah, mm.

D: Um I guess I gave you a pound to still show that I'm, you know, not heartless.

H: Ahem.

D: Uh, you know so, you know I want to keep all of it, but um I guess with the offer of being able to have more, without the choice.

H: Um.

D: Um, it sort of, it was easier for me, to say, I won't feel so guilty, I don't feel.

H: Yeah tempting, isn't it?

D: Feel a bit guilty now, but no I just thought – is, there's no option for her so I might as well keep more of it.

UNIT 8 Recording 5

J = Jim   L = Liz

J: Here's your coffee.

L: Thanks, Jim. Oh, I needed that.

J: No problem. Hey, Liz, there's something I've been meaning to talk to you about.

L: Oh yeah?

J: It's just that … well … you know you borrowed some money from me last week?

L: Oh, right. It was ten euros, wasn't it? I don't actually have that on me at the moment.

J: It's not that, it's … I hope you don't take this the wrong way, but, um …

L: Right.

J: … it's just that this isn't the first time I've lent you money and er, well you haven't paid it back. I mean, I know it's not a lot, just small amounts each time but it kind of adds up quite quickly … I dunno. Do you know what I mean?

L: Yeah. Sorry. I didn't realise. I know I'm terrible with money. I just forget. Look, I promise I'll give it back, but could you wait a week? Until I get paid.

J: Well, actually, you've said that once before. I don't want you to get the wrong idea, but … it, you know, never happened. And it makes things slightly awkward. It makes me feel just a bit annoyed. Do you see where I'm coming from?

L: Oh. Yeah. I suppose so.

J: Look, I've got a suggestion. I'd feel better if we could work out how much is owed and then you could pay me back a little each week, you know, however much you can afford. How does that sound?

L: Yeah, yeah. That sounds reasonable.

J: OK, great so …

UNIT 8 Recording 8

OK, here are some things that I think would be useful if you're visiting the States, especially if you're coming here to do business.

So first of all, with names. When you first meet someone, it's considered good manners to use a title along with their surname, you know like Mr Smith or Ms Jones, and so on. But the funny thing is that in fact people will in most cases want to use first names, you know be on a first-name basis, like 'Hey call me "Bob"' and all that. That might not be comfortable for you but in fact if you stick to a more formal Mr Smith sort of thing, it's not going to be comfortable for them. I also think that once they know your name you'll find people use it a lot, so they'll say it periodically in a conversation. If you're not used to it, it can seem strange at first.

Now with meeting people for the first time … It's pretty normal for people to shake hands, or at least guys do. Women usually do, certainly in business, but not always. On the whole, Americans tend to avoid greetings that involve hugging and other close physical contact, except with family members and friends. Having said that, don't be surprised if someone gives you a hug the first time you meet them, either as a hello or a goodbye. You sort of have to keep your eyes open and try to anticipate what they'll do.

When people sit down, like in a meeting, people like to get comfortable, so people cross their legs with one ankle on the other knee. I know this is rude in some countries but it's normal here. That reminds me, if you're chatting with someone in an office, standing up, they might sit on a desk, which I know is a big no-no in places like Japan. Other gestures? Well, if an American wants to show agreement, they'll sometimes give the thumbs up sign or they'll make a circle out of their thumb and index finger. Don't be offended if in your culture this isn't polite. It just means 'A OK' in the States.

Last of all, timing: punctuality is very important for business occasions and it's unacceptable to be late, and if you are late it will be appreciated if you let your contact know if you are going to be late. It's the same for social occasions, you need to arrive on time.

Of course, having said all this, it's important to remember that the United States is huge and there's a lot of variety in what's acceptable in different places. Anyway, I hope this advice helps.

UNIT 9 Recording 2

Conversation 1

L = Lise   J = Jeff

L: So what happened was, I was sitting in a café and this young couple – they looked like tourists – asked me to take a photo of them. And I took their photo, and they thanked me and left and then I looked at my seat and realised my handbag had gone, with my mobile, wallet, credit card, keys, everything.

J: No! What did you do?

L: Well, there was a guy on the next table and he saw I was really upset and I explained about the bag and he asked me which bank I was with and he said he worked for that bank and gave me a phone number and let me use his mobile to phone them and stop my credit card.

J: And you believed him?

L: Yeah, I mean I was in a real panic. I was really grateful for his help. Anyway, I phoned the number and talked to a woman from 'the bank' and gave her my name and address and my account number.

J: She sounded genuine?

L: Yeah, completely. I could hear the sounds of the call centre behind her. And she asked me to key in my PIN on the phone and she said they'd stop my card.

J: Wow. And you did? You punched in your PIN?

L: Yeah, unfortunately.

J: So it was a double scam. They got your bag and your bank account details.

L: I felt so stupid.

J: So who actually took your bag?

L: Well, it can't have been the young couple because I was looking at them all the time I was taking the photo. Their job was just to distract me. So it must have been stolen when I was taking the photo.

J: Was it the guy at the next table, then? The fake banker?

L: I think so. He must have taken my bag when I wasn't looking. Then he could have hidden it in his case or maybe he gave it to another member of the gang.

J: And then he gave you a fake phone number to call the bank.

L: Yeah, and they probably used a recording of a call centre so that it sounded like the real bank.

Conversation 2

D = Dan   I = Ingrid

D: I was badly tricked a few years ago when I was working in a jewellery shop.

I: You never told me about that. What happened?

D: Well, this woman came in and was looking at necklaces. She was young, attractive, well dressed, and then a guy came in shortly afterwards and he was just looking around. But then the woman went to pay for a very expensive necklace that she'd picked out, and when she was counting out the money onto the counter, the guy grabbed her, flashed his police ID and said he was

arresting her for paying with counterfeit money.

I: Fake money! Wow!

D: So he took the cash and the necklace as evidence, wrote down his contact details, and promised me he'd bring the necklace back by the end of the day. I didn't suspect anything. Then he took the woman away, presumably to book her at the police station.

I: And he didn't come back?

D: No, and stupid me, I didn't even begin to suspect anything until it was closing time, so then I phoned the police and they had no idea what I was talking about. That was it, end of story.

I: How much was the necklace worth?

D: £600. And my boss took it out of my salary. That's why I quit.

I: So the police ID was a fake.

D: Must have been. I just didn't check it.

I: And wait a second, was the woman a real customer?

D: No, the woman must have been working with the guy. She couldn't have been a real customer or she wouldn't have gone with him …

I: But she might have had fake money.

D: I really don't think so.

I: Talk about an ingenious scam …

UNIT 9 Recording 5

P = Police officer   A = Alain

P: Hello, police. Can I help you?

A: Yes, I'd like to report a crime. I've been robbed.

P: I'm very sorry to hear that, Sir. OK, I'll need to take a statement.

A: A statement?

P: To write down some details, if that's all right.

A: Yes, sure.

P: Could you give me your name please, Sir?

A: Alain Girard.

P: Right. That's Girard with a J?

A: No, G, and it's Alain spelled A-l-a-i-n.

P: Right, Mr Girard. Could you tell me exactly when the incident happened?

A: Just now. About an hour ago.

P: Could you be more precise?

A: Excuse me?

P: Could you give me the exact time?

A: I think at 2.50 or 2.55.

P: That's about 2.50 on the seventh of June. And where did it happen?

A: Park Avenue.

P: Can you pinpoint the exact location?

A: Pinpoint?

P: Tell me exactly where.

A: Oh. It was near the entrance to the park. Just about fifty metres inside.

P: OK. Could you tell me what happened?

A: I was walking out of the park, and a man was running towards me and he hit into me hard –

P: He collided with you?

A: Yes and he said 'sorry' and something else, then before I realised what had happened, he had run on. It was only about

AUDIO SCRIPTS

thirty seconds later that I realised my wallet had gone and that he must have taken it when he hit me, collided with me.

P: But did it cross your mind that it wasn't just an accident?

A: No, it never occurred to me that he'd done it on purpose.

P: Did you run after him?

A: No, my mind just went blank and I stood there not knowing what to do.

P: But you were OK? Not hurt?

A: No, just very shocked.

P: OK. Could you tell me exactly what your wallet looked like and what was in it?

A: It's brown leather and it has my credit card and about 250 euros and –

P: Hold on a minute, credit card … about 250 euros, yes?

A: And a photo of my girlfriend.

P: OK. So you saw the man. Can you give me a description?

A: Erm, about twenty, white, quite tall. And he was wearing a sweater, grey colour with a … you know … erm, something you put over your head …

P: A hood? He was wearing a hoodie?

A: Yes, that's the word. So I didn't see his face, not clearly. But he looked as if he was just out jogging, you know, he was wearing some sort of dark trousers, for running or for the gym.

P: Tracksuit bottoms?

A: Yeah. I can't remember anything else, it all happened so quickly.

P: So that's a tall white male, about twenty, wearing a grey hoodie and dark tracksuit bottoms?

A: That's right.

P: And did he have any other distinguishing marks or features?

A: Sorry?

P: Anything special or different from normal? For example, a scar on his face or anything like that?

A: No, he just seemed like a normal guy, out running. Nothing special. Except …

P: Yes?

A: He reminded me a bit of that actor, Vin Diesel. But younger. Do you know who I mean?

P: Vin Diesel, yeah. I'll put it down. And you said he said something to you.

A: Yeah, but I didn't catch what he said. It was too quick.

P: Right, one last question and then I'll take your contact details. Were there any other people in the vicinity?

A: Vicinity?

P: In the surrounding area – nearby. Any witnesses who saw what had happened?

A: No, there was no one nearby, in the … vicinity.

P: Right, now I just need to take your contact details, Mr Girard, and I can also give you a phone number to ring if …

UNIT 9 Recording 8

W1 = Woman 1   M = Man   W2 = Woman 2

W1: So, we really need to decide then what it is we get rid of and what is absolutely essential to keep on the life raft, I think that's probably the most important thing, isn't it?

M: I'm sure it's easy to get rid of a few things, isn't it?

W2: Like what?

M: Well, I'm not sure about the lighter. I mean, we can't really start a fire on a raft, can we?

W2: No.

W1: I suppose it depends on what the life raft is made out of, doesn't it?

M: Yeah, but it's not exactly top priority to be able to cook a hot meal, you know, when you really just need to survive.

W1: So no lighter?

M and W2: OK.

W1: OK. So what do you think is important?

W2: I'd say that a blanket is essential.

W1: Interesting choice. What for?

W2: Well, you can use it for a lot of different things. To keep you warm obviously, but you can use a blanket as a towel if you get wet –

W1: If you fall in the water.

W2: … for example. And a blanket can protect you from the sun.

M: That hadn't occurred to me. OK, I'm convinced. So what else?

W1: Well I can't see the point of taking the hand mirror can you?

M: Actually, I can. Because if …

UNIT 10 Recording 1

A: So come on then, favourite movie of all time.

B: Um, I would have to say, cos I love action films, uh, that it would be *Speed* – have you ever seen that?

A: *Speed*?

B: Yeah it's with Keanu Reeves and Sandra Bullock.

A: Oh, I like her.

B: She's very good isn't she? Um, so yeah, I just love any kind of action film. And I remember watching it when I was really young and watching it with my dad. And it's the sort of, like, a family-friendly action film, because it's not too violent, it's not too gory but it's just really tense. And I remember just like watching it, we had a cushion, me and my dad, and I was just like what's gonna happen next? Um, have you seen it?

A: No! I haven't I, I think I've seen bits of it, like trailers and things but …

B: OK, it's um …

A: No, I knew she was in it.

B: Yeah, so basically, he, uh, there's a baddy in it, as every action film it has a good baddy, and he's got no thumb. I remember that, that was like a memorable bit of it, he had no thumb. And so they sort of highjack this … this bus. And it's set that it can only drive at a certain speed – hence the name. And so it's just basically driving through,

through the city and it can't stop otherwise there's a bomb and it's gonna blow it up. Um, so, and there's a, Keanu Reeves he's, um, he's the goody he's uh a policeman. And he's … he jumps on board the bus to try and stop this bomb from going off. And, uh, it's just all the different characters on the bus. It's just really …

A: The whole film is on the bus?

B: Yeah and, but it's, it's, well not at the beginning, it sort of goes onto the bus. But uh, it's just I remember it being so tense and gripping, 'cos you just didn't know what was gonna happen. You didn't know.

A: It sounds really uncomfortable to watch, was it not?

B: It … it's … I just like that kind of that feeling of like pure suspense 'cos you just have no idea if it's gonna end well or not. And it did end very well. You have to watch it.

A: Well yeah, as long as there's, you know, a point when you can relax, 'cos I don't like feeling like that the whole way through a movie, anxiety.

B: Yeah, because you know when it's like driving along, and it, 'cos I think it has to stay at fifty miles per hour. And uh, so uh, if there's, driving along a motorway and it's, there's traffic and stuff you have to change the route and things, so you just don't know where its gonna go.

A: Oh, OK.

B: And then they get to a bridge that's um, hasn't finished being built. Uh so you're not sure how they're gonna get over the bridge and stuff like that. So there's lots of moments where you just think, I have no clue what's gonna happen.

A: Good stunts?

B: Very good, and I heard that he did all his stunts himself, Keanu Reeves.

A: Yes, they always say that.

B: He likes a bit of action, doesn't he? So, and I think it always helps to have a very good heroine in a film and she's, she's beautiful, don't you think?

A: Yes, I love her. I think she's very funny, but tell me there's some comedy in there.

B: Um, there's not a huge amount of comedy. Uh, it's one of your traditional sort of American blockbuster action films. So yeah but it's, it's just, it's – there's not many action films with comedy in though are there?

A: I think that's why I don't watch them.

B: Oh really?

A: Yeah.

B: What's your sort of, your favourite type of film?

A: I don't like to feel uncomfortable so it's just comedy.

B: Watch *Speed*.

A: Mm mm OK.

UNIT 10 Recording 5

Conversation 1

W = Woman   M = Man

W: So here we are in Greenwich Village.

M: It looks very different from the rest of New York.

W: Yeah, the streets are quite narrow and the buildings aren't as high.

M: It does look quite village-like.

W: Yeah, but it's quite big. It extends out west that way to the Hudson River, north above Washington Square. We'll go up there in a bit.

M: And you lived here?

W: When I first came to New York, yeah. In an apartment just around the corner, on West Third Street. Actually, you can see the building over there.

M: Near The Blue Note Jazz Club?

W: Yeah.

M: I've heard of The Blue Note.

W: It's pretty famous. There are some great jazz clubs around the neighbourhood, and that's one of the best. We can see a show there one night if you want.

M: That'd be great.

W: Now up here on the left is the Café Reggio. It's where I used to hang out and read when I wasn't working.

M: Looks good.

W: Their cappuccino is great. The story goes that the original owner brought cappuccino to America. You can see the original cappuccino machine inside.

M: Cool. We could stop and have a coffee.

W: Maybe a bit later? Let's head over to Washington Square Park and then circle back.

M: OK – lead the way!

…

W: A lot of these clubs we're walking by have a real history. As I'm sure you know, Greenwich Village has always been a centre of artistic life – very bohemian. It's always attracted famous writers, dancers and poets. And in the sixties, it was a big part of the folk music scene: Simon and Garfunkel, Joni Mitchell, Bob Dylan, you know.

M: Before my time! Now what's this?

W: This is Washington Square Park. We'll walk into the park on this side. Can you play chess?

M: A bit, yeah.

W: Any of these guys here would be happy to challenge you to a game of chess. They're here all day, every day.

M: Maybe next time – I'm not that good! What's the arch over there? It looks like the Arc de Triomphe in Paris.

W: Well it should, that's the Washington Square arch. It was modelled on the Arc de Triomphe and built in 1889 to celebrate the hundredth anniversary of the inauguration of George Washington as president.

M: Could we sit down a second? I need a break.

W: Why don't we retrace our steps and go back to the Café Reggio?

M: Sounds good. I could really do with a coffee.

Conversation 2

M1 = Man 1   W = Woman   M2 = Man 2

M1: So, this is Radcliffe Square.

W: Wow! Is this right in the centre then?

M1: Pretty much.

M2: What's that?

M1: Hold on. Let's just get off our bikes … Right, so that building in front of us is the Bodleian, named after the founder – Thomas Bodley. Believe it or not, despite the fact that it's circular, it's actually a library.

W: Cool!

M1: Yeah, it gets a copy of every book published in the UK.

M2: Who can use it?

M1: Any student at the university. Of course, each college also has its own library – you know the university's divided into colleges, right?

M2: Right. How many colleges are there?

M1: Just under forty. Well, thirty-eight to be exact.

W: So that means thirty-eight libraries?!

M1: Mm but they're not all as big as the Bodleian. Anyway, we'll need to get back on our bikes for the next bit.

…

M1: Can you hear me if I talk as we cycle along?

M2: Yeah.

W: OK, but don't go too fast. I'm not very steady on this thing!

M1: So, here's the famous Bridge of Sighs, connecting two sides of Hertford College.

M2: I've seen the original.

M1: What, of the bridge? In Italy, you mean?

M2: Ja, it's in Venice. Beautiful.

M1: OK. We'll go past New College and then onto the High Street.

M2: Is that New College there?

M1: Yep.

W: How 'new' is new?

M1: Roughly 1370.

W: You're kidding!

M1: No, really! Interestingly, the oldest college was actually only founded a hundred or so years earlier! Uh-oh, watch out on this corner …

M1: That's the 'Schools'. It's where the students take their exams. Apparently, the biggest room can seat somewhere in the region of 500 students although I haven't seen it myself. Anyway, we're turning right here. The street's cobbled, so be careful.

M2: How many students are there at the university in total?

M1: To be honest, it depends. In term time, you'd probably get upwards of 20,000.

M2: Many international students?

M1: Some, but most are from the UK. We'll finish by cycling down this way to Christ Church. We can actually go inside if we're quick. It's well worth a visit.

M2: Christ Church is another college?

M1: Yeah, the biggest and probably the most famous. Have you seen any of the Harry Potter films?

M2: No …

W: I have!

M1: Oh, well, you'll recognise the Great Hall. It's where they have the feasts in Hogwarts School. You know that bit when Harry …

① fewer than (<)
   just under forty

② more than (>)
   upwards of twenty thousand

③ about / around / approximately
   Roughly 1370   (≐)
   a hundred or so years earlier
   somewhere in the region
   five hundred students

153

AUDIO SCRIPTS

S = Sarah   T = Tim   N = Nigel

S: Right, well, we have our shortlist for the new feature that we're going to put into the town centre, which one gets your vote, Tim?

T: I'm really in favour of the – the state-of-the-art multiplex cinema. I think that it would be most useful and beneficial for the community. I think it will be used a great deal, I think it would bring jobs to the area, and I think it would provide entertainment and activities for young people.

N: The only thing that would concern me though is that that's going to be very, very expensive.

T: Um hm.

S: I mean, I personally would prefer the botanical garden.

T: Oh.

S: Because I think that that will satisfy the needs of many different age groups. I think it would be very good for wheelchairs, for … for blind people, for people with disabilities, there would be areas that would be excellent for young people, and lots of learning opportunitie in the education centre. And we know from past experience that the older age group certainly enjoy gardens.

T: The only thing that would concern me on that is that you mention youth, but I don't think that you're going to get as many young people involved in a botanical garden. I think if it was interactive then it would be … but just as a thing that was showing I'm, I'm not so sure.

N: Well, I don't want to harp on about costs again but we have to consider the maintenance of this botanical garden. There are very high maintenance costs involved.

S: Oh, so, Nigel what, what would you prefer?

N: Well, my vote would go to the theatre workshop space for young people. And I know we said we don't want to discriminate against any … we don't want to leave out certain members of our society, but I think we've got a problem in this town about kids getting bored, hanging around on street corners, they need something to do and a theatre workshop space is going to get them … it's going to give them a routine, it's going to give them a motivation, and then when they do their shows, they're bringing along their grandparents, their parents, I feel it's very inclusive.

T: Can you see the older generation wanting it, liking it?

N: I think the older generation want to be sure that kids aren't hanging about the streets with nothing to do.

S: And could that theatre workshop space be used for other things as well?

N: Absolutely.

S: Could it be used for meetings, for other sections of society?

N: … Aerobics … there's going to be a sprung wooden floor so there'll be dance classes, yoga, pilates, multi-purpose …

speakout 2ND EDITION

Upper Intermediate
Workbook

with key

Frances Eales • Steve Oakes
Louis Harrison

Pearson Education Limited
Edinburgh Gate
Harlow
Essex CM20 2JE
England
and Associated Companies throughout the world.

www.pearsonelt.com

First published 2015
Fifth impression 2019
This edition published 2016
ISBN: 978-1-292-14938-7

Set in Aptifer sans 10/12 pt
Printed in Slovakia by Neografia

Illustration acknowledgements
Illustrated by Eric@kja-artists

Photo acknowledgements
The publisher would like to thank the following for their kind permission to reproduce
their photographs:

(Key: b-bottom; c-centre; l-left; r-right; t-top)

123RF.com: 9bl, 9br, 35, 51 (tea), 51tl, 51tr, Natalia Lisovskaya 30b, Raman Maisei 8b,
Maridav 8c, Wavebreak Media Ltd 48, Nils Weymann 68t, 68b; **Alamy Images:** Ashley
Cooper 28, Cultura Creative 8t, Natural Visions 50, PhotoAlto 23; **Fotolia.com:**
MasterLu 69; **Getty Images:** Elie Bernager 47, Michael Blann 15, Domen Colja 29, John
Lund / Sam Diephuis 61, Trevor Williams 25; **Press Association Images:** Tsvangirai
Mukwazhi 21; **Shutterstock.com:** Diego Cervo 62, d13 44b, Jack.Q 24, Kavram 30t,
Kurhan 44t, Nejron Photo's 41, Nikkos 38, PhotoBarmaley 51 (coffee); **The Kobal
Collection:** Paramount 65

All other images © Pearson Education

Every effort has been made to trace the copyright holders and we apologise
in advance for any unintentional omissions. We would be pleased to insert the
appropriate acknowledgement in any subsequent edition of this publication.

CONTENTS

VOCABULARY

AGE

1 A Correct B's sentences by changing one word.

1 A: I'm going to play on the swings …

B: Behave your age! They're meant for kids.

2 A: Mina seems very sensible for a sixteen-year-old.

B: I'm continually surprised by her maternity.

3 A: I can't believe he's seventy!

B: Yes, he looks very young than his age.

4 A: What are you doing this weekend?

B: We're visiting an elder aunt of Simon's.

5 A: I think Hugh is too young to become a manager.

B: Careful – that could be seen as age judgement.

6 A: In her forties, Madonna is attracting even more crowds.

B: Yes, she's definitely in her time.

7 A: You could say that social networking sites have 'grown up'.

B: I agree – they've certainly reached of age now.

8 A: I can't believe what he just said!

B: Yeah, he's so unmature. He really needs to grow up.

B Are the age-related phrases in B's responses positive (+), negative (-) or neutral (N)?

GRAMMAR

MODAL VERBS AND RELATED PHRASES

2 Complete the article with the words and phrases in the box. You do not need to use one of the words or phrases.

can	could	are able	being able to	managed to	couldn't
should	had to	don't have to	are supposed to	made	
wasn't allowed	let				

WHAT WAS LIFE LIKE BEFORE THE INTERNET?

- If you wanted to keep in touch with friends, you [1] should *couldn't* just visit a social networking site. You [2] *can* ___ phone or talk to friends face to face. *had to*

- To sell something, you paid for an advert in the local paper. These days you [3] *are able* to reach thousands of potential buyers through sites such as Craigslist or eBay. Before you buy you [4] *are supposed* read the conditions thoroughly. *should* If someone else is bidding for you, don't [5] *let* them bid without giving them a limit.

- Online encyclopedias didn't exist. As a student, once I only [6] *managed to* find information for an assignment by spending two days in a library.

- Music came from shops in the form of CDs. Nowadays it [7] *could* *can* be downloaded online. Obviously a good thing? Well, you [8] *had to* pay for it but many people download illegally. *are supposed to*

- Before life online, as a kid I was [9] *made* to write long thank-you letters for birthday presents instead of [10] *being able to* send a quick email. My parents were really strict. I [11] *wasn't allowed* to play with any new toys until I'd written to everyone.

- You used to go to friends' homes to watch their holiday videos. Thankfully, you [12] *don't have to* do this anymore. A quick look on a video-sharing site is enough!

3 Complete the second sentence so that it has a similar meaning to the first. Use between two and five words including the word given.

1 There's no obligation for the company to provide training. HAVE
The company _____ training.

2 It's impossible to force kids to eat vegetables. MAKE
You _____ vegetables.

3 We weren't able to see the supervisor. MANAGE
We _____ see the supervisor.

4 He was allowed to go after he'd been questioned for three hours. LET
The police _____ after he'd been questioned for three hours.

5 I'm afraid I can't make the meeting. ABLE
I'm afraid I _____ make the meeting.

6 This area is forbidden. Get out immediately. SUPPOSED
You _____ in this area. Get out immediately.

LISTENING

4 A How would you answer questions 1–8?

WHAT'S THE BEST AGE . . .

1 to choose a career?
2 to get married?
3 to have a baby?
4 to start a sport?
5 to learn a musical instrument?
6 to learn a new language?
7 to become president or prime minister?
8 to retire?

B ▶ 6.1 Listen to four speakers. Which question above does each person answer?

Speaker 1: _____
Speaker 2: _____
Speaker 3: _____
Speaker 4: _____

C Listen again and answer the questions.

Speaker 1
1 What age does the speaker think is best?
2 What three factors are important?

Speaker 2
3 What does the speaker think the minimum and maximum age should be?
4 What two factors need to be balanced?

Speaker 3
5 Why do you need to understand yourself and your relationship?
6 What is the wrong age, according to the speaker?

Speaker 4
7 When does the speaker think it's OK for a young person to make a choice?
8 What advice does the speaker give to other people?

D Match the phrases in bold with the meanings a)–e).

1 I don't think there's any **hard and fast** rule.
2 She's **still going strong** now she's over seventy.
3 You have to **strike a balance** between maturity and energy.
4 It **has to do with** giving yourself enough time to get to know yourself.
5 That **worked for** me.

a) was successful
b) choose a moderate way, compromise
c) fixed, definite
d) is connected to
e) continuing to be successful

VOCABULARY PLUS
WORD-BUILDING: PREFIXES

5 A Put the words in the correct group according to the negative prefix they take.

realistic   satisfied   behave   secure   familiar
predictable   logical   patient   mortal   willing
interpret   relevant   healthy

1 un: *realistic* _____ _____
    _____ _____ _____
2 im: _____ _____
3 mis: _____ _____
4 il: _____
5 ir: _____
6 dis: _____
7 in: _____

B Complete the text with the negative form of words in Exercise 5A. You do not need three of the words.

Dealing with difficult students

Students are motivated to learn by a variety of factors. Some look for a sense of personal achievement while others enjoy being involved as a member of a learning group.

Teachers sometimes make the mistake of having [1] _____ expectations of students. It is better to be patient with their progress rather than being [2] _____ because being [3] _____ to let students learn from their own mistakes can be demotivating.

Students often have a lot to deal with, particularly if they are moving from an environment they know to an [4] _____ learning environment. They may feel unsure and [5] _____ because they are not used to the new systems and may become [6] _____ with their new school and way of life. These feelings can take many forms of expression such as sadness or attention-seeking and a tendency to [7] _____.

Whatever form of behaviour this takes the teacher can show understanding by responding to students using expressions such as 'I understand why you feel like that, but …'. The teacher should pay attention to what the student is really saying, even if it sometimes seems to be [8] _____ and unconnected the subject.

It is easy to [9] _____ the new students' actions and statements so it is important to keep listening and communicating with them and letting them know that you are there to support them and not simply to judge them. Start by telling them this and your relationship will soon change from an [10] _____ and harmful one into one that is happy and motivating.

C Write the negative form of words in Exercise 5A in the correct group according to the stress pattern.

oooOo _____
ooOoo _____ _____
oOoo _____ _____ _____
oOo _____ _____ _____
      _____
ooO _____ _____
ooOo _____

D ▶ 6.2 Listen and check. Then listen and repeat.

READING

1 A Read the article. Which of the following topics are not mentioned?

work   transport   clothes   food   relationships   shopping
energy   social networking   newspapers   radio and television

B Six sentences have been removed from the article. Complete the article with sentences a)–f).

a) Work comes to you.

b) Now the restaurant's bioprinter starts to produce the raw ingredients for the restaurant AIPA to cook and bring to the table.

c) Some do accounting, some write letters.

d) You have instant video chat, internet browsing and can do many other things you needed a smartphone for previously.

e) You control what happens in the whole house from here, so you remotely switch on the lights and the shower and tell the kitchen you'll be ready for breakfast in 20 minutes.

f) Computers inside your car take away the need for manual driving.

C Read the article again. Are the statements true (T), false (F) or is the information not given (NG)?

1 You are woken up early because of an important news bulletin.

2 Your artificially intelligent personal assistant has checked your health.

3 Your clothes are newly made as soon as you have decided what to wear.

4 Cars are designed to be energy efficient.

5 The ingredients for your food are produced at the restaurant by a bioprinter.

6 Flying machines make deliveries to your home.

7 Smart glasses save everything you do during the day so that you can play it back later.

8 Your own home contributes fifteen per cent of the electricity you use.

2030 VISION

Smartphones are museum pieces and cable TV – well what was that? The world will be very different in the future but what will everyday life be like in 2030?

06.45

You're gently woken up in your sleep pod – you don't sleep in a bed, they've developed dramatically into sleep pods. [1]_____ Meanwhile your artificially intelligent personal assistant (AIPA) has started work monitoring your body functions and making sure you're fit and well for the day ahead.

07.50

You're ready for work but you don't need to go anywhere. [2]_____ You enter your virtual office and greet co-workers from around the world in your virtual work environment. You and your colleague in Singapore look at the live data feeds and make real-time decisions about your work. Then a workmate nearby asks for a face-to-face meeting over lunch. You decide what to wear and an army of nanobots make the clothes for you.

12.30

Your journey is still by car – but you don't drive it. It drives. [3]_____ They talk to the smart road which is regulating the flow of traffic so that cars are travelling at maximum speed and efficiency. You know there won't be a delay because of a car accident – there hasn't been a car crash for ten years now.

12.45

You arrive for your meal. Your car has already suggested a menu – beef goulash. [4]_____ During the meal your workmate mentions her new smart glasses and this reminds you that a drone will deliver yours later today.

15.30

Work's finished. You have a lot more leisure time now because AIPAs can do a lot of the work for us and a lot quicker. [5]_____ Not all AIPA's have human form, some are simply computer programmes with human-like intelligence and understanding. Right on time the drone arrives with your smart glasses.

19.00

In the evening you see what your new smart glasses can do. Smart glasses have replaced the smartphone because they are a lot easier to use and have a lot more functions. [6]_____ Even better, they record every minute of your day for you so that you can watch your day again – speeded up this time.

22.00

As you sleep the smart electricity grid and your smart electrical appliances are saving electricity and sending it to where it is needed most. In fact, it has been doing this 24/7 but at night it becomes very noticeable as your fridge powers down and the street lights dim. We can finally see the stars from our cities again.

GRAMMAR

FUTURE PERFECT AND CONTINUOUS

2 Underline the correct alternative.

1 Nine o'clock's too late to arrive. The concert *will start/will be starting/will have started* by then.

2 You can use my desk. I *won't use/won't be using/won't have used* it tomorrow as I'm away.

3 Dr Sawali will be happy to lead a discussion during the conference as she*'ll attend/'ll be attending/ 'll have attended* it anyway.

4 Will you still *need/be needing/have needed* me when I'm sixty-four?   *[handwritten: stare verb]*

5 Your two-day visit *will involve/will be involving/ will have involved* a factory tour and several meetings.

6 By this time tomorrow the championship draw *will happen/will be happening/will have happened* and we'll know who we're playing.   *[handwritten: Complete]*

3 **A** Complete the predictions made in the 1950s about life in 2020. Use the future perfect or future continuous.

1 The world / experience / mini ice-age / at that time.
The world will be experiencing a mini ice-age at that time.

2 The average weight / adult male / go down / to seventy kilos.
[handwritten: The average weight adult male will have gotten down to seventy kilos.]

3 Smoking / ban / completely / in all public areas.
[handwritten: Smoking will completely have banned]   *[handwritten: in all public areas]*

4 Everyone / drive / flying cars.
[handwritten: Everyone will be driving flying cars.]

5 Men and women / wear / same clothes.
[handwritten: Men and women will be wearing same clothes.]

6 Poverty and famine / halve.
[handwritten: Poverty and famine will have halved.]

B Which predictions above have already come true (✓), which may well come true (?) and which are unlikely to come true (✗)?

[handwritten: 3. Smoking will have been completly banned in all public areas.]

VOCABULARY

OPTIMISM/PESSIMISM

4 Write letters to complete the words.

1 feel good about a future event
= look **f o r w a r d   t o**

2 have good and bad experiences
= have u**p s   a n d   d o w n s**

3 make no progress = **g o   n o w h e r e**

4 have emotions which are both positive and negative
= have m**i x e d   f e e l i n g s**

5 see the positive side of things
= **l o o k   o n   t h e   b r i g h t** side

6 positive = up**b e a t**

7 fear = dr**e a d**

8 create a feeling of hopelessness
= fill with de**s p a i r**   *[handwritten: "hopelessness]*

WRITING

AN INFORMAL EMAIL; LEARN TO FOCUS ON INFORMAL STYLE

5 **A** Complete the sentences with the words in the box.

for	all	about	to	know	rather	get	'd	let	be

1 April is *a great time* _____ visiting Budapest – the spring festival is on.

2 Now, _____ your idea of travelling to New York. *I* _____ *love* to come along.

3 Sheila was *happy to* _____ an email from her friend in Indonesia.

4 It'd _____ *great* if we could get free tickets to the concert. I'll _____ *you know* when it starts.

5 I'm really excited about planning our holiday together, *I can't wait* _____ meet again and plan it in more detail. See you again soon. _____ *the best!*

6 *Do you* _____ which is the closest airport to Brighton? *I'd* _____ land as near to the city as possible.

B Complete the emails words and phrases in *italics* from Exercise 5A.

Hi Levent!

I was really [1]_____ your text. I can't believe you're finally coming to Liverpool! I knew the information [2]_____ the music festival, in fact I was planning to go myself. If you're going too, why don't we go together? It'd [3]_____ to hang out for a while. In fact, you could come earlier and stay with us for a few days. You always said you'd like to spend some time in the city and this would be [4]_____ it. What do you know about Liverpool – [5]_____ what you'd like to see? [6]_____,

Tim

Hello Tim,

What a surprise that you're going too! [7]_____ to see you and your family but it's difficult to visit you before the festival – [8]_____ come after, if that's OK. Do you have any details about the festival? Can you send them to me? I'll [9]_____ what my plans are next week. [10]_____ hear more about the festival.

All the best,
Levent

VOCABULARY

COLLOCATIONS

1 A Complete the questions with the correct collocations.

1 How long have you had your current cr_____ ca_____?
2 Do you mind st_____ home al_____?
3 Have you ever ri_____ a sc_____? If not, would you like to?
4 Do you think it's OK for men to we_____ make-up?
5 How la_____ do you think parents should let children st_____ up?
6 Have you ever ru_____ your own bu_____? If not, would you enjoy it?
7 How many smartphones have you ow_____?
8 How many so_____ ne_____ websites have you used, if any?
9 Have you ever done a pa_____-ti_____ job?
10 Would you feel safe tr_____ so_____ around another country?
11 When you were younger did you ever ba_____ for a toddler?
12 Should children be allowed to get their ears pi_____?

B Answer each question using no more than three words.

FUNCTION

PERSUADING

2 A Correct the mistakes in A's sentences.

1 A: Look at this picture. Isn't that it time they banned 'size zero' models?
  B: Well, clothes do look quite good on them.
  A: But it sends a terrible message to young girls. Shouldn't they be knowing it isn't normal to be so skinny?
  B: I've never really thought about it much.
  A: Well, you should. Clearly so, these images add to the pressure on young girls.
  B: Yeah, you're probably right.

2 A: Aren't you thinking that they should use technology in football games?
  B: What, you mean instead of referees?
  A: Yeah, to make decisions. No one can't see it would be fairer.
  B: But you need referees for all sorts of reasons.
  A: Yeah, but sure it's more important that decisions are correct.
  B: Hmm. I suppose you have a point.

B ▶ 6.3 Listen and mark the main stresses in A's sentences.

C ▶ 6.4 Listen and repeat A's sentences. Pay attention to stress and intonation.

LEARN TO

CLARIFY IDEAS

3 A Put the phrases in bold in the correct order.

1 A: Do you like me in this dress?
  B: I prefer the white one.
  A: **you / is / so / saying / what / 're** this one, which cost a fortune, looks terrible.
  _____
  B: No, I mean the white one makes you look slimmer.
  A: **other / so, / words / in**, I look fat!
  _____
  B: No, no, you're twisting my words. I just meant that you look *even* slimmer in the white one.

2 A: Don't you think we should pay a decorator to do it?
  B: **you / so / think / basically** I can't do it.
  _____
  A: I didn't mean that. It's just that it might be quicker and save us money.
  B: **what / you / so / mean / is** I might mess it up.
  _____
  A: No, but you're a perfectionist and you know how long it takes you to do things.
  B: So, you'd rather spend money and end up with a worse job!
  A: Not exactly …

B ▶ 6.5 Listen and check.

VOCABULARY OPTIMISM/PESSIMISM

1 Complete the underlined phrases.

A: So, how are you getting on with the course?

B: [1]I / mix / feeling / it. I'm finding the module on statistics very difficult. It feels like I'm [2]nowhere / going, but I'm enjoying the other modules.

A: That's not surprising. Everyone [3]have / their / up / down when they start university.

B: Yeah, but [4]I / dread the exams.

A: Nobody [5]look / forward / take / exams but I'm sure you'll do fine. [6]Look / bright / side. This time next month, they'll all be over.

1 *I have mixed feelings about it*
2 *going nowhere*
3 *has their ups and downs*
4 *I'm dreading for*
5 *looks forward to taking exams*
6 *Look on the bright side.*

GRAMMAR MODAL VERBS AND RELATED PHRASES

2 Complete the conversations with a modal verb or phrase.

A: Did you do the whole walk?   / managed to

B: We [1] could we able to climb to the top, but we [2] couldn't /weren't stay long because of the weather.   able to

A: Were you [3] able to see much of the view?

A: You really [4] ought not fly when you've got such bad flu.

B: But if I don't get on that plane I [5] won't be able to go to the wedding.

A: But when you try to check in, they might not [6] allow you to fly. The rules are quite strict.

A: What time do your parents say you [7] must have to / should go to bed?

B: I'm [8] supposed used to be in bed by ten but I often stay up till eleven. What about you?

A: I'm [9] allowed used to stay up till ten at the weekend but my parents [10] have make me go to bed at nine during the week.

FUNCTION PERSUADING

3 Complete the conversation with the words in the box. You do not need to use three words.

| shouldn't surely doesn't wouldn't haven't |
| aren't clearly don't isn't |

A: Tom, [1] don't you think we should start packing?

B: [2] ~~Clearly~~ Surely it won't take all night to pack. We don't leave till noon.   shouldn't

A: [3] ~~Wouldn't~~ we at least begin? Last time it took ages – [4] we didn't allow enough time then.   clearly

B: Only because I couldn't find my glasses!

A: Exactly. So [5] isn't it better to do it now to give ourselves plenty of time?

B: You could start. I'll just throw in a few things later.

A: But [6] ~~shouldn't~~ it be quicker if we did it together?   wouldn't

GRAMMAR FUTURE PERFECT AND CONTINUOUS

4 Complete the articles with the future perfect or continuous form of the verbs in the boxes. If neither is possible, use the future simple.

| not save discuss pay face double |

By 2025

By 2025 in many countries the number of people over sixty-five [1]_____ and far fewer people of working age [2]_____ taxes to support them. It is almost certainly the case that many older people [3]_____ enough for their old age and [4]_____ an uncertain future or one of poverty. Experts from many different countries [5]_____ the issue in Stockholm over the course of the next week.

| work have replace not drive live |

By 2050

Sixty percent of humanity [6]_____ in cities. They [7]_____ petrol or diesel cars. All cars [8]_____ hybrid engines so that they run on electricity as well as a more traditional fuel. Robots [9]_____ humans in all boring, mundane jobs and as a result, people [10]_____ in more stimulating jobs but with fewer hours.

VOCABULARY PLUS WORD BUILDING: PREFIXES

5 A Find ten words with negative prefixes in the word square.

H	C	K	P	D	O	K	H	K	H	Y	F	N	U	S
X	J	A	Z	I	K	T	T	I	L	C	J	T	J	R
L	T	I	U	S	Y	U	N	V	U	A	U	V	V	V
G	H	N	N	S	Q	N	Q	X	N	T	E	G	I	Y
B	P	S	W	A	M	F	F	C	H	I	H	C	M	S
Z	I	E	I	T	E	A	A	Z	E	I	H	W	P	U
Y	R	C	L	I	D	M	L	X	A	L	G	M	A	P
I	R	U	L	S	L	I	Y	G	L	Q	Q	J	T	T
V	E	R	I	F	F	L	K	M	T	I	H	E	I	L
Y	L	E	N	I	A	I	P	O	H	N	V	E	E	S
L	E	H	G	E	Y	A	F	D	Y	V	D	V	N	U
B	V	X	I	D	S	R	I	Q	Z	X	R	C	T	B
E	A	U	U	N	R	E	A	L	I	S	T	I	C	K
M	N	M	I	S	B	E	H	A	V	E	N	T	Y	R
L	T	Y	M	I	S	I	N	T	E	R	P	R	E	T

B Complete the sentences with the words from Exercise 10A.

1 You eat three burgers and a pizza everyday? That's the most _unhealthy_ diet I've ever heard of.

2 I'm sorry but your point about aliens living on the moon is completely _unrealistic_ to our discussion about science. _irrelevant_

3 We asked for more money for the charity, but the government was _unwilling_ to help.

4 Many of our customers are very _____ with the new product. _dissatisfied_

5 Please don't _misinterpret_ what Ahmet is trying to say.

6 Judy is really _insecure_ – you can tell by the way she bites her nails.

7 Wait a minute for me to find the right TV channel – you're so _impatient_.

8 It's just _insecure_ to think that we can score three goals in five minutes. _unrealistic_

9 Cem's such a naughty boy – I can't believe how often I saw him _misbehave_.

10 Can you help me with the new software? I'm _____ with this programme. _unfamiliar_

Circle the correct option to complete the sentences.

1 I don't think he feels very safe, he seems very _____.
a) unrealistic   b) irrelevant   c) insecure

2 Caroline didn't want to go to university and went to work instead. Now she is _____ her first business.
a) making   b) taking   c) running

3 Is it _____ to eat so much?
a) unhealthy   b) insecure   c) unfamiliar

4 I think we're _____ nowhere here.
a) coming   b) going   c) taking

5 Children under thirteen _____ join social networking sites, but they often do.
a) aren't supposed to   b) don't have to   c) aren't allowed

6 Are you allowed to _____ make-up at school?
a) put   b) get   c) wear

7 Don't phone me until the afternoon. _____ to our Washington office by then.
a) I'll be speaking   b) I'll speak   c) I'll have spoken

8 _____ your headphones today? I've broken mine.
a) Will you be using   b) Will you use
c) Will you have used

9 A third runway has been approved at the airport. What _____ for local residents over the next few years?
a) will that be meaning   b) will that mean
c) will that have meant

10 _____ unfair that wealthy people pay a smaller proportion of taxes than those with less money?
a) Don't you think   b) Isn't   c) Doesn't it seem

11 So _____ that no one knows the answer, they're just guessing?
a) what you're saying is   b) what you're getting is
c) basically you

12 The whole feel of the website is very _____ and positive.
a) upbeat   b) despairing   c) dreadful

13 At school they _____ three hours' homework a night.
a) let us do   b) made us do   c) allowed us to do

14 He's amazing. He looks really _____.
a) his prime   b) young for his age   c) immature

15 The rise of drug abuse fills me with _____.
a) upbeat   b) despair   c) mixed feeling

16 Last Tuesday for the first time, scientists _____ communicate with a patient in a deep coma.
a) could   b) were able   c) managed to

RESULT _____ /16

VOCABULARY

TELEVISION

1 Complete the crossword with types of TV programme.

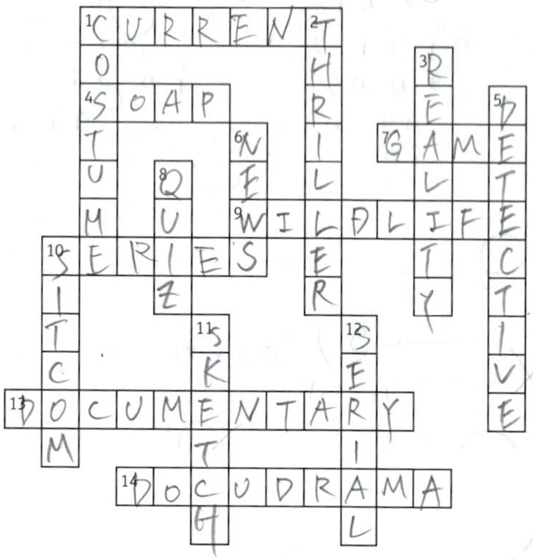

Across

1 A ________ affairs programme covers up-to-date social and political stories.
4 A ________ opera has romance and drama and is on regularly.
7 Number 8 down is one kind of ________ show.
9 This programme features animals.
10 A set of programmes, for example, a new ________ of *Strictly Come Dancing*.
13 A programme about something real.
14 This programme mixes reality and fiction.

Down

1 Actors wear clothes from the past in a ________ drama.
2 It's full of suspense.
3 This type of show often puts ordinary people in extraordinary situations.
5 A private eye solves a murder every week in a ________ series.
6 Find out what happened today on the ________.
8 Competitors answer questions on a ________ show.
10 This has the same characters each week in funny situations.
11 Short funny pieces are acted out on a ________ show.
12 It's a story or drama broadcast in different parts.

GRAMMAR

QUANTIFIERS

2 Cross out the incorrect alternative in each sentence.

1 He's got *quite a few/many/little* English-speaking friends.
2 *Several/Every/Each* room has a whiteboard.
3 We have *a little/a small amount of/little* money left, so we can afford a coffee.
4 *Much/A small number of/A great deal of* time was spent explaining the error.
5 I'll buy *either of/all of/both of* them, I like them so much.
6 *A few/A little/Several* books are missing from the library.
7 I've got *no/any/some* idea what to do if the car breaks down.
8 I can't see *any/many/no* reasons for sleeping here tonight.

3 Complete the report with the quantifiers in the box.

several	another	a large number
a few	no	quite a few	every
plenty of	each	a good deal of

WHAT'S YOUR MEDIUM?

We asked you how you prefer to get information: via the internet, TV, radio, or newspapers and magazines? Here are the results.

Internet: 67%

Unsurprisingly, [1] ________ people said that the internet is their primary source of information, although [2] ________ respondents said they never used it. Two main advantages of the internet were mentioned by [3] ________ people, indeed by most of them. One was easy access. [4] ________ was up-to-date content. Both of these features were given as problems with newspapers and magazines.

TV: 21%

Surprisingly, [5] ________ of respondents, more than 94%, say they spend more time watching TV than they used to although about a quarter of TV viewing is done through the internet. Both normal and internet-based TV remain important sources of information and [6] ________ of them has maintained healthy audience figures.

Radio: 7%

Just as internet TV has been a boost to that medium, the internet has helped radio maintain its status as a preferred source of information for at least [7] ________ respondents who spend [8] ________ time listening to their radios.

Newspapers and magazines: 5%

Most respondents commented that although newspapers and magazines were more reliable than [9] ________ one of the electronic sources, TV, radio and the internet were all more convenient. Four people said that they use [10] ________ other source apart from newspapers and magazines.

LISTENING

4 A ▶ **7.1** Listen to four people talk about their favourite childhood TV programme and complete the table.

Speaker	Programme name	Programme type
1		
2		
3		
4		

B Listen again. Which speaker (1–4) thinks:

a) Kids learnt how to make things.
b) It was something kids understood better than their parents.
c) Every episode took kids on a journey.
d) If you made an effort you could win a prize.
e) Kids learnt a lot that helped them with growing up.
f) Kids enjoyed the unconventional nature of it.
g) It involved a strong element of fantasy.
h) It was very realistic and right for the age group.

C Match the words in bold with meanings a)–f).

1 He's then transported to a world that **corresponds with** the outfit that he's wearing. *seem*
2 It's hard to underestimate its cultural **impact**.
3 It kind of **bridges the gap between** the two.
4 It deals with issues … in an **unpatronising, non-condescending** way.
5 One sketch would **morph** into another.
6 We'd spend our entire lunch break … remembering all the **catchphrases**.

a) expressions which are linked to a performer or programme and are very recognisable
b) appropriately intelligent
c) matches
d) connects
e) influence or effect
f) change

VOCABULARY PLUS

MULTI-WORD VERBS
10/3 HW

5 A Complete the sentences with the words in the box.

across   out (x 2)   up   back   *p82*

攻略了4

1 If I say something offensive, I'm often too stubborn to take it ⎵back⎵ .   *B24/79?*   *神同了d*
2 If a homeless person knocked on my door in the middle of winter, I would put them ⎵up⎵ for the night. *= to provide someone with a place to stay temporarily*
3 Hard work brings ⎵out⎵ the best in me. *以达到*   *To make notice*
4 I come ⎵across⎵ as being more sociable than I really am. *seem*
5 If it turned ⎵out⎵ that my partner had lied to me, I would be disappointed in him. *to be known or discovered finally and suprisingly*

B ▶ **7.2** Listen to the sentences in Exercie 5A and underline the stressed part of the multi-word verb. Then listen and repeat.

C Complete the sentences with a multi-word verb from Exercise 5A but with a different or slightly different meaning.

1 I always buy a new version of a product as soon as it is ⎵brought⎵ ⎵out⎵ . *produce* — *が発売.*
2 I can ⎵put⎵ ⎵up⎵ with a noisy hotel room more easily than a dirty one.
3 Smells rather than images ⎵take⎵ me ⎵back⎵ to my childhood. *remember memory*
4 If I ⎵come⎵ ⎵across⎵ a large amount of money in the street, I would hand it into the police. *find*
5 When a lot of people ⎵turn⎵ ⎵out⎵ for a political demonstration, I'm usually not one of them. *to happen*

D Tick the sentences in Exercises 5A and C that are true for you.

READING

1 **A** Read the article about unauthorised use of photos. Which of the following are mentioned as using photographs without permission?

a professional photographer
an electronics shop
a social networking website
a telephone company
a newspaper
a city transport company
a travel agency

B Five sentences have been removed from the article. Complete the article using sentences a)–f). There is one sentence you do not need to use.

a) 'The value of my work drops every time someone uses it without paying,' he said. 'I can't describe the anger I feel.'

b) Who in the UK would ever find out that their image appears in a billboard advert somewhere in New Zealand?

c) 'We think that amateur photographers should be happy for their work to gain so much exposure,' said a company representative.

d) Or furniture. Or electronic appliances. Or cars …

e) 'In fact it didn't really bother us,' he added. 'But I can imagine someone else being very upset.'

f) There are cases where the courts have not looked favourably upon the photographer's claim.

SAY 'CHEESE' NOW ... SUE LATER

The McGraw family of Dublin expected their visit to Poland to be full of adventure and surprises. But they never expected to find themselves four metres high, beaming at the world from the wall of an underground station.

'We turned a corner onto the platform, and there we were in living colour,' said Paul McGraw. 'It was a family photo that I'd posted on our family blog last year but in the middle of an advertisement for an electronics appliance chain. No one ever asked us for permission,' added McGraw. 'Someone obviously downloaded it off our blog.' ^1_____

The unauthorised use of photographs downloaded from internet photo albums is not uncommon, and it would be impossible to count how many local advertising agencies have avoided costly photography and copyright fees by simply downloading material they find on the internet.

'It's simply too tempting for them,' said advertising lawyer Lee Szymanski. 'In most cases, where the advertisement is going to appear in a small geographical area, the chances of getting caught are almost zero. ^2_____ And if they do get caught, the legal process is too complicated, expensive, and frankly unclear for it to be worth pursuing.'

As rarely as the culprits are caught, there are countless known cases of such 'borrowing'. In one case, a major mobile phone provider used photographs taken from an internet photo album site in one of its campaigns, and justified it by saying that it was 'promoting creative freedom'. ^3_____

Professional photographers have also been affected, and the law has not been clear in deciding if unauthorised use is legal or not. A California newspaper used a copyrighted photo taken by a professional photographer without seeking his permission, and when he sued them, the jury decided it was a case of 'fair use' – leaving the photographer with nothing but legal fees and frustration. On the other hand, a New York judge awarded a Quebec-based photographer over $60,000 in damages when he sued an online travel agency for their use of four photos he had shot in Ghana. Meanwhile, the photos had been duplicated and used on at least 200 other websites, according to the photographer. ^4_____

'Professional photographers are in a better position to seek damages because they copyright their work,' said Szymanski. 'But for most people who simply upload snapshots to share with friends, there's very little they can do.'

So the next time you upload a photo of yourself with a big grin, don't be surprised if you find yourself advertising toothpaste somewhere in the world. ^5_____

GRAMMAR

REPORTED SPEECH

15th March

2 Underline the correct alternatives.

THE WORST INTERVIEW
I EVER HAD – BY ACTOR RUDY SEARS

It was with a young journalist and he started out by asking me normal questions. He asked how long it [1]*took/had taken* me to become successful as an actor and I told him that I [2]*didn't remember/ hadn't remembered* a particular point where I could say I was successful. He asked who [3]*did have/had had* the greatest influence on my acting style and I said that my mother [4]*has/had* – she was an amateur actress. Then he started on the personal questions: he asked if my marriage [5]*was breaking down/broke down* and if it was true that my wife [6]*wanted/wants* a divorce. I said I [7]*won't/wouldn't* discuss that and that I [8]*must/had to* go. In the end he wrote a very negative article about me, but it actually helped my career.

better *had broken down*

3 Change the sentences to reported speech.

1 A: Why did you come here today? *me*
He wanted to know why ~~I had come there~~ *I came there that day.*

2 B: I've been trying to see you since yesterday.
I said that I had been trying to see *him since* *the day before.* *Previous day*

3 A: Please close the door and have a seat.
He asked *me to close the door and* *to have a seat.*

4 B: How can I help you?
He enquired *how he could help me.*

5 A: I have information that Mario the Snitch will be killed tomorrow.
I told ~~him I had information~~ *him I had information* *that Mario the Snitch would be* *killed the* *following* *day*

6 B: What makes you think (this might happen?)
He wanted to know *what made me think* *that might* *happen.*

7 A: Don't waste time asking me questions.
I told him *not to waste time* *asking me* *questions*

8 B: Shall I let the cops know?
He asked ~~he/shall let the cops~~ *me if he should* *let the cops* *know.*
and I told him it was up to him.

VOCABULARY

REPORTING VERBS

4 A Complete the interviewer's questions (1–6) and the answers a)–f) with the correct forms of the verbs.

Have you ever
1 been persuaded *to take* (take part) in a film you didn't want to? *participate in* *part*
2 threatened *to walk out* (walk out) of a film?
3 suggested *making* (make) changes to a film?
4 been accused *of lying* (lie)?
5 apologised *for doing* (do) something when you didn't mean it?
6 admitted *doing* (do) something that you didn't do?

a) No, but sometimes I've refused *to say* (say) 'sorry'.
b) Not usually, but once I told them *to change* (change) my script in a key scene.
c) No, but I've done the opposite: denied *doing* (do) something that I *did* do.
d) No, once I've agreed *to take on* (take on) a job, I would never leave halfway through.
e) No, not even when they've offered *to pay* (pay) me a fortune.
f) No, and in fact I always advise people *to be* (be) honest.

B Match questions 1–6 with answers a)–f).

WRITING

A DISCURSIVE ESSAY; LEARN TO USE LINKERS OF CONTRAST

5 A Look at the sentences from an essay on the topic below. Are they for (✓) or against (✗) the topic?

Topic: Most information on the internet is unreliable.

1 Most internet writers are amateurs, but many give objective information.
2 The internet is a convenient source of information, but its accessibility can also mean that this information is not trustworthy.
3 Of course there's some inaccurate content, but it's the reader's responsibility to identify the reliable information.
4 Wiki contributors try to give accurate information but too many don't use reliable sources.
5 Many amateur news websites look serious, but that doesn't make them accurate.
6 These weaknesses exist, but there are reasons to trust much internet content as well.

B Rewrite each sentence in Exercise 5A with the linker given. Pay attention to punctuation.

1 (although) _____
2 (while) _____
3 (however) _____
4 (despite) _____
5 (although) _____
6 (while) _____

VOCABULARY

THE PRESS

1 A Add vowels to make words.

1 s u pple m ent
2 c i rcul a ti o n
3 s ens a ti o nal i sm
4 e d i ti o n

5 b i a s e d
6 e d i t o r i al pag e
7 f e at u re
8 t a bl e a d
   o i

B Complete the letter with the words in Exercise 1A.

To the Editor,

I am writing to complain about recent changes to your newspaper in the new ¹ *edition* .

I believe I am typical of the paper's readers in that I am an ordinary working person and I strongly object to the ~~feature~~ *sensationalism* of some of your recent headlines and stories, which does not suit a serious newspaper like yours. This style of reporting and the new colour ³ *supplement* are more typical of ⁴ *tabloid* newspapers. Also, the recent ⁵ *editorial page* *feature* on the public transport system was full of the reporter's own opinion and was very ⁶ *biased* . I think you should save your opinions for the ⁷ _____ as that's what it is for. *sensationalism* *editorial page*

I am sure the reason for these changes was to increase ⁸ *circulation* , but it has made me decide to cancel my subscription.

FUNCTION

ADDING EMPHASIS

2 Rewrite the sentences using one of the emphasising structures: **pronoun/noun + be + the one who** or **the + adjective + thing is.**

1 He's always watching the news channel, not me.
   He's the one who's always watching the news channel, not me.

2 You were asking about the celebrity news.
   You were the one who was asking about the celebrity news.

3 The story is incredible because all the people escaped safely.
   The incredible thing about the story is that all the people escaped safely.

4 The fact that people want to buy this paper is remarkable.
   The remarkable thing is that people want to buy this paper.

5 They want to have a big magazine launch party, not us.
   They're the ones who want to have a big magazine launch party, not us.

6 The number of adverts is ridiculous.
   The ridiculous thing is the number of adverts.

3 A Correct the mistakes in the underlined parts of the conversation.

A: ¹This is total <u>outrageous</u>. *totally* Your questions are very biased against the government. I've never heard such biased statements from a journalist before. ²<u>Absolute incredibly.</u> *Absolutely incredible*

B: Well, minister, ³<u>you're the one who always telling the people that we're getting richer</u> *are ↓s ('s)* when the cost of living is increasing and our wages are staying the same. ⁴<u>What on earth do you justify that?</u> *How*

A: Look, ⁵<u>there isn't a way I'd say</u> *is no way* that if the data didn't agree! Having said that, ⁶<u>I be think we can do better to help ordinary people</u> and so we're going to cut petrol tax.

B: ⁷<u>That are a good idea</u>, *is* minister, but why are you introducing it now? Is it because the election is in two months?

A: ⁸<u>That is so wrongly!</u> *wrong* Are you suggesting that we're making up policies to gain votes?

B: To be honest minister, ⁹<u>the amazed thing is that</u> *amazing* you're denying making policies to win votes.

B ▷ 7.3 Listen and circle the stressed words in the underlined parts of the conversation.

C ▷ 7.4 Listen and repeat the phrases.

LEARN TO

MAKE GUESSES

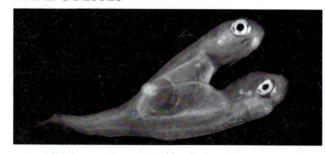

4 A Put the words in the correct order.

1 it's / reckon / I / fish / Siamese / a
   I reckon it's a Siamese fish

2 it's / photo / hoax / a / surely
   Surely it's a hoax photo. / photo hoax.

3 upstream / plant / perhaps / nuclear / a / there's
   Perhaps there's a nuclear plant upstream.

4 might / fish / be / it / two
   It might be two fish.

5 imagine / it's / say / I'd / genuine / to / but / it's / hard
   It's hard to say but I'd imagine it's genuine

B Match sentence beginnings 1–5 in Exercise 4A with endings a)–e).

a) 2̶ ⁵ – why would anyone fake it?
b) 3̶ ¹ just like twins who are connected.
c) ✗3 and this is a genetic mutation.
d) 4 with one on top of the other.
e) ✗ ² and someone's just playing a joke.

VOCABULARY

COLLOCATIONS: DECISIONS

1 Complete the sentences. The first letter of each word has been given.

1 Lying to him will g_____ a_____ all my principles.

2 I intend to s_____ t_____ my principles.

3 We're trying to a_____ the situation to see what went wrong.

4 They can't p_____ o_____ the decision any longer. We need an answer.

5 The committee have agreed to p_____ their decision until they have more facts.

6 Are you asking me to b_____ all my principles?

7 You should f_____ your principles rather than chase fame and fortune.

8 Sue's asked us to e_____ the situation and give a recommendation.

9 He'll need to e_____ the situation and get all the information about it.

10 When do you think the government will a_____ a_____ a decision?

11 We will have to l_____ i_____ the situation in detail.

12 At the end of this long discussion we can finally r_____ a decision.

VOCABULARY PLUS

COMPOUND ADJECTIVES

2 Complete the newspaper headlines. Form compound adjectives with one word from box A and one from box B.

A

| time | life | long | 15-metre | third | record |
| five-year | twenty-storey | | | | |

B

| consuming | time | long | high | changing |
| running | high | breaking | | |

1 Kidnappers given _____ jail sentences.

2 Woman survives fall from _____ building.

3 No solution to Russia and China's _____ argument over oil.

4 Jules Fane wins cycle tour for _____ tenth time.

5 Voting too _____ for young people – survey reveals under-18s won't vote.

6 Prisoners escape over _____ wall.

7 Two million dollars for _____ lucky lottery winner.

8 Shirley Grey has _____ experience: singer leaves stage for charity work.

LISTENING

3 A You are going to listen to a lecture about an experiment to test people's behaviour. Look at the posters. What do you think the experiment was about?

| Coffee | Tea | Coffee | Tea |
| €3 | €2 | €3 | €2 |

B ▶ 8.1 Listen to Part 1 and check your ideas.

C Listen again. Complete the summary using no more than three words for each answer.

The lecture is about differences between people's behaviour when they [1] _____ and how they behave when they [2] _____.

It is in three parts:

1 A description of [3] _____ at Newcastle University.

2 What this tells us about [4] _____ and behaviour.

3 A comparison with other key findings in the area.

The aim of the experiment was to discover whether the [5] _____ that you are being watched can alter your behaviour.

The scientists monitored [6] _____ in a staff room to see how much people paid for their tea and coffee. Above it was a poster with the prices. Each week they [7] _____ on the poster. They found that people were [8] _____ when they were watched by eyes than when there were pictures of flowers. They put [9] _____ as much money in.

D ▶ 8.2 Listen to Part 2 and answer the questions.

1 Why is it important that our brains respond to faces and eyes?

2 How do people behave if they think they are being watched?

3 How did the researchers feel about the results?

4 How could a similar poster be used for speed cameras?

5 Where else could a poster be put?

GRAMMAR
PAST AND MIXED CONDITIONALS

4 A Read the articles and find the mistake in each picture.

EURO-MILLION DILEMMA

One morning in 2014, Jim Farley was outside a Dublin bank when five bundles of cash fell from a security van which was driving away. He took them home and kept them for two days before phoning the bank. He rang from a payphone in a terrible state of anxiety as he didn't know what to do. The security director persuaded him to hand in the money. It came to almost €1,000,000.

PARIS MÉTRO RESCUE

Jean LeBois was waiting for his métro train with his son, Roger, aged four. Suddenly, a man collapsed on the platform and then fell onto the tracks. A train was approaching and LeBois had to make a split-second decision whether to help. He leapt off the platform and pressed the man into the space between the tracks. Five carriages went overhead before the train stopped. Both men emerged safe to the applause of the onlookers.

B Read the articles again and complete the sentences.

1 If Jim _____ (not walk) by the bank that day, he _____ (not see) the money.

2 His call _____ (trace) if he _____ (phone) from a mobile.

3 If he _____ (not come forward) with the money, it's possible that the police _____ (never find) it.

4 He _____ (keep) the money if he _____ (not speak) to the security director.

5 Jim _____ (be) rich now if he _____ (keep) the money.

6 The man _____ (not fall) off the platform if he _____ (not collapse).

7 If the train _____ (stop), Jean _____ (not leap) onto the tracks.

8 The man _____ (be) dead now if Jean _____ (not jump) onto the tracks.

9 If the space _____ (not be) quite deep, both men _____ (kill) by the train.

10 If Jean _____ (have) more time to think, he probably _____ (not jump).

5 Complete the second sentence so that it has a similar meaning to the first. Use between two and five words including the word given.

1 I didn't know who he was so I didn't ask him for an autograph.   HIM
If I'd known who he was, I _____ for an autograph.

2 You feel sick now because you ate too much.   SICK
You _____ if you had eaten less.

3 Anya's skis weren't very good and this could be the reason she didn't win the race.   MIGHT
Anya _____ if she'd had better skis.

4 The ambulance took a long time. Is that why they couldn't save him?   COULD
If the ambulance had got here sooner, _____ saved?

5 You're living in a one-bedroom flat today because you didn't take my advice.   LIVING
If you'd taken my advice, _____ in a one-bedroom flat today.

6 You weren't paying attention and so you didn't hear what I said.   IF
You would have heard what I said _____ attention.

7 Angie left the sat-nav behind and we're lost.   LOST
We wouldn't _____ remembered the sat-nav!

8 In my situation, what other choices were there?   YOU
What _____ if you'd been in my situation?

6 A ▶ 8.3 Listen and write the phrases you hear.

1 _____
_____

2 _____
_____

3 _____
_____

B Listen again and mark the stressed words and any examples of weak forms with /əv/. Then listen and repeat.

READING

1 A Look at the picture. Which position do you usually sleep in?

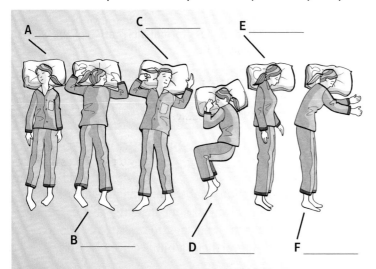

A _____
C _____
E _____
B _____
D _____
F _____

SLEEP POSITIONS GIVE CLUE TO THE NATION'S PERSONALITY

1 Some of Britain's best-known body language experts have been studying the four most common sleep positions for a well-known hotel chain. They think that our sleeping posture shows something about our character and how we see life. They believe that how we sleep reflects how we spent our day – under stress, relaxed and happy, bored and uncomfortable, feeling in or out of control. Here are the findings from the study.

2 Over half of people in Britain sleep with our knees up and our head down. It's called the Foetal position and more women than men sleep like this. People sleeping in this position are seeking comfort from the stresses and worries of their day. They are often shy and sensitive to others and like their lives to be ordered and under control.

3 The next most common position is the Log. As the saying goes, people who 'sleep like a log' lie on their side with their body straight and their arms down by their side. These people are trusting, easy-going and likely to be popular and part of the in-crowd. Unfortunately they often tend to be too trusting of other people, even to the point of being gullible. Around one third of British people adopt this sleep position. This position needs to be contrasted with the Soldier position in which people sleep on their back with their arms very close to them. It is said that people who sleep in this position are quiet perfectionists who have high expectations of themselves and others and really don't like to make a fuss about things.

4 A significant number of people in the UK sleep in the Yearner position with their arms out in front of them, as if they are chasing something. People who sleep in this position are open to possibilities but can be cynical. Worse still, once they make a decision – a good one or a bad one – they are not going to change their mind. Two similar positions are the Starfish and the Freefaller. People sleeping in the Starfish posture, lie on their back with both their hands above their heads. These people make great friends because they are good listeners and tend to be very supportive.

5 Freefallers make up the fourth major group of British people. Freefallers sleep lying on their front with their arms outstretched, as if they are falling through the sky. They feel that they are not in control of their lives and although they tend to be gregarious, below the surface they are nervy and thin-skinned.

6 So, with over 70% of British people sleeping in the Foetus or Freefall positions, the picture indicates that the UK is a worried and anxious nation.

B Read the article and label the pictures of the sleeping positions with the names.

C Which type of person are the quotes 1–6 about? Underline the part of the article which helped you decide.

1 'Freida is always talking to people and gossiping, but if you say anything bad about her, she really doesn't like it.'
2 'Go and talk to Sarah, she always makes time to listen to people.'
3 'We threw a surprise party for him and he almost died of embarrassment.'
4 'No, you can't persuade him. He's decided what he wants.'
5 'Yeah, he wants everything to be perfect, so we're always working late.'
6 'He loves a good party and he's so laid back.'

D Find words in the article which mean:

1 physical position (paragraph 1)
2 a small group of people seen by others to be particularly popular or fashionable (paragraph 3)
3 ready to believe anything (paragraph 3)
4 anxious or excited behaviour often about unimportant things (paragraph 3)
5 someone who likes being with other people (paragraph 5)
6 too sensitive (paragraph 5)

VOCABULARY

VALUES

2 Rearrange the letters in bold to make words. The first letter is underlined.

1 Dave really lost **o_clntor** of the meeting when the staff members started to shout.
2 Our company is very proud of its strong policies on **ulity_eaq**.
3 My football team really shouldn't have lost the match – there's no **cu_jstie** sometimes.
4 Anyone with a sense of **rsne_fais** would say that Renata was the better player even though she lost.
5 PC games are really bad for young people – they fill them with **gres_agsino**.
6 Demet's **re_egd** made her spend all the prize money instead of sharing it with her family.
7 I find **osiyg_tener** one of the most appealing characteristics in a person.
8 You'll need to ask the boss – she's the one with all the **w_pore** in this organisation.

GRAMMAR

-ING FORM AND INFINITIVE

3 A Underline the correct alternatives.

Scientists are learning more and more about sleeping and waking states. For example, did you know that [1]*daydream/daydreaming* can help you [2]*to solve/solving* complex tasks? This is because it activates the part of the brain associated with [3]*tackle/tackling* difficult problems. Also [4]*take/taking* a nap in the middle of the day refreshes your brain. It's like [5]*to clear/clearing* your email inbox so that there's room for new information. Interestingly, [6]*stay up/staying up* all night, as many students do before exams, increases the ability to hold new facts by forty percent. Some people don't seem [7]*to need/need* much sleep. UK prime minister Margaret Thatcher was famous for [8]*be able/being able* to run the country on just four hours sleep a night. However, the great scientist Albert Einstein tended [9]*require/to require* ten hours a night, perhaps because he solved problems by [10]*sleep/sleeping* on them.

B Which fact in the text above do you think is incorrect?

4 Write sentences. Use an *-ing* form, an infinitive or an infinitive + *to*.

1 When / I / be / young, my father / teach / me / work hard / play hard.

When I was young, my father taught me to work hard and play hard.

2 Jake / hate / not / able / play / football / because of his bad leg.

_____

3 They / have / invite / Guido / give / talk / at / the conference.

_____

4 Olga / have / suggest / go for / picnic.

_____

5 What / you / want / me / do?

_____

6 Would / you / mind / tell / us / how old / you / be?

_____

7 The firm / not / expect / have to / pay for / the damage.

_____

8 Can / I / persuade / you / change / your mind?

_____

9 It / not be / worth / wait / any longer.

_____

WRITING

AN INFORMAL ARTICLE; LEARN TO USE LINKERS OF PURPOSE

5 A Underline the less formal alternative of the words and phrases in bold.

CUTTING IT SHORT

Have you ever wondered why some people are always late?

[1]**It is a question/That's something** I often ask myself. [2]**I'm always/I am constantly** late for trains, for concerts, for weddings, for everything! I do try, honestly, [3]**nevertheless/but** I've been like this all my life.

People hate latecomers. If you arrive late at a meeting [4]**it is thought/people think** you're lazy or disorganised or you don't actually [5]**think much of/respect** the other people there. But that isn't true. We time-challenged people live a life of constant anxiety and stress. I can't begin to count the money [6]**that has been wasted/I've wasted** by missing planes, classes, hair appointments, not to mention the stress of continually apologising for messing up other people's schedules.

However, help is at hand. If you're someone who always cuts things short, here are some suggestions to help you [7]**get over/recover from** this chronic problem. First of all …

B Do you identify with the writer of the article?

C Correct the mistakes with linkers of purpose in the sentences.

1 Sara was late because of her alarm clock wasn't working properly.

2 You should make sure you put things in your calendar in order remind you to do them.

3 Yuan went to the cinema early to getting a good seat.

4 Take your car keys so that as you can drive if you get tired of walking.

5 You need to study hard so to get a good test result.

6 Because I was late, I waited until the break to go into class so as to upset the other students.

7 On order not to disturb the boss, don't talk outside that room – she's in an important meeting.

8 We use an online meeting maker so as get agreement from everyone on the best time to meet.

D Complete the article in Exercise 5A with three suggestions and a conclusion (150–200 words).

VOCABULARY

BEHAVIOUR

1 A Add vowels to make words.

1 diplomatic
2 confrontational
3 sensible
4 supportive
5 collaborative
6 sensitive
7 unhelpful
8 assertive
9 focused
10 tactful
11 aggressive
12 direct

B Which adjectives above are positive (+), negative (-) or can be either (+/-)?

C Match the adjectives in Exercise 1A with quotes 1–10. Sometimes two adjectives are possible.

1 'You're late again, Jones! Get into my office and sit down! Now!' _____

2 'Oh, you look really tired. Lie down and rest. I'll bring you a cup of tea.' _____

3 'I prefer you in the other dress. This one makes you look overweight.' _____

4 'You touched the ball! You cheat!' _____

5 'I'll work on the charts for the report while you edit the text.' _____

6 'Look, I'm not angry but just tell me, why did Louise get a pay rise when I didn't?' _____

7 'OK, everyone. I think we're straying from the point. We need to get back to the main issue.' _____

8 'We don't deal with problems with your connection. You need to phone your broadband provider. You've already tried them? Well, it's nothing to do with us.' _____

9 'It's true that I don't have the receipt, but I only bought it here last week. Could I speak to your supervisor. She's at lunch? No problem, I'll wait.' _____

10 'If you want to lose weight, don't go on an extreme diet. Just eat slightly less and try and walk for half an hour a day.' _____

FUNCTION

HANDLING AN AWKWARD SITUATION

2 A Put the words in the correct order to complete B's part of the conversation.

A: Is everything OK?

B: ¹I've / to / talk / something / about / been / there's / to / you / Actually, / meaning / .

_____

A: Oh, is there a problem?

B: ²you / get / the / to / want / wrong / I / don't / idea, / but / …

_____

A: That sounds bad.

B: ³you / just / mobile / leave / on / that / often / It's / your / .

_____

A: I don't understand.

B: ⁴you're / annoying / And / it / and / that's / not / rings / when / here / .

_____

A: But I need to keep it on in case my son phones.

B: ⁵disturbing / trying / but / Yes, / people / are / work / when / to / it's / .

_____

A: It's important that he can get straight through to me.

B: ⁶I'm / understand / from / see / but / you / where / I / do / coming / ?

_____

A: I suppose so.

B: ⁷set / it / silent / you / when / could / not / to / here / Maybe / you're / .

_____

A: What you mean just the 'vibrate' setting?

B: ⁸feel / about / you / Yes, / how / would / that / ?

_____

A: OK, that sounds reasonable. I'll do that from now on. Sorry about that.

B: Thanks, I'd appreciate it.

B ▶ 8.4 Listen to the conversation and repeat B's part. Pay attention to the stress and intonation.

LEARN TO

SOFTEN A MESSAGE

3 ▶ 8.5 Listen to B's part of the conversation and add the extra words you hear to the conversation in Exercise 2A.

GRAMMAR QUANTIFIERS

1 A Read the descriptions and correct a quantifier in each sentence by crossing out, changing or adding one word.

1 Floor-to-ceiling windows allow you to enjoy lots of fantastic views of the city whilst the city enjoys plenty ~~of~~ fantastic views of you.

2 The flat is in need of a little redecoration and lighting but it benefits from a large ~~amount~~ *number* of walls, floors and ceilings.

3 A few flats with such excellent views *barames* ever come on the market and, as it is currently owned by an artist, each room is uniquely decorated.

4 The flat would be suitable for either a mushroom grower or someone who loves caves, as quite a few *of* the rooms are on the lower ground floor.

5 The flat is in a lively area, close to a large number of shops and several of clubs, so it would benefit from some double glazing in the windows.

B Read the descriptions again. What is the problem with each flat?

VOCABULARY REVIEW

2 A Look at the underlined sounds in each group. Circle the word with the different sound.

1 biased, deny, promise
2 reality, threaten, sketch
3 serial, circulation, generosity
4 persuade, tabloid, sensationalism
5 focused, confrontational, control
6 sensible, aggressive, assess

B ▶ R4.1 Listen and check. Then listen and repeat.

P801A, P952A

3 Complete the sentences with the correct word or phrase. *separate parts*

1 series/serial
  a) I can't wait for the next episode of the *serial ~~series~~* to find out what happens next.
  b) They're doing a *~~serial~~ series* on eastern cuisine; last week's was about Thai cooking and next week's is from Malaysia.

2 sitcom/sketch show
  a) Al Shaw stars in this *sitcom* about a high-flying executive who suddenly finds himself out of work.
  b) Dean Murray is back in the *sketch show* playing his familiar roles as the farmer who can't stand animals, the one-armed dentist and the policeman who can only speak in rhyme.

3 equality/greed
  a) He was surprised at his own *~~equality~~ greed*. There was enough to share but he had eaten all the cake.
  b) She was made *~~greed~~ equality* officer in the company after she complained that women were not being promoted.

4 power/fairness
  a) There's no *~~power~~ fairness* in the referee's decision to send another Italian player off the pitch.
  b) The problem with concentrating all the financial *~~fairness~~ power* in one position is that no one else can make decisions.

5 explored/reached
  a) They *explored* the options and decided to sell the hotel.
  b) They evaluated the situation carefully before they *reached* a decision.

6 sticking to/assessing
  a) He's *sticking to* his principles and refusing to reveal the name of his informer.
  b) He's *assessing* the situation at the moment.

7 sensitive/sensible
  a) She's very *sensitive* to other people's needs.
  b) It's *sensible* to keep a note of your passport number.

8 assertive/tactful
  a) You need to be *tactful* when dealing with him so as not to upset him.
  b) You should be more *assertive*. Don't let her bully you.

[bully]
V. いじめる。
おどす

彼は自分の主張を貫き、情報提供者の名前を明かすことを拒否している

VOCABULARY PLUS   MULTI-WORD VERBS

4 Complete the sentences by adding *across*, *back*, *out* or *up* in the correct place.

1 I'll have to take ~back~ everything I said about the film. It was brilliant!
2 I don't like her in person, but she comes ~across~ well on TV.
3 They're bringing ~out~ a new version of the game next March.
4 Some old friends in San Francisco put me ~up~ for the night.
5 The concert turned ~out~ to be disappointing.

GRAMMAR   REPORTED SPEECH

5 Complete the reported speech sentences. Use between two and five words including the word given.

1 'I want to leave school,' Emilio said to his father.
TOLD
Emilio _told his father he wanted_ to leave school.

2 'Could you sing something for us?' the guys in the band asked me.
WANTED
The guys in the band _wanted me if I could sing_ something for them. _to sing_

3 'You didn't give me your phone number,' Ben said.
HIM
Ben explained that I _hadn't given him my_ phone number.

4 'Why don't you like computer games?' Jane asked Rick.
HE
Jane asked Rick _why he didn't like_ computer games.

5 'Were you working for Sarah at that time?' Harry asked.
WORKING
Harry asked me _if I had been working_ for Sarah at that time. _; whether_ _was working_

6 'I won't be seeing Katya until tomorrow,' she said.
KATYA
She said she _wouldn't be seeing Katya_ until the next day.

VOCABULARY   REPORTING VERBS

6 A Match the reporting verbs to the sentences.

agree   admit   apologise   promise   offer
suggest   deny   threaten   ~refuse~   accuse

1 No, I'm paying for the meal. I won't let you.   *refuse*
2 I'm sorry if I have caused any embarrassment. _apologise_
3 We'll reduce taxes if you vote for us. _promise_
4 Unless I get more money, I'm going to quit the show. _threaten_
5 You did it, Leona! You stole my wallet! _accuse_
6 We'll share the information with you. _offer_
7 Let's take a break for a few minutes. _suggest_
8 OK, I stole €5,000 from the bank. ~agree~ _admit_
9 I've never had cosmetic surgery. _deny_
10 You want me to make a speech? OK, no problem. ~admit~ _agree_

B Write reported speech sentences using the reporting verbs for each of the sentences in Exercise 6A.

1 He _refused to let me pay for the meal_.
2 I _apologised to have caused any embarrass-_ _for causing_ _ment._
3 We _promised to reduce taxes if you —_
4 She _threatened to quit the show_.
5 He _accused to Leona stole his wallet._ _of stealing_
6 They _offered to share information with you._
7 She _suggested to take a break for a —_ _taking_
8 He ~agreed to stole €5000~ from the bank.
9 He _denied to have cosmetic surgery._ _even having had_
10 She _admitted to make a speech_.

8. admitted stealing   10. agreed to make

FUNCTION   ADDING EMPHASIS

7 Complete the email extract with different words to complete the phrases that add emphasis.

The people in the flat below us are driving us
1 _totally_ / _absolutely_ / _completely_ crazy. Last Friday they had an all-night party. I wouldn't have minded but the thing
2 _is_ / _was_ that they didn't warn us in advance and there was no 3 _way_ we could sleep through it. Why 4 _on_ earth do people need to have music so loud? I 5 _really_ / _absolutely_ hate it when people are 6 _so_ thoughtless. I had 7 _such_ a sleepless night that I was in a bad mood all day and had a 8 _really_ awful argument with Jack. It ended up with him shouting, 'Well, you're the 9 _one_ who wanted to move here in the first place!' and walking out. Then the woman downstairs complained to me about the shouting! That made me 10 _absolutely_ furious! _really_

55

GRAMMAR PAST AND MIXED CONDITIONALS

8 Complete the phrases. Sometimes there is more than one possibility.

A: Looking back over your career so far, ¹you / do / things / differently if you could start again?

B: I'm very happy with my choices so even if I could, ²I / not / want / change / anything professionally. As far as my personal life is concerned, I do wish I'd waited before settling down. ³If / Angela and I / not / get married so young, then ⁴we / still / be / together.

A: And ⁵if / you / were / give / advice to me as an up-and-coming actor, ⁶what / you / say?

B: ⁷If / I / start / again now, ⁸I / still / think / I / choose to work in the theatre to get as much basic experience as possible.

1 *would you have done things differently*
2 *I wouldn't want to change anything*
3 *If Angela and I hadn't got married*
4 *We might / could / would still be together*
5 *If you were to give advice / giving advice*
6 *what would you say*
7 *If I started / were starting again*
8 *I still think I would chose*

1. would you do things differently
2. I would have wanted to change anything

VOCABULARY PLUS COMPOUND ADJECTIVES

9 Rewrite the sentences with the compound adjectives in brackets.

1 I'm sorry but I'll have to get back to work – this project takes a lot of time. (time-consuming)

2 In a race that broke all records, Daniel Nduka wins the London marathon. (record breaking)

3 The company tries to save money then suddenly come up with the funds when they're really needed. (money-saving)

4 I had to close my eyes before going into the room – it was so bright in there. (brightly lit)

5 I had to wait for five months before I had an operation to repair my knee. (five-month)

GRAMMAR -ING FORM AND INFINITIVE

10 Complete the articles with the correct form of the verbs in the boxes.

express do look recognise be

Right or Left: 1

Researchers in the UK have discovered that dogs tend ¹*to look* at the right side of human faces. The right side is known ²*to be* better at ³*being* (*expressing*) emotional states. Interestingly, dogs don't seem ⁴*to do* this when they look at other animals. ⁵*Recognising* human emotions is an important skill for a pet.

have watch process give sit

Right or Left: 2

In an experiment, 74% of cinema goers would rather ⁶*give* (*sit*) to the right of the screen. The right side of the brain is important for ⁷*having* (*processing*) emotional information. By ⁸*watching* the film from the right, people are choosing ⁹*to process* (*give*) themselves the best viewing experience. Interestingly, when told the film was poor, people didn't mind ¹⁰*sitting* (*having*) a seat anywhere.

FUNCTION HANDLING AN AWKWARD SITUATION

11 Underline the correct alternatives. In one case both are possible.

A: Ingrid, there's something I've ¹*meant/been meaning* to talk to you about.

B: Sure, Cristina. What's up?

A: I ²*don't want you/hope you don't* take this ³*a wrong/ the wrong* way but you often look very tired.

B: What do you mean?

A: ⁴*It's just that/It's that just* I've noticed you yawning sometimes and, well, a receptionist needs to look more welcoming to clients. ⁵*Do you know/Do you see* what I mean? (Both)

B: You're right. I have been having difficulties sleeping recently.

A: How ⁶*would you feel/are you feeling* about getting some advice? From your doctor?

B: Yes, that's probably a good idea. Sorry about this, Cristina.

CHECK

Circle the correct option to complete the sentences.

1 That's not very _____ – telling her she's put on weight!
   a) collaborative   b) unhelpful   **c) tactful**

2 There were _____ things I would have changed but not many.
   a) quite few   **b) a few**   c) very few

3 The doctor told _____ to bed.
   a) that I should go   **b) me to go**   c) me going

4 I asked them to clean up the mess but they _____ to do it.
   a) refused   b) threatened   c) apologised

5 Companies should have rules about _____ so that no one is discriminated against.
   a) power   b) control   **c) equality**

6 My grandfather asked me _____ recently.
   a) what had I been doing   **b) what I'd been doing**
   c) if I'd been doing

7 It's _____, but it looks like some kind of animal.
   a) difficult to say   b) imagine   c) seems to say

8 It was _____ fantastic news that I couldn't believe it at first.
   a) such   b) so   **c) such a**

9 You need to _____ the situation.
   a) follow   b) go against   **c) assess**

10 If Tom hadn't acted so quickly they _____ now.
   a) might have been killed   b) weren't alive
   c) could be dead

11 I'm trying to go to the gym twice a week _____ get fitter.
   a) so   b) for   **c) in order to**

12 _____ do it slowly or you could cut yourself.
   a) You should learn   **b) You'd better**   c) Practise

13 I like factual programmes so I don't watch _____.
   a) documentaries   b) current affairs programmes
   c) reality shows

14 There is _____ traffic on the road because of the weather.
   a) hardly   **b) very little**   **c) a small number of**

15 Thousands of people _____ to vote.
   a) turned out   b) brought out   **c) pulled out**

16 Margit said _____ the next day.
   a) she'll do it   **b) she'd do it**   c) she's doing it

17 You often _____ good websites while you're looking for something else.
   a) put up with   **b) come across**   c) break into

18 I _____ him to phone Washington.
   a) suggested   b) offered   **c) reminded**

19 There's a difficult situation I've _____ to talk to Kurt about.
   a) what I mean   **b) been meaning**   **c) taken the wrong way**

20 Louise Becker's _____ is read by millions of people every day.
   a) sensationalism   **b) editorial page**   c) biased

21 You're _____ wanted to come!
   a) one who   **b) the one who**   c) the one

22 I don't want _____ get the wrong idea, but …
   a) that you   **b) you to**   c) you

23 The paper has been accused of being _____.
   a) biased   **b) tabloid**   c) sensationalism

24 How long do you think it will take for them to _____ a decision?
   a) come to   b) arrive   c) stick to

25 If you _____ the lottery ticket, we'd be rich now.
   a) don't lose   b) didn't lose   **c) hadn't lost**

26 I really lost _____ of my temper when I saw that man kick his dog.
   a) control   b) fairness   c) aggression

27 If you'd been in my situation, what _____?
   a) would you do   **b) would you have done**   c) did you do

28 Hurry up. We've got to run _____ to get to the concert on time.
   a) for   **b) in order**   c) so

29 _____ ticket costs €20.
   a) Each   b) Few   c) All

30 It's OK to speak your mind, but why are you always so _____?
   a) focused   b) assertive   **c) confrontational**

RESULT   /30

9.

1. I'm sorry but I'll have to get back to work – this project is (very) time-consuming.

2. In a record-breaking race, Daniel Nduka wins the London marathon.

3. The company tries money-saving techiques then suddenly come up with the funds when they're really needed.

4. I had to close my eyes before going into the ~~room~~ brightly-lit room.

5. I had a five-month wait before I had the operation to repair my knee.

9) TROUBLE

LISTENING

1 A Look at the pictures. Can you think of a reason why you might NOT notice the animals?

B ▶ **9.1** Listen to the first part of a radio programme and answer the questions.

1 What is the best definition of 'inattentional blindness'?
 a) Losing your eyesight because of someone's carelessness
 b) Failing to see things that are obvious because you are stressed
 c) Not seeing one thing because you are focused on something else

2 Were your ideas about the pictures right?

C ▶ **9.2** Listen to the rest of the programme and put the topics in the correct order. One topic is mentioned twice and one is not mentioned.

a) pilots
b) motorcycles
c) drivers
d) footballers
e) store security guards

D Listen again to the whole programme. Are the statements true (T), false (F) or is the information not given (NG)?

1 A quarter of the people who did the gorilla experiment didn't notice the gorilla.
2 If you're looking for someone with glasses, you might not notice someone with a parrot.
3 Drivers who are sending text messages might not notice a car stopping in front of them.
4 If you expect to see a particular word or name on a sign, you might not notice a synonym.
5 In a simulation, trained pilots were better at seeing unusual things on the runway than non-pilots.
6 A thief is more likely to fool a guard in a store by stealing openly.
7 It's safer to drive a car than to ride a motorcycle.
8 The expert gives the advice 'Expect the unexpected'.

GRAMMAR

-ING FORM AND INFINITIVE

2 A Underline the correct alternative.

1 a) After high school, I went on *finding/to find* work in order to earn money.
 b) After high school, I went on *studying/to study* and attended university because that was expected.

2 a) I remember *locking/to lock* my flat when I left it today, but it's possible that I didn't do it.
 b) I remembered *locking/to lock* my flat when I left it today, I'm 100 percent sure.

3 a) I'm trying *learning/to learn* English well enough to pass an advanced exam.
 b) I tried *speaking/to speak* English in case they understood it but they didn't.

4 a) I'll never forget *meeting/to meet* my English teacher for the first time.
 b) I've forgotten *doing/to do* my homework many times.

5 a) I had to stop *thinking/to think* about all of these sentences before answering.
 b) I've had to stop *thinking/to think* about my other work so that I could concentrate on this exercise.

6 a) I like *studying/to study* English at least fifteen minutes a day even if I'm not in the mood.
 b) I like *travelling/to travel* more than anything else.

B Tick the sentences above that are true for you.

3 Complete the story with the correct form of the verbs in brackets.

MY DAY AS A POLICE WITNESS

It was 2014 and I had witnessed a theft – in fact, I'd tried ¹_____ (catch) the thief, but when I caught up with him he pulled out a knife, so I stopped ²_____ (chase) him and walked away. I remember ³_____ (stand) there, thinking how silly the situation was, before I gave up. I like ⁴_____ (be) helpful even when it's unpleasant or dangerous, so I didn't mind. Before I walked away though, I remembered ⁵_____ (memorise) his face, in case the police asked me for a description; but I made a mistake, because I forgot ⁶_____ (pay) attention to his height. Well, the police did call me a few days later and said they'd caught the guy and needed me to identify him in a line-up. So I went in, and looked at the eight faces … they asked me which was the thief, but I just went on ⁷_____ (look) at the faces, because they ALL looked like the thief. I tried ⁸_____ (picture) him with my eyes closed, but it didn't work. In the end I picked someone – the biggest, tallest one – because that was my recollection, that the guy was big and threatening. The one I picked turned out to be a police officer himself (who later went on ⁹_____ (become) the chief of police), and the real thief was the shortest guy in the line-up. On my way out, I stopped ¹⁰_____ (say) goodbye to the head detective, and he just said 'Don't call us, we'll call you.'

VOCABULARY

CRIME

4 Find ten words for crimes in the wordsearch.

A	M	C	A	I	P	R	I	C	B	C	H	L	S
R	V	A	N	D	A	L	I	S	M	K	Q	V	H
S	R	K	I	D	N	A	P	P	I	N	G	A	O
O	L	T	I	S	N	V	M	U	C	M	Q	Q	P
N	P	X	X	A	Z	Y	Q	H	L	N	K	R	L
Y	S	R	K	V	H	W	C	K	O	J	J	P	I
S	T	A	L	K	I	N	G	X	K	V	T	S	F
Q	Z	Z	W	A	V	P	S	H	E	C	V	D	T
W	L	P	S	V	S	H	A	C	K	I	N	G	I
L	V	Y	Y	L	C	B	R	I	B	E	R	Y	N
I	D	E	N	T	I	T	Y	T	H	E	F	T	G
C	O	U	N	T	E	R	F	E	I	T	I	N	G
W	Q	J	L	F	Q	B	M	U	G	G	I	N	G
F	U	Q	E	Y	J	R	N	V	P	W	C	O	H

VOCABULARY PLUS

DEPENDENT PREPOSITIONS

5 A Complete the news stories by adding the dependent prepositions *for, from, with* or *of* to the verbs in bold. The prepositions don't always follow the verbs immediately.

5th February – An Edinburgh man was ¹**charged** murder today. Police say they ²**suspect** 48-year-old Bill Haller committing a series of murders, but a senior police officer says they will only ³**accuse** Haller one, the famous Scarsdale murder.

9th February – A police car transporting prisoner Bill Haller crashed on the motorway today and burst into flames. Haller managed to ⁴**rescue** the driver the burning vehicle just before it exploded. The mayor ⁵**thanked** the prisoner ⁶**saving** the driver (who by coincidence is the mayor's son) certain death.

11th February – Bill Haller was ⁷**cleared** the Scarsdale murder today as police ⁸**arrested** another suspect the murder. The mayor praised the police for their detective work and ⁹**apologised** to Haller the mistake. Haller made a statement ¹⁰**criticising** the police their actions and ¹¹**blamed** an ambitious senior police officer charging him without evidence.

B Read the stories again. Why do you think the man was released?

READING

1 A Complete the article with the words in the box.

pride   greed   sympathy   fear   curiosity

B The quotes are from people who fell for one of the scams in the article. Write the correct number of each scam next to the sentences.

a) That's strange, I can't access my email anymore.

b) I sent the subscription form in and the money last week. They haven't replied yet.

c) Everyone should give something, we can't just let them starve.

d) Look at this. I've got an uncle in Italy. Or I used to have one.

e) Excuse me, I'm here for the awards. I believe there's a room booked in my name.

C Match the meanings 1–8 with the words and phrases in bold in the article.

1 takes advantage of

2 it really exists and it's legal

3 unfortunate situation

4 fame

5 clever and indirect

6 you can't check it

7 weakness

8 fake

FIVE REASONS YOU'LL FALL FOR AN INTERNET SCAM

Most of us think we're too clever to be caught by an email scam, but hustlers know they can always find someone naive enough to fall for their tricks. They also know five key facts about human nature, and one of these is behind every email scam you'll come across.

1 _____ : You would think people would learn, but the desire for more money is our greatest **vulnerability**. From the instant lottery ('You've already won!') to an inheritance from the relative you never knew you had, the scam always aims at the same thing: to get you to pay in advance in the hope that you'll get back ten or a hundred times that much later.

2 _____ : It's amazing how many of us imagine we've written a great novel, or at least a good poem, and have such a strong desire for **recognition** that we'd actually pay for it. The publishing scam works in clever stages, starting with a simple request to submit your poem. You then find out it's been chosen as a semi-finalist in a poetry contest; you only need to send in some money to register. Eventually you're asked for a large amount of cash to cover travel costs so that you can go and receive your prize at the (non-existent) presentation ceremony!

3 _____ : If you find yourself paying for a 'premium subscription' to a service that promises to give you access to information – about yourself or someone else – you might be paying for a genuine, functioning service, but it might just be another scam that **preys on** your desire to know more. These often start out by telling you that THEY have information about YOU and that you can protect that information by subscribing; or they offer information about anyone you want. There <u>are</u> agencies that really do sell personal information (for example, credit ratings), but many of these offers are **bogus**.

4 _____ : The email may contain a direct threat with an equally direct demand for money or it may be more **subtle** and tell you that your bank account has been attacked and you need to enter your personal details, including your PIN, to protect it; or that your email account will be cancelled unless you verify your password. Of course, once the scammers have this information, they can get to your money or pretend they're you and use that disguise to get money.

5 _____ : Who can ignore a photograph of a suffering child or the **plight** of disaster victims in need? Sadly, for every **legitimate** charity in operation there are probably dozens of fake charities using our natural kindness and compassion to get us to transfer money to a bank account somewhere, but the end result is that we're just making millionaires out of the scammers.

So, if you've received an email from an **unverifiable** source and you're feeling greed, pride, curiosity, fear or sympathy, you're probably being scammed.

VOCABULARY
SYNONYMS

2 A Read the forum entries. Which thing do you think is the worst?

WHAT'S THE WORST THING YOU DID WHEN YOU WERE A KID?

- We went door to door and we would ¹**pose as** boy scouts raising money for a charity. We used to ²**fool** everyone, but it wasn't hard – we had the right uniforms.

- I used to ³**swap** my neighbour's newspaper every day for the previous day's paper. He never noticed.

- My friend and I took sweets from the local shop. One of us would ⁴**divert** the shopkeeper's **attention** while the other filled her bag.

- I used to ask people for change and when they took it out of their pocket I'd ⁵**snatch** it and run away.

- I told people I'd been robbed and needed two euros to get home. They used to ⁶**fall for it** every time and I made at least ten euros an hour.

B Put the letters in order to make synonyms. The first letter is underlined.

a) sadttric — _drastic_   _distract_ ≐ divert
b) cedivee — _deceive_ ≐ fool
c) nedterp ot eb — _pretend to be_ ≐ pose as
d) brag — _grab_ ≐ snatch
e) cwiths — _switch_ = swap
f) eb keant ni — _be taken in_ ≐ fall for it

C Match the words and phrases in bold in Exercise 2A with the synonyms a)–f) in Exercise 2B.

GRAMMAR
PAST MODALS OF DEDUCTION

3 Underline the correct alternatives. Sometimes there is more than one possibility.

A: Oh no! It ¹*can't have/might have/must have* gone!

B: What's up?

A: You ²*might have/must have/should have* left the car unlocked. The doors are open, no windows are broken and my bag's gone!

B: I thought I'd locked it, but I ³*might have/can't have/shouldn't have* left it open. I clearly remember locking it.

A: Or the thief ⁴*could have/must have/should have* been good at picking locks.

B: No, I ⁵*can't have/might have/shouldn't have* left it unlocked. I'm certain I did lock it. They ⁶*could have/must have/might have* picked the lock somehow.

A: Well, whatever happened, they ⁷*must have/can't have/might have* gone far. We've only been gone for ten minutes. Call the police.

4 Complete the sentences with a past modal of deduction and a suitable verb.

1 They _____ home yet – they only left half an hour ago and it's 60 km away.

2 Ali and Fatima _____ each other in college; they're always talking about their time there.

3 You _____ your keys when you took out your wallet or maybe you left them in the café.

4 This essay is too good to be Leila's own work; it _____ from the internet.

5 I _____ my hand while I was peeling the potatoes or maybe later.

6 But you _____ him in town yesterday – he's been abroad all week.

7 You _____ all my chocolate. There's no one here except me and you and I haven't had any of it!

8 I think we're on the wrong road. We _____ a turning somewhere.

5 ▶ 9.3 Listen and complete the sentences with a past modal of deduction and a verb. Then listen and repeat.

1 It _____ you.
2 It _____ me.
3 You _____ her.
4 They _____ there.
5 We _____ them.

WRITING
A 'HOW TO' LEAFLET; LEARN TO AVOID REPETITION

6 A Put the words in order to complete the tips for how to keep secure at an ATM.

1 nearby / you / make / characters / sure / check / suspicious / that / there / no / are / .

_____

2 your / your / entering / be / cover / fingers / careful / PIN / when / particularly / to / .

_____

3 count / to / try / quickly / money / the / .

_____

4 your / put / to / time / take / safely / away / card / .

_____

5 if / to / attention / around / tries / your / turn / someone / get / never / .

_____

6 be / nearby / always / people / of / aware / .

_____

B Write six tips for a leaflet: *How to avoid being a victim of identity theft.* Use a variety of ways to give the advice.

FUNCTION

REPORTING AN INCIDENT

1 A Find the mistakes in the underlined phrases and write the correct versions below.

A: I've just been robbed, on the underground, by a pickpocket.

B: What happened?

A: Well, this guy got on the train and ¹he reminded me to that English football player ... ²wait, my mind's gone blink. Oh yeah, David Beckham.

B: David Beckham? Didn't you wonder why he was travelling on the underground?

A: ³It never occupied me, no. Well, then everyone crowded round with their phonecams.

B: Typical!

A: I had to push my way past them and ⁴before I was realising what was happening, my wallet was gone, right out of my bag.

B: Did you see or feel anyone take it?

A: ⁵No, in fact only it was a minute later that I realised they'd done it. ⁶It was all happened so fast and I was in a hurry anyway.

B: So the David Beckham lookalike must have been a distraction.

A: Yeah, and he must have had someone working with him.

B: Well, the people with phonecams, maybe they ...

A: Do you think so? ⁷They seemed to like students, but ...

B: Oh, definitely, it was a pickpocket gang. That's how they work.

1 _____

2 _____

3 _____

4 _____

5 _____

6 _____

7 _____

B ▶ **9.4** Listen and check. Then listen and say A's part at the same time as the recording.

VOCABULARY

INCIDENTS

2 Complete the account of a bad dream with one word in each gap.

I was cooking when I heard a loud crash outside. I went out to see what it was – a driver had tried to avoid knocking ¹ ~~out~~ over a penguin crossing the road and had run ² over a second penguin who was just behind the first one. I was trying to help when the driver pointed at my window and I saw that the frying pan was on ³ fire . I tried the door but I realised I'd locked myself ⁴ out so I picked up the first penguin and tried to use it to break ⁵ ~~through~~ down the door. Its wings suddenly grew huge and it flew off so then I tried to climb in through the bathroom window but I got ⁶ stuck . The driver pulled me out and for some reason I then decided to climb onto the roof but I lost my balance and fell ⁷ ~~down~~ off . I must have got knocked ⁸ out because the next thing I remember was opening my eyes and seeing Brad Pitt standing there with an empty bottle saying, 'Sorry, we've run out of water'. Then I woke up!

LEARN TO

REPHRASE

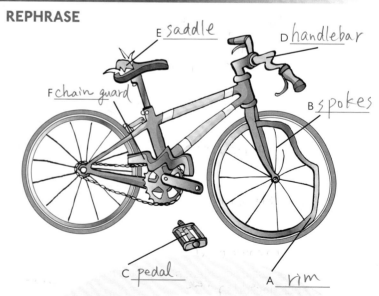

E saddle
D handlebar
F chain guard
B spokes
C pedal
A rim

3 A Label the parts of the bicycle A–F with the words in the box.

pedal   chain guard   handlebar   spokes   rim   saddle

B ▶ **9.5** Listen to the conversation or read the audio script on page 74 to check.

10)) CULTURE

READING

1 A Look at the photo and read the question on the forum. How would you answer it? Can you give an example?

B Read the forum and match comments 1–7 with categories a)–d).

a) sound   *1, 6*
b) image   *7*
c) situation   *2, 5*
d) other   *3, 4*

C Seven sentences have been removed from the article. Complete the article with sentences a)–g).

2 **a)** I guess I identify with the character from the start and so it feels like it's me who's <u>trapped</u>.

6 **b)** Maybe it reminds me of my early childhood, that feeling of being lost, of hearing my own voice crying out for help.

1 **c)** And then there's that fast bit in *Friday the 13th*, they have the whole orchestra playing …

7 **d)** Darkness and shadow can have the same effect – the effect of hiding the evil character but letting you see just enough to imagine its shape and form.

5 **e)** You know that partly because they're not a main character and they're not needed to play the story out.

4 **f)** It's similar, I guess, when there's a <u>sinister</u> little boy or girl, or twins in old-fashioned clothes …

3 **g)** Some are also made from made-up compound nouns, like *Cloverfield*, *Skinwalkers*, *Wickerhouse*.

D Find words in the forum that mean:

1 make a high-pitched sound (paragraph 1)
~~creepy music~~ *Shriek*

2 strange and frightening (paragraph 3)
eerie 得体のしれない

3 damaged or made immoral (paragraph 4)
~~evil~~ *corrupted*

4 talking quickly (paragraph 6)
chattering

5 quick moment (paragraph 7)
flash

FILM FAN FORUM

This week we asked:
What makes a horror film scary for you?

1 I'm a big fan of horror film music and I think that's the thing that really carries the fear factor for me. You get slow creepy music like in *Jaws*, you know buh-dup-buh-dup-buh-dup-buh-dup, … ¹_____, or the screaming shock music like in *Psycho*, where suddenly when the shower curtain opens, the violins (shriek) 悲鳴 incredibly loudly. Every time I see that scene I jump out of my seat and it's the music that does it.

2 Vulnerability is what gets me. A character is put into a position where they can't really protect themselves against something terrible, whether they're alone, trapped in a closed space, or walking down a dark stairway or narrow hallway, or in a forest that's overgrown and hard to walk through, and basically not knowing what's going on, but knowing it's not good. ²_____

3 I think the title of a film has quite an impact. If it's good, it somehow captures the whole experience of the film, so even years after seeing *The Omen*, if I heard that title, I'd relive the feeling. The really good titles seem to follow a pattern, for example, 'the' followed by a word ending with *-ing*, for example, *The Haunting, The Shining, The Vanishing*. ³_____ Or you get odd, (eerie) words after 'the': *The Ring, The Uninvited* and, of course, *The Omen*. Very scary, I don't know why.

4 A kid's bicycle upside-down with one of its wheels turning. A broken doll. A child's shoe. I see a shot of one of those and I hide under my seat. ⁴_____ I think it has to do with the innocence of childhood being (corrupted) by evil. 邪悪

5 There's a kind of scene in a lot of horror films that always gets me. I call it the 'innocent victim' scene. You'll have a character who's often a very likeable old guy or old lady who does a simple job like running a shop or working in a restaurant. What happens is something like they close up the shop, get into their car, drive home in darkness, pull into their driveway … and so on, and you know that at any moment something very bad is going to happen to them, but you don't know exactly when. ⁵_____

6 When the sound track has sound effects that sound a bit like human voices, that really scares me. So like religious chants or women's voices (chattering.) You almost hear words but not quite. Or a child's voice, that gives me the shivers. ⁶_____

7 When you get just a glimpse of the villain or evil being. So he or she walks by a window or is spotted by a character just for a (flash) and then is out of sight. ⁷_____ It really makes the evil come alive in your mind because your imagination starts racing, generating images.

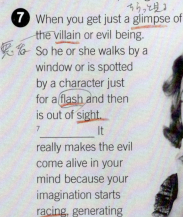

VOCABULARY

ADJECTIVES TO DESCRIBE FILMS

2 Add vowels to make words.

1 f**a**st-p**a**c**e**d
2 g**o**ry
3 hyst**e**r**i**c**a**l
4 c**o**ntr**o**v**e**rs**i**al
5 f**u**ll **o**f s**u**sp**e**ns**e**

6 gr**i**pp**i**ng
7 t**o**uch**i**ng
8 cr**e**py
9 **o**utst**a**nd**i**ng
10 th**o**ught-pr**o**v**o**ki**n**g

GRAMMAR

RELATIVE CLAUSES

3 A Underline the correct alternatives.

THE PROBLEM WITH
CINEMAS

[1]What/<u>When</u>/Whose I was younger, one thing I used to do was to go and see new films as soon as they came out but I've stopped because of the way [2]who/what/<u>that</u> people behave there. The cinema should be a place [3]which/<u>where</u>/when you are transported to another world but this is impossible because:

- a mobile phone rings, [4]when/<u>which</u>/what completely kills the moment. People [5]<u>who</u>/whose/what leave their mobile phones on are thoughtless; people [6]who/<u>whose</u>/when phones ring should be sent out.

- people act like they're at home, by [7]whom/where/<u>which</u> I mean they have conversations, sometimes [8]where/<u>when</u>/which there's something really moving happening on screen. You hear about times in the day [9]what/<u>when</u>/which something went wrong instead of the dialogue.

- children, [10]which/who's/<u>whose</u> parents should control them better, kick your seat every time they laugh.

B In which examples above is it possible to leave out the relative pronoun?

4 Make sentences containing relative clauses with the prompts. The word in bold immediately follows the relative pronoun.

1 A biopic / be / a film / **tells** / the life story / famous person.
   A biopic is a film which tells the life story of a famous person.

2 The biopic / I want to review today / be / *Raging Bull,* / **be** / the story of a famous boxer.

3 Robert de Niro, / **play** / the part of Jake La Motta, / be / absolutely extraordinary.

4 The film / be / made at a time / **most** biopics / be of heroic figures.

5 The film, / **be** / directed by Martin Scorsese, / be / now recognised as a masterpiece.

6 De Niro / become / interested when he read the book / on / **story** / be / based.

WRITING

A REVIEW; LEARN TO USE ADVERB + PAST PARTICIPLE COMBINATIONS

5 A Rearrange the letters to make adverbs that collocate with the past participles.

1 ghlhyi <u>highly</u> / ylediw <u>widely</u> praised
2 hyhlars <u>harshly</u> / oyghlwelrminve _____ / eahvliy <u>heavily</u> criticised — over whelmingly
3 klulfysil <u>skilfully</u> / iisetvsynle <u>sensitively</u> directed
4 ptlnnoagyi _____ / nlngvnoiicyc _____ acted — poignantly — convincingly

B Complete the sentences with one of the collocations above.

1 a) Audiences all over the world have applauded the film.
   The film has been <u>widely praised</u>.
 b) Critics have given it very positive reviews.
   It has been <u>highly praised</u>.

2 a) There wasn't a critic who said a positive thing about his last movie.
   His last movie was <u>overwhelmingly criticised</u>.
 b) The reviews weren't just negative, they were <u>very</u> negative.
   The film was <u>heavily criticised</u>. harshly

3 a) It wasn't an easy script, but Spielberg showed his talent in the way he directed it.
   The script was <u>skilfully directed</u>.
 b) The topic is a delicate one, but Bigelow showed she could handle this in her direction of the film.
   The film was <u>sensitively directed</u>.

4 a) The acting in that scene made me cry.
   That scene was <u>poignantly acted</u>.
 b) Morgan Freeman's acting was so good, I actually believed he was the real Nelson Mandela.
   The role of Nelson Mandela was <u>convincingly</u> acted.

GRAMMAR

PARTICIPLE CLAUSES

1 A Read the article and circle one mistake in each picture.

DAMAGED GOODS

When a woman ¹*took/taking* an art class at a New York museum tripped and fell into a Picasso painting, ²*tear/tearing* a fifteen-centimetre hole in the canvas, the public gasped and giggled, ³*shocked/shocking* at how anyone could get so close to a valuable work of art. But museums, ⁴*pressed/pressing* to attract as many paying customers as possible, often give visitors considerable access to works of art and this can carry risks. Similar incidents have happened in other collections.

- A visitor ⁵*walked/walking* down the stairs in a Cambridge museum stumbled into some 17th-century Chinese vases, ⁶*shattered/shattering* the vases into hundreds of pieces.

- A drawing by a famous artist, ⁷*valued/valuing* at over £80,000, was put through a paper shredder by a worker at a London auction house. The worker, deeply ⁸*embarrassed/embarrassing* by the incident, has managed to keep his (or her) identity a secret.

- A housekeeper ⁹*employed/employing* by a wealthy German family ¹⁰*lived/living* in a villa near Berlin knocked down a Ming dynasty plate.

- A painting by the Italian, Giorgio de Chirico, ¹¹*displayed/displaying* in a house in the Netherlands, was damaged when a demolition ball came through the wall, ¹²*put/putting* a large hole through the painting.

- At the London National Gallery a painting ¹³*was/being* removed from a wall was broken in two. Apparently the glue ¹⁴*used/using* to hold sections of the frame wasn't strong enough.

B Underline the correct alternatives in the article in Exercise 1A.

2 A Replace the underlined phrases with phrases with participles. Make changes to the rest of the sentence where necessary.

1 The people <u>who lived</u> on the other side of the river were trapped.
   The people living on the other side of the river were trapped.

2 Anyone <u>who is planning</u> to go home early or <u>who wants to take a break</u> should let us know.
   Anyone planning to go home early or wanting

3 <u>As I walked</u> out of the restaurant, I ran into my old boss, <u>who was coming</u> in.
   Walking out of the restaurant, I ran into my old boss, comming in.

4 I used to work with the woman <u>who lives</u> next door.
   I used to work with the woman living next door.

5 I left the party quickly <u>and didn't tell</u> anyone that I was unwell.

6 <u>She carried</u> a child under each arm and ran out of the blazing building.

7 He jumped up <u>because he was frightened</u> by the loud bang, <u>as he mistook</u> the door for a gun.

8 Walls <u>which have been painted</u> white tend to attract more graffiti.

B ▶ **10.1** Listen and check. Then listen and say the sentences at the same time as the recording, paying attention to stress and intonation.

VOCABULARY

THE ARTS

3 Add vowels to make words.

1 We couldn't get tickets, the show was a s**e**ll-**o**u**t.
2 He's what they call an '**a**lt**e**rn**a**t**i**v**e' comedian, which means I wouldn't take my grandmother to see him!
3 The film has got r**a**v**e** r**e**v**i**ews in most papers.
4 It was a gr**o**u**nd-br**e**ak**i**ng performance, completely different from anything I've seen before.
5 The show is amazing! A real m**u**st-s**ee**!
6 Her interpretation of the role of Juliet has cr**e**at**e**d **a** st**i**r amongst the critics.
7 They stopped playing small clubs once they went m**a**i**nstr**e**am and became popular.
8 The musical was a fl**o**p and closed after one week.
9 I don't know what all the hyp**e** was about. She was awful!
10 The main dancer was ill and someone else took his place, which was a real l**e**td**o**wn.

LISTENING

4 A Look at the photos. Which one do you think is better and why? Think of three reasons.

B ▶ 10.2 Listen to Part 1 of a talk about how to take a good photo and circle the best alternative.

1 The main problem with the light is that …
   a) it's behind the photographer.
   b) it's shining into the lens.
   c) it's too direct and creates a flat effect.
2 The fact that the subject is in the centre …
   a) is good because it's in sharp focus.
   b) is bad because it leaves space at either side of her.
   c) is bad because it cuts off her legs.
3 The problem with the background is that …
   a) it's not interesting.
   b) it's not completely in focus.
   c) it's a missed opportunity.
4 The person taking the picture …
   a) zoomed in too close.
   b) is standing too far away.
   c) didn't look at the woman's face carefully.
5 The last problem the speaker mentions …
   a) is that the woman is looking at the camera.
   b) is that the photographer is too tall.
   c) doesn't apply to this photograph.

C ▶ 10.3 Listen to Part 2 and complete the notes. Use no more than three words for each gap.

THE FIVE RULES

1 Position yourself so that the light is coming
_____.

2 Divide the screen into _____
and place the subject at one of the
_____.

3 Make sure the background is _____
_____.

4 You should be _____ to the
subject.

5 Adjust your _____
so that the lens and the subject's eyes are at
_____.

VOCABULARY PLUS

TWO-PART PHRASES

5 A Complete the advice for studying English.

Do you ever get sick and [1]_____ **of feeling you're not making progress?**

Everybody who learns a language has their ups and [2]_____ along the way. Follow our dos and [3]_____ for language study and we guarantee your English will improve in leaps and [4]_____!

DO find a place with peace and [5]_____ to do your studying.

DON'T study off and [6]_____, skipping days, or you'll make much slower progress. Spend at least ten minutes a day doing something in English, even just studying words.

DO watch a film in English now and [7]_____, at least once a month, and don't worry about understanding every word – just enjoy it!

DO record yourself in English once in a while and listen to the recording. Most mobile phones can make a rough and [8]_____ recording that's good enough for this task.

DO speak English with anyone who will speak English with you, even if their English is not as good as yours. There are pros and [9]_____ to practising with someone below your level, but in fact it can be very valuable because you'll be thinking in English.

DON'T cram! When you've got an exam, look at the test date and plan your revision. Make sure you've completed what you need to do within your plan, give or [10]_____ a few days.

DO learn from your mistakes. When you do a test or exam, go back and study the exam through and [11]_____ and think about how to improve weak areas.

There's lots more advice, we could go on and [12]_____, but you should really get back to studying!

B Tick which advice you think is good.

FUNCTION
GIVING A TOUR

1 A Put the words in the correct order.

1 visit / worth / it's / a / well
  It's well worth a visit.

2 the / over / let's / to / head
  Let's ~~head~~ over to the ~~head~~. (head)

3 to / they / interrupt / had / supposedly,
  Supposedly, they had to interrupt.

4 not, / or / it / believe / took / it
  Believe it or not, it took

5 was / as / originally / it / built
  It was ~~built as~~ (originally)

6 were / well, / founded / they / in
  Well, they were founded in.

7 he / that / goes / story / the / used
  ~~He used that the story goes.~~
  The story goes that he used

B ▶ **10.4** Listen and draw any links between the words in the phrases. Then listen and repeat.

It's well worth a visit

C Complete the conversation with phrases from Exercise 1A. Write the number of the phrase in the correct place.

A: Here we are at the famous Leaning Tower of Pisa. (a) _5_ a bell-tower for the cathedral.

B: It looks like it's going to fall over!

A: It won't. Not today. (b) _4_ 177 years to build.

B: Why did it take so long?

A: (c) _3_ its construction because Pisa was constantly at war.

B: Didn't Galileo live in Pisa?

A: Yes. (d) _7_ the leaning tower to demonstrate the rules of gravity, by dropping things off the top.

B: Is that true?

A: Who knows, really. (e) _2_ Piazza dei Cavalieri.

B: Oh yes, that's such a beautiful square.

A: Well, my favourite restaurant, Ristorante alle Bandierine, is on the way. (f) _1_.

B: Sounds good to me.

VOCABULARY
DIMENSIONS

2 A Write the noun and verb forms of each adjective.

1 long _length_ _lengthen_
2 short _shortness_ _shorten_
3 narrow _narrowness_ _narrow_
4 wide _width_ _widen_
5 broad _breadth_ _broaden_
6 thick _thickness_ ~~enthick~~ _thicken_
7 deep _depth_ _deepen_
8 high ~~hightheight~~ _height_ ~~raise~~ / _heighten_
9 large _largeness_ _enlarge_

B Complete the sentences with the correct form of words from Exercise 2A.

1 The jury needs to _narrow_ down its choices before choosing the finalists.

2 He doesn't have much experience in other companies. He's a good candidate, but I think he needs to ~~deepen~~ his work experience. _broaden_

3 The mystery of strange lights appearing in the sky in Russia ~~enlarge~~ today as scientists said they couldn't explain them. _deepened_

4 The _thickness_ of the mixture is important – it shouldn't be too thin, so when you mix together the flour and water, wait for it to _thicken_ before pouring it into the pan.

5 The _width_ of the road isn't enough to add another lane – they'll have to _widen_ it.

6 We need to check the _length_ of the sofa to make sure it's not too long.

7 Lessons should be shorter and they should ~~enlarge~~ the breaks in between. _lengthen_

8 This video tutorial will show you how to ~~broaden~~ a small photo. _enlarge_

9 The bridge was ~~lengthen~~ _high_ enough for normal trucks to go underneath, but the _height_ of those particular lorries was above the legal limit.

10 This exercise is too long – it needs to be _shortened_

lower part of the bottom surface of something

LEARN TO
EXPRESS ESTIMATES

3 Correct the mistakes in the sentences.

1 There were ~~under~~ just _~~200~~_ people at the party. (under)

2 The homework should take you ~~rough~~ an hour to do. _roughly_

3 We'll be arriving at 4 o'clock or so ~~what?~~ _when_

4 The renovations cost ~~downwards~~ of one million euros. _upwards_

5 We're expecting somewhere ~~on~~ a region of a _in the_ thousand people for the conference.

GRAMMAR   -ING FORM AND INFINITIVE

1 Underline the correct alternatives.

The rules of dinner party etiquette for women (1950)

Dining in high society can be stressful if you don't know the rules. Study these and you'll survive any dinner party.

✗ 1 When you are about to sit down, stop *letting*/*to let* the man next to you hold the chair for you.

2 Once seated, remember *turning*/*to turn* to your right and start a conversation with the man next to you.

✗ 3 If the man has forgotten *turning*/*to turn* to his left, gracefully join the conversation on your left and always try *looking*/*to look* interested even if you are not.

✗ 4 If another guest tells you they remember *meeting*/*to meet* you before, agree with them even you don't remember them.

5 If someone drops a dish, don't stop *talking*/*to talk*, just go on *having*/*to have* the conversation you were having.

✗ 6 If the person you're talking to doesn't seem to be listening, try *asking*/*to ask* questions – people love talking about themselves!

VOCABULARY PLUS   DEPENDENT PREPOSITIONS

✗ Complete the second sentence so that it has a similar meaning to the first. Use between two and five words including the word given.

1 He said he was sorry because he hadn't listened to her. **APOLOGISED**
   He ~~apologised not to listened to her~~ *for not listening*
   to her.

2 People think that the website encourages bad behaviour. **BLAME**
   People blame the website ~~encourage~~ *to/for encouraging*
   bad behaviour.

3 TV companies will no longer be allowed to show adverts for fattening foods before 9p.m. **BANNED**
   TV companies will ~~ban to show~~ *be banned*
   adverts for fattening foods before 9p.m. *from showing*

4 Because of his quick reactions the plane didn't crash. **SAVED**
   His quick reactions saved ~~the plane's crash~~ *the plane from crashing*

5 Kelly had always wanted to be an astronaut. **DREAMT**
   Kelly had always ~~dreaamt to be~~
   an astronaut. *dreamt of being*

6 The police think Jim helped the robbers escape. **SUSPECTED**
   Jim ~~was~~ *is* suspected ~~to help~~ *of helping*
   the robbers escape.

7 She thinks I don't help enough. **CRITICISING**
   She's always criticising ~~my help not~~
   enough. *me for not helping*

VOCABULARY   REVIEW

3 Complete the sentences with the correct word or phrase.

1 deceive/fall for
   a) I always fall for his compliments even though I know he just wants a favour.
   b) It's not difficult to deceive people because most of us want to believe that everyone's intentions are good.

2 taken in/distracted
   a) They were taken in by us pretending to have a fight.
   b) Everyone was distracted by the trick and no one saw the guy robbing the cash register.

3 ground-breaking/sell-out
   a) It was a ground-breaking performance and changed the way people saw the character of Hamlet forever.
   b) It was a sell-out performance and impossible to get tickets for.

4 letdown/flop
   ✗ a) After the success of their first album, the mild response to their second one was a ~~flop~~ *letdown*
   b) They were booked for five shows but the first was a total letdown so the rest were cancelled. *flop*

✗ 5 bribery/shoplifting
   a) ~~Shoplifting~~ *Bribery* is common in the country, which is why if you have money you can get anything done.
   b) ~~Bribery~~ *Shoplifting* costs supermarkets and other stores a lot of money. For this reason shops have increased security and made it more difficult for people to take things.

6 hacking/vandalism
   a) People in public life have to be careful of journalists hacking into their email accounts and publishing private messages.
   b) Examples of vandalism are spraying graffiti on walls and breaking shop windows.

7 narrow/shorten
   a) We'll need to shorten the time it takes to get the produce from the farm to the supermarket.
   b) Either I've put on weight or this door is very narrow – I had to squeeze through it.

✗ 8 gory/gripping
   a) I find the plot of all of his books so ~~gory~~ *gripping* that I can't put them down once I start reading.
   b) I never expected a film about animals to be so ~~gripping~~ – I felt quite ill at the sight of so much blood. *gory*

9 knocked out/knocked over
   a) He got knocked out when his head hit the ice; he had to be taken to hospital.
   b) He got knocked over during the football match but he picked himself up straightaway and carried on.

4 A Look at the underlined sounds in each group. Circle the word with the different sound.

1 (rescue) touching, mugging
2 hype, height, (gory)
3 thought-provoking, now and then, ground-breaking
4 rave reviews, accuse, (full) of suspense
5 (hacking) cause, fall for
6 hysterical, (bribery) deceive

B ▶ R5.1 Listen and check. Listen again and repeat.

GRAMMAR   PAST MODALS OF DEDUCTION

5 A Read the two puzzles. What do you think the answers are? Write two ideas for each.

> **PUZZLE 1** A fully booked 747 took off from Hong Kong, bound for London Heathrow. When it arrived in London, there were no passengers on board.
>
> **PUZZLE 2** There were two men who were born on the same day in the same hospital. They had the same mother and the same last name. They looked exactly alike but they weren't twins.

B Complete the conversation about the puzzles with *must/might/could/can't/couldn't have* and the correct form of the verbs in brackets.

A: OK, so what about the plane puzzle?
B: The people ¹ _couldn't have got / can't_ (get) on the plane.
A: They did get on.
B: Then I'm not sure, but the plane ² _could have experienced_ (experience) a problem and everyone had to get off.
A: No, there was no problem with the plane. I'll give you a hint: it wasn't a non-stop flight.
B: Got it! The plane ³ _might / must have made_ (make) a stop on the way and all the passengers got off there.
A: That's right. So what about the second puzzle?
B: That can't be right, the woman ⁴ _must give / have given_ (give) birth to twins!
A: No, as it says, they weren't twins.
B: Oh. Then they ⁵ _couldn't / can't have had_ (have) the same birthday, it's impossible. Something's not right.
A: No: same birthday, same mother, same name.
B: I suppose there ⁶ _could / might be / have been_ (be) two mothers who were sisters …
A: No. Same mother. One mother.
B: This is only a possibility – they ⁷ _might be / could be have been born_ (be born) a year apart, so they had the same birthday, but were one year apart.
A: No, it was the same year. Just minutes apart. But … they had a sister.
B: Oh! So they ⁸ _must be / have been_ (be) triplets!

FUNCTION   REPORTING AN INCIDENT

6 Underline the correct alternatives.

A: So you let her in your door because she wanted a glass of water?
B: It just didn't ¹*cross/occur/seem* my mind that she was lying.
A: What, a complete stranger coming into your house?
B: She ²*occurred/seemed/reminded* like a nice person.
A: Didn't you see her pick up your mobile?
B: Well it all happened ³*such/with/so* fast, but maybe yes.
A: So you saw it but didn't pay attention?
B: Yes. It was only ⁴*time/much/immediately* later that I realised what had happened.
A: How old was she, would you say?
B: She looked ⁵*as/about/like* she was about forty years old.
A: Can you describe her appearance?
B: She ⁶*reminded/remembered/looked* me of that actress …
A: Which one?
B: I don't recall, my mind's gone ⁷*blink/blind/blank*.
A: Did she introduce herself?
B: I didn't ⁸*cross/grab/catch* her name. It was probably false anyway.

GRAMMAR   RELATIVE CLAUSES

7 Complete the article with *who, which, whom, whose* or *when*.

> Chinese superstar Lang Lang, ¹ _who_ has inspired millions of young pianists and ² _whose_ performance was a highlight of the opening ceremony of the Beijing Olympics, was born in Shenyang in 1982.
>
> From the age of two, ³ _when_ his parents paid half a year's salary to buy him a piano, he was brought up to become the world's number one pianist. Lang Lang, ⁴ _who_ was naturally talented, won his first competition at five ⁵ _whom / when_ he had to stand up to play the piano because his feet couldn't reach the pedals. His father, ⁶ _who_ gave up his job as a police officer, moved with him to Beijing for further studies, during ⁷ _which_ time father and son lived in poverty.
>
> Nowadays, he is a young man for ⁸ _whom_ playing the piano and being a superstar both come naturally. Lang Lang, ⁹ _whose_ work as a Unicef ambassador is dear to his heart, has recently launched a piano competition for children, ¹⁰ _who / which_ is sure to be a great success.

GRAMMAR PARTICIPLE CLAUSES

8 Complete the articles with the present or past participle of the verbs in the boxes.

spend   use   live   find   kill

NUMBERS: people

5.5 litres: the amount of blood [1] _found_ in the human body

13: the percentage of the world's population [2] ~~live~~ _living_ in deserts

25: the number of years [3] ~~spend~~ _spent_ asleep if you live to seventy-five

70: the number of muscles [4] _used_ to say a single word

30,000: the number of people [5] _killed_ each year by cobras and vipers

suffer   send   make   start   arrive

NUMBERS: machines

40: the percentage of spam email [6] ~~suffered~~ _arriving_ at addresses [7] _started_ with A, M, S, R or P

53: the percentage of people [8] ~~arrive~~ _suffering_ from nomophobia (fear of being without their mobiles)

100: the number of cars [9] _made_ every minute

14,528: the number of text messages [10] _sent_ by a Californian girl in one month

VOCABULARY PLUS TWO-PART PHRASES

9 Correct the mistake in each two-part phrase.

1 I only wanted peace and ~~downs~~ _quiet_ and what did I get? A screaming baby!

2 Our relationship has its ups and ~~bounds~~ _downs_, but I'd say we're a solid couple.

3 You have to weigh up the ~~leaps~~ and cons _pros_ and then decide.

4 There's some ~~back~~ and take _give_ in every friendship; don't be so selfish.

5 I'm sick and ~~ready~~ of your complaints. Shut up or leave!
get tired 〜がすっかり例にする。_down_

6 We could go ~~off~~ and on _on_ about this forever, let's just end the conversation now.

7 We only meet ~~rough~~ and then, _now_ but that's enough for me.

8 Our business was going nowhere, now it's improving in leaps and ~~don'ts~~. _bounds_ という熟語に

FUNCTION GIVING A TOUR

10A Add vowels to complete the words and phrases.

a) h e a d o v e r
b) w o rth
c) m o delled
d) a ppa re ntly
e) b u rnt
f) m a y kn e w
g) n a m ed
h) re tr a ce
i) b e l e i e v e
j) s u pp o se dly
k) fo u nd ed
l) st o ry g o e s

10B Use words and phrases a)–f) to complete part 1 of the tour and g)–k) to complete part 2.

Tour of Kyoto, Japan, part 1

The original city of Kyoto was [1] _modelled_ on the ancient Chinese capital Chang'an. Many buildings were [2] _burnt_ down in the 15th-century Onin War, but the city survived the Second World War.

As you [3] _may know_, Kyoto is famous for its geisha. [4] _Apparently_ women who train to be geisha today are not allowed to marry or have mobile phones. The two famous geisha districts, Gion and Pontocho, are well [5] _worth_ a visit, so let's [6] _head over_ there later.

Tour of Kyoto, Japan, part 2

Here we are at the Jishu shrine. See those two stones? The [7] _story goes_ that if you walk from one to the other, you will one day find true love.

And this is Kiyomizu-dera temple, which was [8] _founded_ in 798. It's [9] _named_ after a waterfall nearby. [10] ~~Head over~~ _Believe_ it or not, not one nail was used to build it.

Why don't we [11] _retrace_ our steps to the Manga Museum – [12] ~~apparently~~ _supposedly_ they have over 200,000 titles and we can read as many manga as we want.

CHECK

Circle the correct option to complete the sentences.

1 Her performance was _____, but otherwise the play was rather disappointing.
   a) outstanding   **b)** controversial   **c)** touching

2 That's strange, I remember _____ this letter, but here it is in my bag.
   a) post   **b)** posting   **c)** to post

3 He was _____ for identity theft.
   a) suspected   **b)** arrested   **c)** saved

4 My best _____ lives in Paris, works in advertising.
   a) friend who   **b)** friend, whose   **c)** friend, who

5 There was so much _____ about the new show that it was sure to be a _____.
   a) hype, letdown   **b)** rave reviews, flop
   c) ground-breaking, sell-out

6 The cinema burnt to the ground. Police think it was _____.
   a) hacking   **b)** mugging   **c)** arson

7 He _____ committed the murder. He wasn't even in the country at the time.
   a) may have   **b)** can't have   **c)** mustn't have

8 They'll need to _____ the canal if wider boats are going to sail through it.
   a) broaden   **b)** lengthen   **c)** deepen

9 It didn't _____ my mind to phone you.
   a) catch   **b)** occur to   **c)** cross

10 She was keen to _____ her husband of the crime.
   a) clear   **b)** blame   **c)** save

11 I can't believe you _____ that guy who was _____ a tourist.
   a) deceived, snatching   **b)** were taken in, posing as
   c) were fooled by, pretending to be

12 That's the woman _____ son hit my son.
   a) who   **b)** whose   **c)** who's

13 Here we are at the president's childhood home. _____ it's got two floors and all the other houses around here have one.
   a) Interestingly   **b)** Supposedly   **c)** Apparently

14 I don't think it would have been a _____ if it hadn't created such a _____.
   a) must-see, mainstream   **b)** sell-out, stir
   c) flop, ground-breaking

15 She took her umbrella, _____ that it would rain at some point during the day.
   a) expected   **b)** expecting   **c)** having expected

16 The monument was modelled _____ a well-known ancient Egyptian obelisk.
   a) by   **b)** for   **c)** on

17 People _____ redundant by the economic crisis were happy to get any kind of job.
   a) make   **b)** made   **c)** making

18 The protestors were _____ from marching through the city centre without permission.
   a) accused   **b)** charged   **c)** banned

19 I really didn't hear you ring the doorbell. I _____ been sleeping or maybe I was listening to music.
   a) could have   **b)** can't have   **c)** mightn't have

20 They seemed _____ if they were just having fun.
   a) to be   **b)** like   **c)** as

21 He _____ my wallet and _____ it for an identical one, which he gave back to me.
   a) grabbed, switched   **b)** swapped, snatched
   c) fooled, posed

22 Her first relationship was the one thing _____ she thought more than anything else.
   a) which   **b)** which about   **c)** about which

23 My foot got _____ in a hole and I couldn't get it out.
   a) run over   **b)** stuck   **c)** locked out

24 Look, footprints! Someone _____ got here before us.
   a) could have   **b)** might have   **c)** must have

25 _____ all his life to build his dream house, he decided to travel instead.
   a) Having worked   **b)** Working   **c)** Worked

26 A search engine is a good _____ tool for checking spelling.
   a) off-and-on   **b)** rough-and-ready
   c) now-and-then

27 We stopped on the way up the mountain _____ a break.
   a) to take   **b)** taking   **c)** take

28 The tablet's working and my headache's beginning _____.
   a) going   **b)** go   **c)** to go

29 The book was so _____ that I couldn't put it down.
   a) touching   **b)** creepy   **c)** fast-paced

30 My first girlfriend knew me _____ and no one has understood me as well since.
   a) through and through   **b)** off and on
   c) ups and downs

RESULT   /30

UNIT 6 Recording 1

Speaker 1

I don't think there's any hard and fast rule, so for me, any time is the right time. I began when I was six, but then again I knew someone who started when they were almost fifty and she's still going strong now she's over seventy. You're never too old. I suppose the key is how much time you have to practise and your motivation. My parents let me try out different instruments and eventually I chose the violin. That's important too. I'm not sure my parents were too happy about my choice, though! They had to put up with years of me sounding like a dying cat!

Speaker 2

I think there's actually a legal minimum age in some countries, something like thirty-five, but in my opinion it should be at least fifty. Otherwise you just don't have enough experience to do it. But then of course you have to strike a balance between maturity and energy. You need to be able to react quickly to events and survive sometimes on very little sleep. So yes, someone in their fifties or maybe sixties could manage but no older than that.

Speaker 3

I couldn't really give a number at all, since I can't state what's right for other people. I think it has to do with giving yourself enough time to get to know yourself and to understand your relationship together well enough so that neither of you will create an unhealthy environment for the child. Some people say there's never a right time, but I think there's definitely a wrong time – too soon.

Speaker 4

Lots of people I know didn't know what they wanted to do with their life when they were twenty and they still don't know now they're over forty! But seriously, it's OK to decide young, if you have a real vocation, you know, you've always wanted to be a doctor or an engineer or something like that. But most of us don't have much idea when we leave school. So I reckon the best idea is to try out lots of things to see what you enjoy and develop lots of general skills. That worked for me. Most companies need staff who can get on with other people and can communicate their ideas clearly and who have reasonable computer skills and things like that.

UNIT 6 Recording 2

unrealistic
unfamiliar, unpredictable
dissatisfied, illogical, irrelevant
impatient, immortal, unwilling, unhealthy
misbehave, insecure
misinterpret

UNIT 6 Recording 3

1

A: Look at this picture. Isn't it time they banned 'size zero' models?

B: Well, clothes do look quite good on them.

A: But it sends a terrible message to young girls. Shouldn't they know it isn't normal to be so skinny?

B: I've never really thought about it much.

A: Well you should. Clearly, these images add to the pressure on young girls.

B: Yeah, you're probably right.

2

A: Don't you think that they should use technology in football games?

B: What, you mean instead of referees?

A: Yeah, to make decisions. Anyone can see it would be fairer.

B: But you need referees for all sorts of reasons.

A: Yeah, but surely it's more important that decisions are correct.

B: Hmm. I suppose you have a point.

UNIT 6 Recording 4

A: Look at this picture. Isn't it time they banned 'size zero' models?

A: But it sends a terrible message to young girls. Shouldn't they know it isn't normal to be so skinny?

A: Well you should. Clearly, these images add to the pressure on young girls.

A: Don't you think that they should use technology in football games?

A: Yeah, to make decisions. Anyone can see it would be fairer.

A: Yeah, but surely it's more important that decisions are correct.

UNIT 6 Recording 5

1

A: Do you like me in this dress?

B: I prefer the white one.

A: So what you're saying is this one, which cost a fortune, looks terrible.

B: No, I mean the white one makes you look slimmer.

A: So, in other words, I look fat!

B: No, no, you're twisting my words. I just meant that you look *even* slimmer in the white one.

2

A: Don't you think we should pay a decorator to do it?

B: So basically you think I can't do it.

A: I didn't mean that. It's just that it might be quicker and save us money.

B: So what you mean is that I might mess it up.

A: No, but you're a perfectionist and you know how long it takes you to do things.

B: So you'd rather spend money and end up with a worse job!

A: Not exactly …

UNIT 7 Recording 1

Speaker 1

One of my favourite programmes when I was a kid was a very famous show called *Mister Benn*. I don't really remember that much about it, I know it was my favourite because my mother tells me it was. It was a cartoon and from what I remember it's about a guy who goes into a fancy clothes shop and he puts on a different outfit and then every time he comes out of the clothes shop he's then transported to a world that corresponds with the outfit that he's wearing. I think I liked it because there was this innocent sense of adventure about it. I can't remember much about any individual episodes though.

Speaker 2

The classic for Brits of my generation is *Blue Peter* – it's hard to underestimate its cultural impact. It was a kind of magazine programme for children. Basically, it involved two or three presenters (who also had a dog and a cat) involved in various tasks – demonstrating how to make toys or ornaments out of everyday household objects, short documentary trips to various places of interest and so on. Occasionally they held interviews with famous actors or performers of some sort. They would also bring in people who had some form of talent – musical, for example – to do live studio performances. Everyone wanted a 'Blue Peter badge', the special prize you could be awarded if you wrote in and they read your letter or if you won a competition or something similar – literally a badge of honour.

Speaker 3

I liked this show *Grange Hill* because it was, I think, an accurate representation of what life in an English comprehensive school in a British city is like and it dealt with issues that were interesting for teen … perhaps a bit younger than teenagers … So like when you were from nine to twelve. I think it was a really good show because you're not yet old enough to watch adult TV but you're too old to watch kids' TV and it kind of bridges the gap between the two, and it deals with issues like drugs and sex in an unpatronising, non-condescending way. I suppose it was a kind of soap opera for kids, but quite a serious one.

Speaker 4

When I was a teenager, my favourite show was *Monty Python*. It was different from any other kind of comedy show we'd had before. Instead of separate sketches with proper endings, in *Monty Python* they'd start a sketch and then suddenly stop it halfway or one sketch would morph into another. If a sketch was getting boring there'd be a news announcer coming on and saying 'and now for something completely different!' The links between the sketches would sometimes be cartoons, very surrealistic and weird cartoons of people exploding or strange machines. I suppose one of the main reasons I liked it was because my parents didn't understand it at all, so it was a kind of rebellion. After a Monty Python night we'd spend our entire lunch break at school going through it, remembering all the catchphrases and taking each sketch apart.

UNIT 7 Recording 2

1 If I say something offensive, I'm often too stubborn to take it back.
2 If a homeless person knocked on my door in the middle of winter, I would put them up for the night.
3 Hard work brings out the best in me.
4 I come across as being more sociable than I really am.
5 If it turned out that my partner had lied to me, I would be disappointed in him.

UNIT 7 Recording 3

A: This is totally outrageous. Your questions are very biased against the government. I've never heard such biased statements from a journalist before. Absolutely incredible.
B: Well, minister, you're the one who's always telling the people that we're getting richer when the cost of living is increasing and our wages are staying the same. How on earth do you justify that?
A: Look, there's no way I'd say that if the data didn't agree! Having said that, I do think we can do better to help ordinary people and so we're going to cut petrol tax.
B: That is a good idea, minister, but why are you introducing it now? Is it because the election is in two months?
A: That is so wrong! Are you suggesting that we're making up policies to gain votes?
B: To be honest minister, the amazing thing is that you're denying making policies to win votes.

UNIT 7 Recording 4

A: This is totally outrageous.
A: Absolutely incredible.
B: you're the one who's always telling the people that we're getting richer
B: How on earth do you justify that?
A: Look, there's no way I'd say that if the data didn't agree!

A: Having said that, I do think we can do better to help ordinary people
B: That is a good idea, minister, but why are you introducing it now?
A: That is so wrong!
B: the amazing thing is that you're denying making policies to win votes.

UNIT 8 Recording 1

Part 1

Today, in the third of my lectures on human behaviour, I'm going to talk about the difference between the way people act when they're being watched – or think they're being watched – and how they act when they're unobserved. I'll be describing a recent experiment conducted at Newcastle University. I'll be drawing conclusions from this experiment, to see what it teaches us about psychology and behaviour and finally, I'll be comparing it with other key research findings in the area.

So, what did the team at Newcastle set out to discover? They wanted to find out whether the simple belief that they were being watched would alter people's behaviour. To do this they made use of an 'honesty box' in a staff common room at the university. The idea behind the honesty box was that staff members would pay the correct amount for their coffee and tea. This honesty box had been in there for several years, so no one had any idea that an experiment was taking place.

What they did was to place a small poster at eye-level above the honesty box, listing the prices for the drinks. However, each week the poster alternated between different images of either flowers or of a pair of eyes looking straight at the observer. Here, you can see examples of the kind of pictures they used. At the end of each week the team monitored the amount of money that had been collected and compared this to the volume of milk that had been consumed. They found that people paid nearly three times as much money when the notice included a pair of eyes as when it included an image of flowers.

UNIT 8 Recording 2

Part 2

So what does this experiment tell us? Well, firstly it underlines something we already know – that our brains are hard-wired, are programmed, to respond to faces and eyes. It's important for people to know if they're being watched. Secondly, it shows that people are influenced if they think they're being watched; they behave less selfishly. The team were surprised by the significant difference in the findings. And what implications could this have for the future? Well, the team believe the idea could be applied to public situations where people have to decide whether to

behave well or badly. One example would be for warnings for speed cameras. The team's previous studies show that drivers would react more positively to images of faces and eyes than to a picture of a camera. Another place where a picture of eyes could be placed is near a CCTV camera in town centres.

Now, before I go on to discuss other studies, does anyone have any questions?

UNIT 8 Recording 3

1 What would you have done?
2 I wouldn't have done that.
3 If I'd known when you were coming, I would've met you at the station.

UNIT 8 Recording 4

A: Is everything OK?
B: Actually, there's something I've been meaning to talk to you about.
A: Oh, is there a problem?
B: I don't want you to get the wrong idea, but …
A: That sounds bad.
B: It's just that you often leave your mobile on.
A: I don't understand.
B: And it rings when you're not here and that's annoying.
A: But I need to keep it on in case my son phones.
B: Yes, but it's disturbing when people are trying to work.
A: It's important that he can get straight through to me.
B: I understand, but do you see where I'm coming from?
A: I suppose so.
B: Maybe you could set it to silent when you're not here.
A: What you mean just the 'vibrate' setting?
B: Yes, how would you feel about that?
A: OK, that sounds reasonable. I'll do that from now on. Sorry about that.
B: Thanks, I'd appreciate it.

UNIT 8 Recording 5

1 Actually, there's something I've um been meaning to talk to you about.
2 Well, I don't want you to get the wrong idea, but …
3 It's just that, you know, you often leave your mobile on …
4 And it rings when you're not here and that's slightly annoying.
5 Yes, but it's a bit disturbing when people are trying to work.
6 I understand, but I mean, do you see where I'm coming from?
7 Maybe you could just set it to silent when you're not here.
8 Yes, how would you er feel about that?

AUDIO SCRIPTS

1 biased, deny, promise
2 reality, threaten, sketch
3 serial, circulation, generosity
4 persuade, tabloid, sensationalism
5 focused, confrontational, control
6 sensible, aggressive, assess

UNIT 9 Recording 1

A: … and we're joined today by Alex Temple, a researcher in something called inattentional blindness. Welcome to the show.

B: Thank you.

A: So for starters, can you tell us exactly what is 'inattentional blindness'?

B: Well, the best way I can explain it is through some of the experiments that have been done. The most famous is the gorilla experiment. Subjects are shown a film of two groups throwing around a basketball, one group dressed in white, the other in dark clothes. And the viewer is told to count the number of times the team in white passes the ball. After about ten seconds, someone dressed in a gorilla suit walks out to the middle, faces the camera and then walks off. Most people watching the film don't notice the gorilla.

A: Don't notice it? That's hard to believe.

B: It seems that way till you do it. The point is that it's part of the nature of how we see, or don't see, when we pay attention.

A: You mean when we pay attention we see less.

B: When we pay attention we see what we're paying attention to. If I ask you to go out on Oxford Street and count the number of people with glasses, then when you come back I ask how many teenagers you saw with parrots on their shoulders, we'd get a similar result, even if there were several teenagers with parrots.

A: I suppose so. But why is this so important?

UNIT 9 Recording 2

B: Well, when this happens in everyday life it can have significant consequences – a lot of accidents happen because of inattentional blindness.

A: For example?

B: Well, for example, road accidents. Many accidents happen when a driver is talking on his or her mobile phone, using a hands-free set-up, which is legal. A driver in this situation actually misses a great deal of visual information, or is slower to process it.

A: A car stopping in front of them for instance?

B: Exactly. When there's a smooth flow of traffic and the driver is talking on the phone, some of their ability to process visual information is taken away. A car stops in front of them and it's like the gorilla – it's not what they're concentrating on, or looking for, and so they don't 'see' it. They also tend not to notice advertising hoardings by the road, for instance, even quite striking ones.

A: Maybe this explains why I miss signs when I'm driving.

B: Well, if you're driving in the USA and you're looking for a sign that says 'city centre' you might not notice the one that says 'downtown', even if you're not talking on the phone. That's more about selective seeing, which is related to inattentional blindness.

A: And how is this … information used?

B: In lots of ways. We use simulators to demonstrate to trained pilots that they're less likely to notice something unusual on the airport runway than an untrained person – and this awareness helps them adjust how they use their visual perception and processing, and can prevent accidents.

A: Fascinating.

B: And in more common jobs, like a guard in a store. They expect a thief to try and hide what they're doing, so if someone steals something openly – just smiles, greets the guard and walks out of the store – they might not notice it. We do simulations to train guards not to be blinded by their expectations of how a thief behaves.

A: So it's really about training people not to be blind?

B: Yes. Though we've seen applications in design too. It's happened that a car driver driving at night tried to overtake another car and simply didn't see the motorcycle coming in the other direction – because the headlights didn't look like car headlights. So some motorcycle headlights have been made to look more like car headlights.

A: Any advice for our listeners? Is this something they can use in everyday life?

B: Sure. Aside from not talking on the phone while driving, I'd say that it's important to be aware of how you're looking at things. How your expectations of what you'll see actually blinds you to what's there.

A: So, expect the unexpected?

B: Yes, exactly.

UNIT 9 Recording 3

1 It must have been you.
2 It couldn't have been me.
3 You may not have seen her.
4 They can't have been there.
5 We could have seen them.

UNIT 9 Recording 4

A: I've just been robbed, on the underground, by a pickpocket.

B: What happened?

A: Well, this guy got on the train and he reminded me of that English football player … wait, my mind's gone blank. Oh yeah, David Beckham.

B: David Beckham? Didn't you wonder why he was travelling on the underground?

A: It never occurred to me, no. Well, then everyone crowded round with their phonecams.

B: Typical!

A: I had to push my way past them and before I'd realised what was happening, my wallet was gone, right out of my bag.

B: Did you see or feel anyone take it?

A: No, in fact it was only a minute later that I realised they'd done it. It all happened so fast and I was in a hurry anyway.

B: So the David Beckham lookalike must have been a distraction.

A: Yeah, and he must have had someone working with him.

B: Well, the people with phonecams, maybe they …

A: Do you think so? They seemed like students, but …

B: Oh, definitely, it was a pickpocket gang. That's how they work.

UNIT 9 Recording 5

A: It was a pretty bad accident. The front rim was completely twisted.

B: Rim?

A: The metal part of the wheel. And of course the spokes were broken.

B: Spokes?

A: The wires that go from the centre of the wheel to the rim. The chain guard got dented.

B: Chain guard?

A: The metal thing that covers the chain. One pedal broke off.

B: Pedal?

A: The thing you put your foot in. And the handlebar got bent.

B: Handlebar?

A: The thing you hold when you ride. And somehow the saddle got ripped.

B: Saddle?

A: The thing you sit on when you ride a bike.

B: Oh dear. Did you break any bones?

A: Bones? I cracked my skull.

B: Skull?

A: That's the big bone inside your head.

UNIT 10 Recording 1

1 The people living on the other side of the river were trapped.

2 Anyone planning to go home early or wanting to take a break should let us know.

3 Walking out of the restaurant, I ran into my old boss coming in.

4 I used to work with the woman living next door.

5 I left the party quickly, not telling anyone that I was unwell.

6 Carrying a child under each arm, she ran out of the blazing building.

7 He jumped up, frightened by the loud bang, mistaking the door for a gun.

8 Walls painted white tend to attract more graffiti.

UNIT 10 Recording 2

Part 1

Hello everyone and thank you for coming. This evening I'm going to talk to you about how to take great photographs – the five secrets that every good photographer knows and uses. To be honest, these aren't really secrets, but hopefully, they'll be new to some of you and you'll find them useful.

OK, let's start with a photograph that includes some of the most common mistakes that amateurs make ... As you can see, this photo is a typical snapshot, the sort where someone got the woman to pose for the camera. Nothing against posing, though my preference is for more natural shots, but in any case there are several basic errors.

First of all, the picture-taker made sure the sun was behind him or her, to avoid sun going into the lens and that's good, but this way the subject has the sun blasting on her face, just a flat hard light. It also means that she can't open her eyes properly!

Secondly, the subject has been centred in the frame which leaves a lot of space at either side of her and creates a pretty boring and predictable image.

This leads me to the third common mistake that people make which concerns the background. We can see too much background here – the street scene with parked cars is distracting and unattractive.

Fourthly, overall there's too much space around the subject, the picture taker is either too far away or has used the wrong perspective, or both. Leaving too much space around the subject can make them appear smaller than you'd like and make objects in the background too important. The final thing to check is the angle. Amateur photographers often stand higher than their subject which makes the subject look up – which is not the best angle to see a face, but ... actually, in this case, the photographer has got it right and positioned the camera in line with the subject's eyes.

You might think I'm being unfair, as this is just a quick snapshot. But I want you to see just how simple it is to make even your family snapshots consistently good photos.

UNIT 10 Recording 3

Part 2

OK, so here are the five key rules.

Rule number one: light from the side. So if you're outside, notice where the sun is shining from and position yourself so that it's to your left or right as you're facing your subject. If it's to your side, the subject won't have that flat hard light on them, but much more interesting shadows and shades, which give the image more depth and contour.

Rule number two is the rule of thirds. When you're framing a shot, divide the screen up into thirds both horizontally and vertically, and think of the four points where the lines intersect as centres. If your subject is a face, position the face at one of these four points. In other words, place your subject off-centre to add interest.

Which brings us to rule number three: think about your background. Avoid cluttered backgrounds which distract from the main focus of your photograph. This may mean positioning yourself in a particular way so, for example, there are trees or water or sky behind your subject and not cars. You can then use natural elements in the background to add texture and pattern.

Rule number four is related to this: take three steps closer to your subject. Try to fill the picture with your subject rather than leaving a lot of air around – unless the background or surroundings are important.

And rule number five is to adjust your height to your subject, so if they're much shorter, for example a child, kneel or crouch down. The lens and their eyes should be at about the same level. You'll be amazed at the difference.

So those are the five rules. Let's look at another photo of the same person and see how the rules work in practice.

UNIT 10 Recording 4

1 It's well worth a visit

2 Let's head over to the

3 Supposedly, they had to interrupt

4 Believe it or not, it took

5 It was originally built as

6 Well, they were founded in

7 The story goes that he used

R5 Recording 1

1 rescue, touching, mugging

2 hype, height, gory

3 thought-provoking, now and then, ground-breaking

4 rave reviews, accuse, full of suspense

5 hacking, cause, fall for

6 hysterical, bribery, deceive

UNIT 6

6.1

1A

1 **Act** your age!
2 I'm continually surprised by her **maturity**.
3 Yes, he looks very young **for** his age.
4 We're visiting an **elderly** aunt of Simon's.
5 Careful – that could be seen as age **discrimination**.
6 Yes, she's definitely in her **prime**.
7 I agree – they've certainly **come** of age now.
8 Yeah, he's so **immature**.

B

positive: 2, 3, 6, 7
negative: 1, 5, 8
neutral: 4

2

1 couldn't
2 had to
3 are able
4 should
5 let
6 managed to
7 can
8 are supposed to
9 made
10 being able to
11 wasn't allowed
12 don't have to

3

1 doesn't/don't have to provide
2 can't make kids eat
3 didn't manage to
4 let him go
5 won't be able to/'m not able to
6 aren't supposed to be

4B

Speaker 1: 5
Speaker 2: 7
Speaker 3: 3
Speaker 4: 1

C

1 any age
2 having enough time to practise, motivation, trying out different instruments before choosing
3 50–69
4 maturity and energy
5 so you don't create an unhealthy environment for the child
6 too soon/young
7 when the person has a particular vocation (for example, to be a doctor or an engineer)
8 try out lots of things to see what you enjoy and develop general skills

D

1 c 2 e 3 b 4 d 5 a

5A

1 un: realistic, familiar, predictable, willing, healthy
2 im: patient, mortal
3 mis: behave, interpret
4 il: logical
5 ir: relevant
6 dis: satisfied
7 in: secure

B

1 unrealistic
2 impatient
3 unwilling
4 unfamiliar
5 insecure
6 dissatisfied
7 misbehave
8 irrelevant
9 misinterpret
10 unhealthy

C

oooOo: unrealistic
ooOoo: unfamiliar, unpredictable
oOoo: dissatisfied, illogical, irrelevant
oOo: impatient, immortal, unwilling, unhealthy
ooO: misbehave, insecure
ooOo: misinterpret

6.2

1A

relationships, social networking, newspapers, radio (shopping is referred to indirectly: the drone is bringing new smart glasses which have been bought)

B

1 e 2 a 3 f 4 b 5 c 6 d

C

1 F 2 T 3 T 4 T 5 T 6 T 7 T 8 NG

2

1 will have started
2 won't be using
3 'll be attending
4 need
5 will involve
6 will have happened

3A

2 The average weight of an adult male will have gone down to seventy kilos.
3 Smoking will have been banned completely in all public areas.
4 Everyone will be driving flying cars.
5 Men and women will be wearing the same clothes.
6 Poverty and famine will have halved.

4

1 look forward to
2 have ups and downs
3 go nowhere
4 have mixed feelings
5 look on the bright
6 upbeat
7 dread
8 fill with despair

5A

1 for
2 about, 'd
3 get
4 be, let
5 to, All
6 know, rather

B

1 happy to get
2 about
3 be great
4 a great time for
5 do you know
6 All the best
7 I'd love
8 I'd rather
9 let you know
10 I can't wait to

6.3

1A

1 credit card
2 staying, alone
3 ridden, scooter
4 wear
5 late, stay
6 run, business
7 owned
8 social networking
9 part-time
10 travelling solo
11 babysit
12 pierced

2A

1 Isn't ~~that~~ it time that they banned 'size zero' models?
Shouldn't they ~~be knowing~~ **know** it isn't normal to be so skinny?
Clearly ~~so~~, these images add to the pressure on young girls.
2 ~~Aren't you thinking~~ **Don't you think** that they should use technology in football games?
~~No one can't~~ **Anyone can** see it would be fairer.
Yeah, but ~~sure~~ **surely** it's more important that decisions are correct.

B

1 <u>Look</u> at this <u>picture</u>. Isn't it <u>time</u> that they <u>banned</u> 'size <u>zero</u>' <u>models</u>?

But it sends a <u>terrible</u> message to <u>young girls</u>. Shouldn't they <u>know</u>, it isn't <u>normal</u> to be so <u>skinny</u>?

Well you <u>should</u>. <u>Clearly</u>, these <u>images</u> add to the <u>pressure</u> on <u>young girls</u>.

2 Don't you <u>think</u> that they should use <u>technology</u> in <u>football</u> games?

<u>Yeah</u>, to make <u>decisions</u>. <u>Anyone</u> can <u>see</u> it would be <u>fairer</u>.

Yeah, but <u>surely</u> it's more <u>important</u> that <u>decisions</u> are <u>correct</u>.

3A

1 So what you're saying is
So, in other words,
2 So basically you think
So what you mean is

REVIEW 3

1

2 going nowhere
3 has their ups and downs
4 I'm dreading
5 looks forward to taking exams
6 Look on the bright side.

2

1 were able to/managed to
2 couldn't/weren't able to
3 able to
4 ought not/oughtn't
5 won't be able
6 allow you to/let you
7 have to/should
8 supposed to
9 allowed to
10 make

3

1 don't
2 Surely
3 Shouldn't
4 clearly
5 isn't
6 wouldn't

4

1 will have doubled
2 will be paying
3 will not/won't have saved
4 will be facing
5 will be discussing
6 will be living
7 won't be driving
8 will have
9 will have replaced
10 will be working

5A

H	C	K	P	D	O	K	H	K	H	Y	F	N	U	S
X	J	A	Z	I	K	T	T	I	L	C	J	T	J	R
L	T	I	U	S	Y	U	N	V	U	A	U	V	V	V
G	H	N	N	S	Q	N	Q	X	N	T	E	G	I	Y
B	P	S	W	A	M	F	F	C	H	I	H	C	M	S
Z	I	E	I	T	E	A	A	Z	E	I	H	W	P	U
Y	R	C	L	I	D	M	L	X	A	L	G	M	A	P
I	R	U	L	S	L	I	Y	G	L	Q	Q	J	T	T
V	E	R	I	F	F	L	K	M	T	I	H	E	I	L
Y	L	E	N	I	A	I	P	O	H	N	V	E	E	S
L	E	H	G	E	Y	A	F	D	Y	V	D	V	N	U
B	V	X	I	D	S	R	I	Q	Z	X	R	C	T	B
E	A	U	U	N	R	E	A	L	I	S	T	I	C	K
M	N	M	I	S	B	E	H	A	V	E	N	T	Y	R
L	T	Y	M	I	S	I	N	T	E	R	P	R	E	T

B

1 unhealthy
2 irrelevant
3 unwilling
4 dissatisfied
5 misinterpret
6 insecure
7 impatient
8 unrealistic
9 misbehave
10 unfamiliar

CHECK

1 c **2** c **3** a **4** b **5** a **6** c **7** c
8 a **9** b **10** c **11** a **12** a **13** b
14 b **15** b **16** c

UNIT 7

7.1

1

```
  1C U R R E N 2T
  O           H       3R
 4S O A P     R       E       5D
  T       6N  I   7G A M E    E
  U     8Q E   L   L       T
  M     U  9W I L D L I F E  E
10S E R I E S   E       T   C
  I     Z       R       Y   T
  T    11S     12S           I
  C     K       E           V
13D O C U M E N T A R Y     E
  M     T       I
     14D O C U D R A M A
        H       L
```

2

1 little
2 Several
3 little
4 A small number of
5 either of
6 A little
7 any
8 no

3

1 plenty of
2 several
3 quite a few
4 Another
5 a large number
6 each
7 a few
8 a good deal of
9 every
10 no

4A

Speaker	Programme name	Programme type
1	Mister Benn	cartoon
2	Blue Peter	children's magazine programme
3	Grange Hill	soap opera for children
4	Monty Python	comedy sketch show

B

a) 2 **b)** 4 **c)** 1 **d)** 2 **e)** 3 **f)** 4
g) 1 **h)** 3

C

1 c **2** e **3** d **4** b **5** f **6** a

5A

1 back **2** up **3** out **4** across **5** out

B

1 take it <u>back</u>
2 put them <u>up</u>
3 brings <u>out</u>
4 come <u>across</u>
5 turned <u>out</u>

C

1 brought out
2 put up
3 take (me) back
4 came across
5 turn out

7.2

1A

an electronics shop
a telephone company
a newspaper
a travel agency

B

1 e **2** b **3** c **4** a **5** d

2

1 had taken
2 didn't remember
3 had had
4 had
5 was breaking down
6 wanted
7 wouldn't
8 had to

3

1 why I'd/had come/gone there that day
2 I'd been trying to see him since the day before
3 me to close the door and have a seat
4 how he could help me
5 him (that) I had information that Mario the Snitch would be killed the next/following day
6 what made me think this might happen
7 not to waste time asking me questions
8 (me) if/whether he should let the cops know

ANSWER KEY

4A

1 to take part
2 to walk out
3 making
4 of lying
5 for doing
6 doing

a) to say
b) to change
c) doing/having done
d) to take on
e) to pay
f) to be

B

1 e 2 d 3 b 4 f 5 a 6 c

5A

1 ✗ 2 ✓ 3 ✗ 4 ✓ 5 ✓ 6 ✗

B

1 Although most internet writers are amateurs, many give objective information.
2 While the internet is a convenient source of information, its accessibility can also mean that this information is not trustworthy.
3 Of course there's some inaccurate content. However, it's the reader's responsibility to identify the reliable information.
4 Despite the fact that wiki contributors try to give accurate information, too many don't use reliable sources. OR Despite wiki contributors trying to give …
5 Although many amateur news websites look serious, that doesn't make them accurate.
6 While these weaknesses exist, there are reasons to trust much internet content as well.

7.3

1A

1 supplement
2 circulation
3 sensationalism
4 edition
5 biased
6 editorial page
7 feature
8 tabloid

B

1 edition
2 sensationalism
3 supplement
4 tabloid
5 feature
6 biased
7 editorial page
8 circulation

2

2 You were the one who was asking about the celebrity news.

3 The incredible thing about the story is (that) all the people escaped safely.
4 The remarkable thing is that people want to buy this paper.
5 They're the ones who want to have a big magazine launch party, not us.
6 The ridiculous thing is the number of adverts.

3A

1 This is **totally** outrageous
2 **Absolutely incredible**
3 you're the one **who's** always telling the people that we're getting richer
4 **How** on earth do you justify that?
5 There**'s no** way I'd say
6 I **do** think we can do better to help ordinary people
7 That **is** a good idea
8 That is so **wrong**!
9 the **amazing** thing is that

B

1 This is totally <u>outrageous</u>.
2 Absolutely <u>incredible</u>.
3 <u>you're</u> the one who's always <u>telling</u> the people that we're getting richer
4 How on <u>earth</u> do you justify that?
5 there's <u>no way</u> I'd say
6 I <u>do</u> think we can do better to help ordinary people
7 That <u>is</u> a good idea,
8 That is <u>so</u> wrong!
9 the <u>amazing</u> thing is that

4A

2 Surely it's a hoax photo/photo hoax
3 Perhaps there's a nuclear plant upstream
4 It might be two fish
5 I'd imagine it's genuine but it's hard to say/It's hard to say but I'd imagine it's genuine

B

1 b 2 e 3 c 4 d 5 a

UNIT 8

8.1

1

1 goes against
2 stick to
3 assess
4 put off
5 postpone
6 betray
7 follow
8 evaluate
9 explore
10 arrive at
11 look into
12 reach

2

1 five-year long
2 twenty-storey high
3 long-running
4 record-breaking
5 time-consuming

6 15-metre high
7 third-time
8 life-changing

3A/B

The experiment was about how visual images affect people's behaviour in terms of honesty.

C

1 are being watched
2 are unobserved
3 an experiment/a recent experiment
4 psychology
5 belief
6 an honesty box
7 changed/alternated the image
8 more honest
9 three times

D

1 So that we know if we are being watched.
2 They behave less selfishly.
3 They were surprised.
4 A poster of faces or eyes could be used for the warnings about speed cameras instead of a picture of a camera.
5 Near CCTV cameras in town centres.

4A

In the first picture, the man is phoning from home; in the article, he phones from a payphone.
In the second picture, the man is saving a boy; in the article, he saves another man.

B

1 hadn't walked/hadn't been walking, wouldn't have seen
2 would/might/could have been traced, had/'d phoned
3 hadn't come forward, might never have found/would never have found
4 would/might have kept, hadn't spoken
5 would be, had/'d kept
6 wouldn't have fallen, hadn't collapsed
7 had stopped, wouldn't have leapt
8 would be, hadn't jumped
9 hadn't been, would have been killed
10 had had, wouldn't have jumped

5

1 would have asked him
2 wouldn't feel/be feeling sick (now)
3 might have won (the race)
4 could he have been
5 you wouldn't/would not be living
6 if you had/'d been paying
7 be lost if Angie had
8 would you have done

6A/B

             /əʊ/
1 What would <u>you</u> have <u>done</u>?
        /əʊ/
2 I <u>wouldn't</u> have done <u>that</u>.
3 If I'd <u>known</u> when you were <u>coming</u>,
         /əʊ/
  I would've <u>met</u> you at the <u>station</u>.

8.2

1B

A soldier
B freefaller
C starfish
D foetus
E log
F yearner

C

1 Freefaller (although they tend to be gregarious, below the surface they are nervy and thin-skinned)
2 Starfish (they are good listeners)
3 Foetal (They are often shy)
4 Yearner (once they make a decision … they are not going to change their mind)
5 Soldier (perfectionists who have high expectations of themselves and others)
6 Log (easy-going and likely to be popular; freefallers are also sociable but are not laid back)

D

1 posture
2 (the) in-crowd
3 gullible
4 a fuss
5 gregarious
6 thin-skinned

2

1 control
2 equality
3 justice
4 fairness
5 aggression
6 greed
7 generosity
8 power

3A

1 daydreaming
2 to solve
3 tackling
4 taking
5 clearing
6 staying up
7 to need
8 being able
9 to require
10 sleeping

B

Staying up all night **decreases** (not increases) the ability to hold new facts by forty percent.

4

2 Jake hates/hated not being able to play football because of his bad leg.
3 They have invited Guido to give a talk at the conference.
4 Olga has suggested going for a picnic.
5 What do you want me to do?
6 Would you mind telling us how old you are?
7 The firm didn't/doesn't expect to have to pay for the damage.
8 Can I persuade you to change your mind?
9 It isn't/It's not worth waiting any longer.

5A

1 That's something
2 I'm always
3 but
4 people think
5 think much of
6 I've wasted
7 get over

C

1 Sara was late because ~~of~~ her alarm clock wasn't working properly.
2 You should make sure you put things in your calendar in order **to** remind you to do them.
3 Yuan went to the cinema early to **get** a good seat.
4 Take your car keys so that ~~as~~ you can drive if you get tired of walking.
5 You need to study hard so **as** to get a good test result./You need to study hard ~~so~~ to get a good test result.
6 Because I was late, I waited until the break to go into class so as **not** to upset the other students.
7 **In** order not to disturb the boss, don't talk outside that room – she's in an important meeting.
8 We use an online meeting maker so as **to** get agreement from everyone on the best time to meet.

8.3

1A

1 diplomatic
2 confrontational
3 sensible
4 supportive
5 collaborative
6 sensitive
7 unhelpful
8 assertive
9 focused
10 tactful
11 aggressive
12 direct

B

positive: diplomatic, sensible, supportive, collaborative, assertive, focused, tactful
negative: confrontational, unhelpful, aggressive
either: sensitive, direct

C

1 aggressive, confrontational
2 sensitive, supportive
3 direct
4 confrontational, aggressive
5 collaborative, sensible
6 assertive, direct
7 focused
8 unhelpful
9 assertive
10 sensible

2A

1 Actually, there's something I've been meaning to talk to you about.
2 I don't want you to get the wrong idea, but …

3 It's just that (often) you (often) leave your mobile on.
4 And it rings when you're not here and that's annoying./And when you're not here it rings and that's annoying.
5 Yes, but it's disturbing when people are trying to work./Yes, but when people are trying to work, it's disturbing.
6 I understand, but do you see where I'm coming from?
7 Maybe you could set it to silent when you're not here./Maybe when you're not here you could set it to silent.
8 Yes, how would you feel about that?

3

1 Actually, there's something I've **um** been meaning to talk to you about.
2 **Well,** I don't want you to get the wrong idea, but …
3 It's just that, **you know,** you often leave your mobile on …
4 And it rings when you're not here and that's **slightly** annoying.
5 Yes, but it's **a bit** disturbing when people are trying to work.
6 I understand, but **I mean,** do you see where I'm coming from?
7 Maybe you could **just** set it to silent when you're not here.
8 Yes, how would you **er** feel about that?

REVIEW 4

1A

1 plenty **of** fantastic views
2 a large **number** of walls
3 ~~A~~ Few flats with such excellent views
4 as quite a few **of** the rooms are on the lower ground floor
5 close to a large number of shops and several ~~of~~ clubs

B

1 The big windows mean no privacy.
2 The flat is probably badly in need of repair.
3 The rooms are decorated in different styles (uniquely) and probably not to everyone's taste.
4 The flat's likely to be dark and damp.
5 There's likely to be too much noise.

2A

1 promise
2 reality
3 serial
4 tabloid
5 focused
6 aggressive

3

1 a) serial b) series
2 a) sitcom b) sketch show
3 a) greed b) equality
4 a) fairness b) power
5 a) explored b) reached
6 a) sticking to b) assessing
7 a) sensitive b) sensible
8 a) tactful b) assertive

4

1 take back
2 comes across
3 bringing out
4 put me up
5 turned out

5

1 told his father he wanted
2 wanted me to sing
3 hadn't given him my
4 why he didn't like
5 if/whether I had been/I'd been working/I was working
6 wouldn't be seeing Katya

6A

2 apologise 3 promise 4 threaten
5 accuse 6 offer 7 suggest 8 admit
9 deny 10 agree

B

2 I apologised for causing any embarrassment.
3 We promised to reduce taxes if you voted for us.
4 She threatened to quit the show (unless she got more money).
5 He accused Leona of stealing his wallet.
6 They offered to share the information (with me/us).
7 She suggested taking a break (for a few minutes).
8 He admitted stealing €5,000 from the bank.
9 He denied ever having had cosmetic surgery.
10 She agreed to make a speech.

7

1 totally/absolutely/completely
2 is/was
3 way
4 on
5 really/absolutely
6 so
7 such
8 really
9 one
10 absolutely/really

8

1 would you have done things differently/would you do things differently
2 I wouldn't want/have wanted to change anything
3 If Angela and I hadn't/had not got married
4 we might/could/would/'d still be together
5 if you were to give advice/giving advice
6 what would you say
7 If I started/were starting again
8 I still think I would/'d choose

9

1 I'm sorry but I'll have to get back to work – this project is (very) time-consuming.
2 In a record-breaking race, Daniel Nduka wins the London marathon.
3 The company tries money-saving techniques then suddenly comes up with the funds when they're really needed.
4 I had to close my eyes before going into the brightly-lit room.
5 I had a five-month wait before I had the operation to repair my knee.

10

1 to look
2 to be
3 expressing
4 to do
5 Recognising
6 sit
7 processing
8 watching
9 to give
10 having

11

1 been meaning
2 hope you don't
3 the wrong
4 It's just that
5 Do you know/Do you see
6 would you feel

CHECK

1 c 2 b 3 b 4 a 5 c 6 b 7 a 8 a
9 c 10 c 11 c 12 b 13 c 14 b
15 a 16 b 17 b 18 c 19 b 20 b
21 b 22 b 23 a 24 a 25 c 26 a
27 b 28 b 29 a 30 c

UNIT 9

9.1

1B

1 c

C

a) 2 b) 5 c) 1, 4 d) not mentioned
e) 3

D

1 F 2 T 3 NG 4 T 5 F 6 T 7 NG
8 T

2A

1 a) to find   b) studying
2 a) locking   b) to lock
3 a) to learn   b) speaking
4 a) meeting   b) to do
5 a) to think   b) thinking
6 a) to study   b) travelling

3

1 to catch
2 chasing
3 standing

4 to be/being
5 to memorise
6 to pay
7 looking
8 picturing/to picture
9 to become
10 to say

4

A	M	C	A	I	P	R	I	C	B	C	H	L	S
R	V	A	N	D	A	L	I	S	M	K	Q	V	H
S	R	K	I	D	N	A	P	P	I	N	G	A	O
O	L	T	I	S	N	V	M	U	C	M	Q	Q	P
N	P	X	X	A	Z	Y	Q	H	L	N	K	R	L
Y	S	R	K	V	H	W	C	K	O	J	J	P	I
S	T	A	L	K	I	N	G	X	K	V	T	S	F
Q	Z	Z	W	A	V	P	S	H	E	C	V	D	T
W	L	P	S	V	S	H	A	C	K	I	N	G	I
L	V	Y	Y	L	C	B	R	I	B	E	R	Y	N
I	D	E	N	T	I	T	Y	T	H	E	F	T	G
C	O	U	N	T	E	R	F	E	I	T	I	N	G
W	Q	J	L	F	Q	B	M	U	G	G	I	N	G
F	U	Q	E	Y	J	R	N	V	P	W	C	O	H

5A

1 charged with
2 suspect 48-year-old Bill Haller of
3 accuse Haller of
4 rescue the driver from
5 thanked the prisoner for
6 saving the driver (who by coincidence is the mayor's son) from
7 cleared of
8 arrested another suspect for
9 apologised to Haller for
10 criticising the police for
11 blamed an ambitious senior police officer for

5B

Because he saved the mayor's son.

9.2

1A

1 greed 2 pride 3 curiosity 4 fear
5 sympathy

B

a) 4 b) 3 c) 5 d) 1 e) 2

C

1 preys on
2 legitimate
3 plight
4 recognition
5 subtle
6 unverifiable
7 vulnerability
8 bogus

2B

a) distract
b) deceive
c) pretend to be
d) grab
e) switch
f) be taken in

C

a) 4   **b)** 2   **c)** 1   **d)** 5   **e)** 3   **f)** 6

3

1   can't have
2   must have
3   might have
4   could have/must have
5   can't have
6   must have
7   can't have

4

1   can't have got/reached/arrived/got back
2   must have met
3   might/could have dropped/lost
4   must have come/been downloaded/been copied
5   might have/could have cut/hurt
6   can't/couldn't have seen/met
7   must have eaten/taken/had
8   must have/could have/might have missed

5

1   It must have been you.
2   It couldn't have been me.
3   You may not have seen her.
4   They can't have been there.
5   We could have seen them.

6A

1   Make sure you check that there are no suspicious characters nearby.
2   Be particularly careful to cover your fingers when entering your PIN.
3   Try to count the money quickly.
4   Take time to put your card away safely.
5   Never turn around if someone tries to get your attention.
6   Always be aware of people nearby.

9.3

1A

1   he reminded me **of** that English football player
2   wait, my mind's gone **blank**.
3   It never **occurred to** me, no.
4   before I **(had) realised** what was happening, my wallet was gone
5   No, in fact **it was only** a minute later
6   It ~~was~~ all happened so fast
7   They seemed ~~to~~ like students/They **looked** like students

2

1 over   2 over   3 fire   4 out   5 down
6 stuck   7 off   8 out

3A

A   rim
B   spokes
C   pedal
D   handlebar
E   saddle
F   chain guard

UNIT 10

10.1

1B

a) 1, 6   **b)** 4, 7   **c)** 2, 5   **d)** 3

C

1 c   2 a   3 g   4 f   5 e   6 b   7 d

D

1 shriek   2 eerie   3 corrupted
4 chattering   5 flash

2

1   fast-paced
2   gory
3   hysterical
4   controversial
5   full of suspense
6   gripping
7   touching
8   creepy
9   outstanding
10   thought-provoking

3A

1 When   2 that   3 where   4 which
5 who   6 whose   7 which   8 when
9 when   10 whose

B

2, 9

4

2   The biopic (which/that) I want to review today is *Raging Bull*, which is the story of a famous boxer.
3   Robert de Niro, who plays the part of Jake La Motta, is absolutely extraordinary.
4   The film was made at a time when most biopics were of heroic figures.
5   The film, which was directed by Martin Scorsese, is now recognised as a masterpiece.
6   De Niro became interested when he read the book on which the story is based.

5A

1   highly/widely
2   harshly/overwhelmingly/heavily
3   skilfully/sensitively
4   poignantly/convincingly

B

1   **a)** widely praised
     b) highly praised
2   **a)** overwhelmingly criticised
     b) harshly/heavily criticised
3   **a)** skilfully directed
     b) sensitively directed
4   **a)** poignantly acted
     b) convincingly acted

10.2

1A

1   A painting, not a statue, was damaged by a demolition ball.
2   The painting that was damaged was broken in two. It didn't get a hole in it. It was damaged because the glue holding the frame together wasn't strong enough, not because someone put an elbow through it.
3   The vase was broken into hundreds of pieces, not just two.

B

1   taking
2   tearing
3   shocked
4   pressed
5   walking
6   shattering
7   valued
8   embarrassed
9   employed
10   living
11   displayed
12   putting
13   being
14   used

2A

2   Anyone planning to go home early or wanting to take a break should let us know.
3   Walking out of the restaurant, I ran into my old boss coming in.
4   I used to work with the woman living next door.
5   I left the party quickly, not telling anyone that I was unwell.
6   Carrying a child under each arm, she ran out of the blazing building.
7   He jumped up, frightened by the loud bang, mistaking the door for a gun.
8   Walls painted white tend to attract more graffiti.

3

1   sell-out
2   alternative
3   rave reviews
4   ground-breaking
5   must-see
6   created a stir
7   mainstream
8   flop
9   hype
10   letdown

4B

1 c   2 b   3 a   4 b   5 c

C

1   from the side
2   thirds each way, (four) intersecting points
3   interesting
4   (quite/fairly) close
5   height, the same level

5A

1 tired
2 downs
3 don'ts
4 bounds
5 quiet
6 on
7 then
8 ready
9 cons
10 take
11 through
12 on

10.3

1A/B

1 It's well worth a visit
2 Let's head over to the
3 Supposedly, they had to interrupt
4 Believe it or not, it took
5 It was originally built as
6 Well, they were founded in
7 The story goes that he used

C

a) 5   b) 4   c) 3   d) 7   e) 2   f) 1

2A

2 shortness, shorten
3 narrowness, narrow
4 width, widen
5 breadth, broaden
6 thickness, thicken
7 depth, deepen
8 height, heighten/raise*
9 largeness, enlarge
*When we make something higher we usually *raise* it. When feelings or effects become stronger, they are *heightened*.

B

1 narrow
2 broaden
3 deepened
4 thickness, thicken
5 width, widen
6 length
7 lengthen
8 enlarge
9 high, height
10 shortened

3

1 There were **just under** 200 people at the party.
2 The homework should take you **roughly** an hour to do.
3 We'll be arriving at 4 o'clock or so ~~what?.~~
4 The renovations cost **upwards** of one million euros.
5 We're expecting somewhere **in the** region of a thousand people for the conference.

REVIEW 5

1

1 to let
2 to turn
3 to turn, to look
4 meeting
5 talking, having
6 asking

2

1 apologised for not listening
2 blame the website for encouraging
3 be banned from showing
4 saved the plane from crashing
5 dreamt of being
6 is suspected of helping
7 criticising me for not helping

3

1 a) fall for   b) deceive
2 a) taken in   b) distracted
3 a) ground-breaking b) sell-out
4 a) letdown   b) flop
5 a) Bribery   b) Shoplifting
6 a) hacking   b) vandalism
7 a) shorten   b) narrow
8 a) gripping   b) gory
9 a) knocked out   b) knocked over

4A

1 rescue
2 gory
3 thought-provoking
4 full of suspense
5 hacking
6 bribery

5B

1 can't/couldn't have got
2 might/could have experienced
3 must have made
4 must have given
5 can't/couldn't have had
6 could/might have been
7 could/might have been born
8 must have been

6

1 cross
2 seemed
3 so
4 much
5 like
6 reminded
7 blank
8 catch

7

1 who
2 whose
3 when
4 who
5 when
6 who
7 which
8 whom
9 whose
10 which

8

1 found
2 living
3 spent
4 used
5 killed
6 arriving
7 starting
8 suffering
9 made
10 sent

9

2 ups and downs
3 pros and cons
4 give and take
5 sick and tired
6 on and on
7 now and then
8 leaps and bounds

10A

a) head over
b) worth
c) modelled
d) Apparently
e) burnt
f) may know
g) named
h) retrace
i) Believe
j) supposedly
k) founded
l) story goes

B

1 modelled
2 burnt
3 may know
4 Apparently
5 worth
6 head over
7 story goes
8 founded
9 named
10 Believe
11 retrace
12 supposedly

CHECK

1 a   2 b   3 b   4 c   5 a   6 c   7 b
8 a   9 c   10 a   11 c   12 b   13 a
14 b   15 b   16 c   17 b   18 c   19 a
20 c   21 a   22 c   23 b   24 c   25 a
26 b   27 a   28 c   29 c   30 a